From *Follow My Dust*, courtesy Don Uren.
Upfield felt this photo was artificially posed.

Upfield's desired epitaph
ARTHUR W. UPFIELD
His
Epitaph to Be

—

*A boy: every wind blew fair.*
*A youth: he mutinied.*
*A young man: he wrecked the ship.*
*Then he built another.*

(*Follow My Dust*)

# The Spirit of Australia

# The Spirit of Australia:

## The Crime Fiction
## of
## Arthur W. Upfield

### Ray B. Browne

Bowling Green State University Popular Press
Bowling Green, OH 43403

Cover design by Gary Dumm

# Acknowledgments

This book could hardly have been written, and surely not with any strength it might have, without the pioneering work done by Philip Asdell in his *Bony Bulletin*, edited and published at 5719 Jefferson Blvd., Frederick, Maryland 21701, and the various people whose comments he has published. I thank him for permission to quote extensively from the *Bony Bulletin*. I am grateful also to the encouraging words and pioneering work done by Betty Donaldson and to Joe Kovess for setting me straight on several aspects of Upfield's life, as he works diligently on a historical-bibliographical study of Upfield's life and works. I am grateful to Don Uren, Jessica Hawke's son, for permission to reproduce photos from *Follow My Dust*. I appreciate also Mrs. Louise Muller's permission to quote from her extensive recounting of how, often under her suggestions, Upfield changed much of the wording of *The Barrakee Mystery* and many of his other works( *Bony Bulletin*, No. 5, March 1983, and personal correspondence), and Dr. John H. Dirckx's permission to recount his knowledge and investigation of coffin dust (as used by Upfield as his means of dusting off his victim in *An Author Bites the Dust; Bony Bulletin*, No. 7, Oct. 1983), and to *The Armchair Detective* and William A. S. Sarjeant for permission to publish his map of the settings for Upfield's books (Vol. 12, No. 2, 1979) somewhat altered.

I appreciate also the various publishers of Upfield's work from whom I have quoted in this book. Upfield, it seemed to me in making this study, demands much quotation since he was writing pretty much of a distant land and at times an alien world. He needs to be the voice of and the artist at work, illustrating his own work and thoughts.

To all those appreciative people who read and work in Upfield's novels and short stories—my appreciation and empathy.

Finally, to my co-workers although they may not know it, my family: Pat, Alicia, Glenn, Kevin and Mirra.

# Contents

Arthur Upfield when he met Bony.
From *Follow My Dust*, courtesy Don Uren.

# Preface

In the world of crime fiction, Arthur W. Upfield stands among the giants. His work must be ranked among the leaders in crime fiction, and his detective-Inspector Napoleon Bonaparte, called Bony by all, is one of the half dozen most memorable of all crime fighters.

The route Upfield took for the development of Bony was not short and direct. He wandered through the outback of Australia for years, apparently bumming around following the lure of least resistance, until two perceptive people, called simply Mary and Angus by Upfield, pointed out the uselessness of his existence and persuaded him to turn to writing. Literature, and especially crime literature, owes those two individuals a great deal of gratitude.

Because of the nature of his existence, Upfield's life during the early years in Australia has several vacant and hazy spots. The one extended biographical study devoted to him, Jessica Hawke's *Follow My Dust* (1951) is a puzzlement. It leaves out much and is casual with much else. This was an autobiography that Upfield wrote but which he could not market to a publisher and which was subsequently edited by Jessica Hawke. It was either a deliberate attempt to leave much of Upfield's life under the dust or a grand example of how much a person can forget when he writes his autobiography. But the need for a good biographical study of Upfield is now being filled. Joe Kovess, one of Australia's leading authorities on Upfield, is in the final process of gathering information for a biography of the author. It is to be hoped that this book will be published within the next two or three years. Meanwhile, we must get along on what is known.

In brief, it is known that Arthur Upfield went to Australia in 1910 (1911) because his father sent him there thinking that the young man, based on experience, was going to be a trouble maker and should be sent as far away from home as possible. Once arrived

1

in Australia, young Upfield tried out at virtually every kind of job in the Outback. Finally, in 1924 at the insistence, or at the time of the insistence, of Mary and Angus, mentioned before, he decided that he should take up one of the great joys and skills of his life, that of telling stories. Upfield had great ambitions; like all aspiring authors, he wanted to write the best books in his field, in this case the "Great Australian novel." In this vein, and with several false starts, he discovered the model for his great detective-Inspector Napoleon Bonaparte, and wrote 29 books with Bony as the subject. Altogether, Upfield wrote 36 books, leaving one unpublished and one unfinished at his death. The unfinished one was completed by two friends and published in 1966. The unpublished one, lately found among Upfield's papers, is now being readied for publication, possibly in 1987.

What do the facts we know of Upfield's life and his published works all add up to? The answer is full and firm. Upfield was an independent, fiercely self-assertive ex-Britisher who, as a converted Englishman loved Australia above all other countries, especially the Outback—that wonderful and harsh country comprising most of the continent and very few of the population. In many ways Upfield, as he once had Bony say, became Outback Australia. He became the "Spirit of Australia," thus the name of this book. To assert that Upfield was the Voice of Australia does not detract from the works of any of the other fine Australian writers but it merely states how deeply and thoroughly Australia resonated in the heart and works of Arthur Upfield. As Upfield was the Voice of Australia, Australia was the Inspiration of Upfield. The two existed symbiotically. One contained the other.

In many ways the story of Australia of the first half of the twentieth century is the story of Arthur Upfield. In far more ways the story of Upfield and his works was the story of Australia. But each is an honor to the other. The world is surely the richer, and Australia the more widely appreciated, because of the works of this ex-Englishman who lived so hard the Australian life.

The book that follows is an effort to explicate and comment on some of the aspects of Upfield's books that make him and them so important. The comments trace major themes in Upfield's life and philosophy, major attitudes he expressed and developed and the mental and physical setting in which he developed them. Finally, each book is evaluated in light of Upfield's other works, and in light of other, mainly non-Australian, authors. In all aspects Upfield comes out a winner.

The full story is not told in this book. But at least an effort has been made to supplement the scanty scholarship available on the material. Readers who appreciate the author can only look forward to continued research and criticism of this most renowned Australian author.

# Chapter 1
# Life and Philosophy

Arthur William Upfield (1888-1964) was born in Gosport, England, near Portsmouth, the eldest of five boys. He was christened William Arthur, but in order to avoid the confusion of people asking for Little Bill, the order of his names was reversed and as a child he came to be called by the Dickensian name Arker-Willum.

The Upfield house was crowded, and young William was something of a trouble-maker. So, in order to make room for more congenial living for the younger four boys, Arthur was sent to live with his grandparents, on both sides, most of his childhood, returning to his parents' home for brief spells and apparently getting along happily and harmoniously there during these short terms, especially with his siblings. But Arthur was always restless and a practical joker, and during these early years he must have caused his father long moments of apprehension. This anxiety matured into a firm belief on the father's part that his eldest son was nothing but trouble and had to be taken care of in the finest terms—in a permanent exile to Australia.

The man who resulted from this treatment in childhood was one of strong attitudes and convictions. Perhaps he had come by his philosophy naturally. But regardless of the cause, genetic or environmental, he was a born and consistent non-conformist, and remained one throughout life. He was fiercely independent, quick to act, and always followed his own star.

In late 1910 or early 1911 (the exact date seems to be indeterminate) at the age of 22 Arthur Upfield was sent to Australia, where, it was hoped, he would become a respectable farmer. Australia had a population of four million inhabitants, most of whom lived in the coastal cities. His father's words to his son as explanation of the final separation were that Arthur would never amount to any good, Australia was so far away that once there Arthur could not cause the family trouble, and perhaps, best of all, he could never save enough money to get back to England. Such a parental attitude and such an act of expulsion must have cut deeply into Arthur's personality and psyche and left permanent scars.

Upon arrival in Adelaide, Arthur was met by a wheat farmer from Pineroo, South Australia. Young Upfield took his first job in Australia on this farmer's station. But the work and hours were so odious to Arthur, that, having been awakened at 3 A.M. to go to work his first morning there, he quit the job forthwith. In need of another job, Arthur disdained to use the letters of introduction that his father had provided, deciding instead to get along on his own resources and talents. His next job was with a Mr. Fearon, at Mitchum, as a boundary rider. This job lasted four months. Upfield then returned to Adelaide and was given a position as fourth cook at Adelaide's finest hotel. He was successful in this position but left after two days. He reapplied for a job as fence-rider, and although he had been turned down at his first application for this job as being too green and new to Australia, this time he was hired and sent to the outback by train via Broken Hill on his way to Momba Station. He was bewitched by the appearance of Broken Hill as he disembarked from the train and waited hours for the stage coach which would take him the rest of the way.

Broken Hill—named "Wilya-Wilya-Yong," "Place of Youth" by the Aborigines—had been built on a silver mine, and had been named for the small mountain it was adjacent to, which was broken in the middle. This small city represented the outback of Upfield's dreams and later obsession. It had intense desert heat, sidewalks made of planks, hitching-posts for the horses, and a frontier atmosphere that invited one to free himself and his soul from the cares of civilization. As Upfield was about to depart for Momba Station, where he was to work for a year as boundary rider on a fence 80 miles long, he was asked by the driver of the Cobb & Co. stagecoach which was to transport him what he thought of Australia down Adelaide way. Upfield replied that Adelaide was not Australia— "This is it," he insisted, meaning the outback. Thus he early revealed a prejudice toward and a feeling for the outback which was to stick with him throughout his life and would influence and control his literary works through the years.

With this introduction into the Australian outback, Upfield initiated a career that would find him testing all the possibilities of the new land, trying his hand at every unskilled and impermanent job he could find. During his long career in the bush he became boundary-rider, cattle-drover, sheep-herder, rabbit-tracker, opal-gouger, grape-picker, cook and station manager; in 1948 he led an Australian Geographic expedition on a trip of 5000 miles to investigate a portion of the Australian Northwest. As he traveled from job to job, generally pushing his swag on a bicycle from which the pedals had been removed, Upfield read the Book of the Bush, as he consistently called nature in his books, loved what he read about the Australian interior and stuck to it. In *The Mountains Have a Secret*, Upfield says that "nobody knew Australia better" than Bony, his detective (i.e. Upfield himself) and he stayed with it. As he told Pamela Ruskin for her brief sketch of his career published in the May issue of *Walkabout* magazine, the publication of the Australian Geographical Society, "I clung to it till my teeth fell out."

Always as restless as the blowing sand he walked on, Upfield was apparently charged from youth with an idealism and humanitarian impulse to help people which may or may not have resulted from his father's treatment of him but which surely became a salient characteristic later in his books. In nearly all his novels, Upfield has Bony endeavor to help someone in addition to the victims of the crimes. The purpose of Bony's work is, of course, to catch a lawbreaker. But often, too, Bony sets out just gratuitously to assist someone not involved in or victimized by the crime. For example, he is always interested in advancing the career of some country constable who has not received but wants a promotion and a removal to a better assignment. Bony tries to help whites who are caught in the culture of the country. And since he himself is a half-caste, Bony is always trying to assist the Aboriginals who are being abused by the so-called advance of what the whites call civilization.

Undoubtedly because of this instinct to be helpful, as well as to satisfy his moving instinct, on August 23, 1914 Upfield volunteered for military service in World War I and served with the Australian Imperial Force at Gallipoli and in Egypt and France. He was mustered out after five years and stayed in England for another five years, occupying the position of private-secretary to a military officer of high rank. Upfield apparently got along well with his family during these years. He had demonstrated to his father the he could stand steady on his own two feet. In 1915 Upfield married Anne Douglas (who survived him) and fathered a son, named Arthur James Upfield. But congeniality with his family and his marriage and child did not satisfy the restless Upfield who had seen a different kind of life in Australia. He longed for the freedom of life "down-under." So after having been away for ten years Upfield sailed back to the life he had come to love.

Although Upfield was to call his marriage in England a "disaster," it did not end with his leaving England for the second time. Subsequent details, however, are confused or not known. One version has him reconciling with his wife in the early 1930s when Upfield, wife and son lived in Kalamunda, Western Australia, and a second time in the later thirties, when they lived in Mt. Dandenong, Victoria. Another version of the efforts at reconciliation have Upfield bringing his family to Melbourne two years after he accepted a job with the *Melbourne Herald* in 1932, where he became a staff writer and authored *The Great Melbourne Cup Mystery*. Regardless of precise details, the reconciliaton was not a success. Upfield finally left his family for good when they were at Mt. Dandenong. Upfield's wife would not agree to a divorce, so he apparently lived with Jessica Uren at Airey's Inlet, Victoria, and at Bermagui and Bowral, New South Wales, without benefit of clergy.

So in 1919 Upfield's life in Australia began again. He had been lured back by the call of the bush and the way of life that he had experienced earlier. Europe must have seemed far more than half a world away from Australia in character, people, way of life and philosophy of existence. Apparently Upfield had found in Australia during his first visit a society of settlers who were still sufficiently close to their original roots to be democratic. They had a good sense of humor. They drank hard, worked hard, and were "giants," a type not "bred anymore," in Upfield's view. To a man as respectful of the democratic giant as he was, Upfield yearned for traces of greatness in the old European settlers. As he said in *The Battling Prophet*: "This race has not entirely passed away. The last remnants are still to be found living in peaceful old age on the banks on inland rivers and near a township which they visit only on pension days. It was a race the likes of which will never again be seen, for it possessed all the admirable attributes and but few of the human vices."(18) One of the giants still around, John Luton in *The Battling Prophet*, represented that age when "all men were equal" and all were respected because they were not "damned by meanness of thought and of act."

Although he himself seemingly was too independent to fit into groups, Upfield was drawn toward the inter-dependence of one person on another. Those independent giants of old appealed to Upfield's sense of community. In Australian society men and women had to pit their strengths against a nature that was greatly their superior and stood indifferent to or in opposition to them. Experience had taught Upfield that the individual though he stood alone needed to help others and to be helped by his fellow man. As he said in *The Battling Prophet*, the Australians' "dependence on one another in a world of vast, semi-arid distances gave to them a spiritual strength rarely found in city and town even in their own times." (19) These people's motto was simple and generous: "If your neighbor needs a pound, give him five. If a down-and-outer begs for a crust, give him half your loaf." (19) Today the curse was on somebody else; tomorrow it would be on you. Mankind's failure to appreciate that common bond of dependence saddened Upfield, who spoke through his Detective-Inspector: "Bony was sickened by the petty jealousy in human hearts, and by the lack of imagination in men of high estate." (92)

Where they demonstrated any generosity, the white Australians had undoubtedly learned a great deal of it from the Aboriginals, who, according to Upfield, were the most generous people in the world. Upfield's attitude is revealed in the biography of him called *Follow My Dust*. This strange biography, according to Joe Kovess, was written by Upfield in the early thirties but he was unable to get his publishers interested. It was edited by Jessica Hawke and published in 1957. In this book, Upfield praised the Australian aborigine.

In all human history no people are closer to the Christian ideals than the Australian aborigine, and next to him is the white man who is captured by the aborigines' Spirit of the inland. Give an aborigine a pair of trousers, and another is wearing them the next day. Give him a hunk of meat, and he shares it all round. The white man is hungry, hand him a meal. He needs a coat, give him your spare one, and if you haven't a spare one, give him the one you do have. Christlike! It is insurance against you own time of need. And what is the edict 'Love your neighbor,' if it isn't a form of insurance? A greater coverage, anyway, than an armaments race." (96)

This is a philosophy Upfield apparently held all his life. But it was not natural to many Europeans.

This world of Australia in its physical and spiritual conditions required considerable adjustments by European ex-patriots living in the new land. In addition to the physical conditions so unlike those of their European homes, these people had to live next to a primitive society of Aborigines from whom the land had been stolen and who never fully acquiesced in their loss. Upfield may have felt that in Australia he had a better setting for his philosophy about the Aborigines and civilization that he had developed there than he might have had in England had he chosen to live in that country. Mainly, however, he seems to have been unable to resist the call of this wild. Once in his blood, it would not release him. It controlled and directed his every action. At this stage, anyway, it apparently did not admit the concept of wife and family, or at least the wife and family he had.

Just what kind of man did Australia have to work on in Arthur Upfield and what kind of result did it turn out? According to John K. Ewers, Australian writer, in an article in *Walkabout*, the official publication of the Australian Geographic Society, Upfield was somewhat enigmatic. He was generous with his knowledge and experience, though somewhat abrupt in his manner. He was direct and blunt, never one to mince words. He spoke quickly and staccato-like. Ewers said:

When excited he speaks quickly, the syllables hopping out like bullets from a machine-gun. Sometimes his words race ahead of his thoughts, both in his speech and in his writing.

But Upfield was sensitive to what he thought were his short-comings. Once he was what he thought discourteous during one of Ewers' many visits in mentioning that he could have written two thousand words while otherwise using his time in talking to his visitor. Later in a hastily scribbled note, Upfield apologized to Ewers:

Unfortunately my tongue is not always controlled by my mind. There are times when engaged in conversation that my mind is occupied by quite different subjects. . . . I have suspected that this failing has lost me friends.

These characteristics, though different somewhat in detail, remained consistent in generalities. According to Pamela Ruskin, in a brief sketch of his life, Upfield was a tough, irascible, wiry man, with slate-colored eyes and "a thin trap of a mouth and ears like jug handles." He smoked too much. In his early books, Upfield, speaking about his own actions, frequently commented on Bony's smoking habits, severely criticized him for making his own badly-rolled cigarettes and for chain-smoking. Several times he promised that he would give it up; in the later books, Upfield, apparently realizing that he himself could not quit the habit, stopped talking about it. In his own later life Upfield was still trying to give up smoking and welcomed any opportunity to "decarbonize" his lungs, as he called it.

In addition to his irascibility, Upfield was apparently somewhat truculent, a bit of behavior probably stemming from his need to hide shyness, but obviously also useful in an effort to protect his independence. This determination was evidenced in some little symbols which were perhaps as much idiosyncratic show as substance of character. For example, Upfield's stationery in later years, according to his friend Louise Mueller, carried the two declarations "All Fame And No Bloody Money" inscribed at the top, and at the bottom was the sentence "Ill-mannered is he who cometh without invitation," a maxim which he attributed to someone Upfield called "Uppoffski."

According to John Hetherington, who talked with Upfield in his seventies, Upfield's hands were

> those of a man who has done much rough work, and his hazel eyes, netted in fine wrinkles, are a bushman's eyes, but he dresses as conventionally as any retired bank manager or pharmacist. He is equable, tolerant in his judgements, easy in his speech. His nose is short and blunt, and his straight mouth good-humoured. His strong dark hair, although greying, has not begun to thin.

We get a glance at an earlier Upfield in the character of Clarence B. Bagshott, a writer of popular novels in both *The Devil's Steps* and *An Author Bites the Dust* who is a projection Upfield made of himself. According to Upfield, Bagshott was a rare Dickensian giant who talked loud, drank much, liked fishing. He was larger and gustier than life. He was merely ordinary in appearance, with a low and narrow brow but the back of his head exceptionally wide, and with eyes that were constantly alert. In addition, as he says in the first of the two novels, when Bagshott smiled he "seemed human enough." (146) In *An Author Bites the Dust* Upfield fills in Bagshott's character by saying that he is a "born story-teller." In other words, Upfield in the first book of this pair was probably describing himself as he would have liked to be, but in the second book he was describing himself as he really was. He himself was a born story-teller and one who did not like the details of cleaning up his copy, as we shall see later.

But whatever he looked like and however he felt about his abilities, Upfield was made for Australia and Australia for him. He brought with himself from England a propensity for being an Australian—all the raw materials waiting to be molded—and Australia molded it for him. Upfield loved Australia for fifty-four years and reported it as faithfully as he could down to his day of death. When he died he was still thinking positive. Always sickly and asthmatic, Upfield took to his bed as his health declined but still kept his writing pen by his bed. When he died in Bowral, February 13, 1964, while living with Jessica Urens, he had begun his thirty-fourth novel, the twenty-ninth involving Bony, and was apparently still a frustrated, individualistic man not willing to accept the world on its terms. He was an Australian in a strange and alien world. But it was one he fiercely loved

The Australian setting that Upfield loved was not always peaceful and amicable. Tension between the Aborigines and the whites often stretched to the breaking point and occasionally exploded in violence. In so doing, society presented Upfield with a drama fraught with an obvious potential for disaster but with an apparent potential for good also. Though it was hardly the classic case of irresistible force colliding with immovable object (for the power of the white civilization was obviously greater than that of the more primitive and far weaker Aboriginal), the conflict held in its grip the future of Australia—perhaps of mankind itself, at least symbolically for Upfield. Upfield always discussed the Australian situation in terms of the broader concept of primitivism vs. civilization. This Australian cauldron was an excellent place to study the forces that many people, for example American fellow-author of detective fiction a decade after Upfield, Ross Macdonald, realized surface most dramatically and most dangerously when societies get clamped together with no way for one to break the embrace of the other and escape. In Australia this conflict was that between the life-style of the Aborigines and that of the Europeans.

But no matter how profound and sweeping the conflicts might have been in his eyes, Upfield did not write of the development of Australia in epic terms, although he saw it as almost epical and occasionally addressed the problems in near-epic terminology. For example, sometimes the books begin with an epical sweep and flourish that echoes the cosmos and eternity. In speaking of a set of mountains (in *The Mountains Have a Secret*) Upfield writes:

They rose from the vast plain of golden grass; in the beginning, isolated rocks along the north-west horizon, rising to cut sharply into the cobalt sky, the rocks united and upon that quarter of the plain it could be seen that a cosmic hurricane had lashed the earth and created a sea, a sea of blue-black waves poised to crash forward in geographical suds.

But instead of epic, Upfield saw the conflict more nearly resembling tragedy—a tragedy inherent in the conflict of opposites. In the same novel *The Mountains Have a Secret*, (150) for example, after Bony sees where one man has stabbed another, Upfield says of Bony's conclusion "Tragedy was written clearly on this page of the Book of the Bush." The geography of Australia, as Upfield points out in *The Will of the Tribe* (7) joins in the "opposition to man" and thus fuels the tragedy that is evidenced throughout the continent. This landscape consists of a geology and topography as varied and as harsh as that anywhere else in the world and one that is kept fired up with the various nationalities of the people populating Australia. Upfield points out in numerous instances that if the various nationalities living there would forget their homelands and become truly Australian, the country could be made worth living in.

But they cannot. Especially the conflict between the invading Europeans and the resident Aboriginals seems never-ending. This reality causes Upfield much concern, much bitterness and occasional resignation. In *Bushrangers of the Skies* (164), for example, Rex, a half-caste son who should inherit a large cattle station from his white father, says he is determined to fight the whites because money cannot buy equality with them. Bony, himself a half-caste, tends to agree with Rex on this point and gives him a Darwinian observation that in civilization the strong devour the weak, and that he, Bony, is prepared to shoot murderers, whom he despises. Bony also avers that condescension by whites, which so many Aboriginals and half-castes find intolerable, should prove to Aboriginals, as it does to him, the superiority of the native Australians. But the peace such philosophy brings is uneasy at best. Since Upfield's day the newly sensitized Aboriginals have become even more determined to have their place in the sun. They want their rights and they want them now.

Although Upfield wrote in the genre of detective fiction and was limited somewhat to personal conflict and retribution, at least on the surface of his works, he expanded the horizons of the genre into something much greater. Other authors of Australian fiction have been more nearly epical in their sweep. Mary Durack, for example, in her several books about pioneer life on the Australian continent, or the slightly later authors Colleen McCullough, in *The Thornbirds*, and Nevil Shute, in *A Town Called Alice*, broadened their subjects into bona fide epics. Upfield's books were, instead, about the heroic struggle between titanic forces of nature and man that ground mankind and the potential of civilization between them. Upfield was not an idle bystander in this clash of indifferent forces in a sightless world. He threw his strength into the struggle, trying to influence it as he might and to soften the fall of those who had to tumble, the Aboriginals.

In a thoughtful essay John Cawelti once suggested that detective fiction ordinarily is biased with a set of "certain presuppositions about the society, law, and morality from the Anglo-American tradition." Upfield's works, Cawelti pointed out, "illustrate the power of the detective story formula to bring out distinctive qualities of morals and manners" but demonstrate also the limitations of the expression of deeper and more complex issues of culture and society. In point of fact, however, of all authors of crime fiction, Upfield was perhaps least restricted by the rules of the genre. He may have been the first to write crime fiction as a genre larger than detective fiction, a tradition that is growing steadily as authors have gone beyond mere detective fiction to work in crime and suspense fiction and to bring to their work the tools of psychology and culture in general. Upfield's books are works in cultural and philosophical anthropology, which merely use as their *modus operandi* crime fiction worked around a heroic half-caste who dearly loves to solve crimes because they afford his talent, that of tracking criminals and putting together scattered pieces of human action, its fullest play and development. Upfield's works are of heroic forces shaking the world, and they develop on a plane far above the level of mere detective fiction.

There is no doubt that Upfield assumed that he knew Australia physically and spiritually and therefore was capable of speaking of and for it. In one of his early books, *Mr. Jelly's Business*, Upfield personifies Australia in one of his most heroic characters, whom he names "The Spirit of Australia," and describes him as a cultural, spiritual and physical giant. Age "rested on him as a crown of jewels." (32)    Except for the hyperbole, the portrait could have been that of Upfield himself, who surely constituted the Spirit of Australia. In *Bony and the Mouse* Upfield describes another heroic character named Melody Sam—owner of everything in the town of Daybreak—a character that he had studied earlier in at least one short story and who apparently demanded a lot of Upfield's thought and attention. Like "The Spirit of Australia," Melody Sam was a character who defied all time and tradition. He was "A Tycoon! A dictator! A political boss! He was a person who was "an antique, a character, a ruddy legend" who was "universally honoured, if not universally loved." (7)

In *House of Venom* Upfield takes his belief in the hero as spokesman for a nation to its logical conclusion. Bony is asked by one of the characters if he is Australian, if he is a native of the country. Answering with a breadth seldom achieved by a hero in any country or civilization, Bony asserts, as Upfield records: "'I am Australia'," with a pause after each word. Thus he voices the all-inclusive heroic statement "I- *am*-Australia." Although Bony was nearly always arrogant and egotistical in his statements, there was neither attribute in this statement—just the realization that Upfield knew the Australia of the 1930s-40s-50s as few other people had known it. As he had recognized when he first came to the country decades before he felt that the outback was the heart of Australia. In his books he is recording the history of the country heroically.

The essence of frontier heroic literature throughout the world commits a hero against alien and hostile forces in a setting where nature is powerful and is either indifferent or hostile and therefore presents awesome difficulties for the hero. In this setting, the superperson fights for the good of individuals and of society as a whole. Part of the accomplishment of the hero is in triumphing over or in the presence of powerful nature which if not hostile seems to be purposefully throwing obstacles in the part of the hero in his quest.

Since part of the heroic stature of the individual springs from overcoming the forces raised by nature, he becomes a *natural* hero, as opposed to a *social* hero who arises as society becomes more the battleground. For the natural hero the forces of nature extend beyond mere earthly setting, of course, and rise to the supernatural in the shape of evil or indifferent gods who may or may not be interested in the fate of man.

Bony very much fits the mold of this classical natural hero. He is heroic in every way. Though small of stature, he has a keen intellect and is physically strong. He is able to outwalk, outthink, outfight, out-heroize all other men and women that he meets. He is the hero's hero. Generally he uses "civilized" means but he has been known to revert to "primitive" methods if pushed too far. He must win.

But in addition to Bony, Upfield has a Trojan horse filled with other heroes. The setting is heroic. Australia is a land of giants. As Upfield says in *Wings Above the Diamantina* (9) when he comments on a physical setting:

An amazing place, this. It was the studio of the Wind King who had chiselled the sand hummocks into fantastic shapes, a veritable hell when the hot westerlies blew in November and March.''

Most of the heroes who inhabit this country are physical giants. Many are, of course, Aboriginals. In *Wings Above the Diamantina*, again, the hero is Illawalli, who calls Bony his father, mother, friend and son, in the strange complicated racial relationships endemic to the Aboriginals. Illawalli looks like a superman as he is "Standing apart with arms folded, his majestic face calm in repose." (212) And he demonstrates his superiority by literally talking a dying woman back into consciousness and life. Australia is a heroic land filled with heroic people accomplishing heroic deeds.

Upfield's fiction is very much in the tradition of heroic literature, in general, especially as his works remind us of various American heroic writers. His use of the natural world is similar to that of such authors as Frank Norris and Jack London in their man-animal clashes with nature and with the Canadian Robert W. Service in his use of the physical world in his poems about Canadian adventures.

But the two classic American writers who perhaps most clearly exemplify these two aspects of the hero are James Fenimore Cooper in his Leatherstocking Tales, in the person of Natty Bumppo (in his various names), and Herman Melville in at least a half dozen characters, the most notable of whom are the three heroic figures of *Moby-Dick*—Ishmael, Queequeg, Ahab—and Billy Budd in the short novel of the same name.

Natty Bumppo, as a white man who is not quite respectable and who serves as a kind of go-between bridging the gap between civilized whites and the Indians (as Bony does with the Whites and Aboriginals in Australia) combats evil Indians and treacherous whites for the benefit of individuals and through them society as a whole. But his battles are waged in the presence of a second powerful force—nature—which although at times benign or indifferent nevertheless constitutes a force that often becomes hostile and must always be reckoned with.

In Melville's works the frontier is of a somewhat different kind; it is a transcendental nature sometimes embued with a supernatural spirit which seems to combat the godliness in mankind. When Melville's heroes struggle for themselves and mankind they must fight on at least two levels and sometimes against three foes: man, nature and God.

Thus, on two levels the battles of these two authors exemplify the essence of the heroic, frontier struggle. They are concerned with the hero in epical battles, in essence the battle of mankind against alien and hostile forces.

Upfield's settings resemble the American authors'. His is a wild and unsettled country. His working area is the whole of the continent of Australia outside the urban areas, as Cooper's was the whole American frontier and Melville's the frontier of transcendentalism and the limits of the human imagination.

Upfield's antagonists are nature against man, and Australian nature, often more terrible than man in its manifestations, is always heroic. Nature is the test of mankind. As Upfield says in *Bony and the Black Virgin*:

This Australia does strange things to men. Some men it frightens to death, and drives them back to the coastal cities where they can browse like steers in a herd. Other men it cures. With the heat of the sun, and the abrasive action of the wind and sand grains, it cures as smoke will cure sides of bacon. (13)

Not all could stand the conditions of the outback. In *Bony and the Mouse*, Upfield attributed the testing power to the outback in general: "It must be the flaming bush that did certain things to certain men, making some and destroying others."

On the subject Upfield wrote 34 books and numerous short stories (some of which are not available in this country, though the canon is being republished in two or three places now). Some of the subjects are narrow, almost ordinary detection and conventional accomplishments, though they present little-known and interesting aspects of exotic Australian life. But all—the weakest and the strongest—have moments that could have been created only when the subject was Australia and the author Arthur Upfield. At his strongest, moreover, Upfield in his concept of his detective and the challenge of detective against nature and man, and the power of his accomplishment in working the story can be compared only with the absolute strongest of other authors.

Upfield's protagonist is Detective-Inspector Napoleon Bonaparte—called Bony by himself, his friends in the books and Upfield's readers. Bony appears in 29 of Upfield's 34 books. In these books Bony faces the awesome continent of Australia in all her manifestations of stark nature: deserts of sand hundreds of miles across, sand spouts fifty miles wide rising to blot out the sun, rabbits in the millions, mad camels, the terrifying loneliness that comes from complete isolation, and, of course, the hostility between people generated by such a country. "Common to all settings," Upfield says in *Man of Two Tribes*, (7) "is the force of opposition to man." This country, he adds, "will destroy any man who goes out alone." (7) In his treatment of the conflict between man and nature, Bony is never solemn—his disposition is sunny until he gets into the final stages of a contest or when he is trailing people who have abused or murdered women and children—but is always serious. "I never joke," he said once. "Life is too serious to joke."

Upfield makes it clear from the beginning of his series that Bony, a half-caste, walks between two cultures, at times blessed by his mixed blood, at times cursed:

He walked the soft tread of the Australian aboriginal.... By birth he was a composite of the two. His mother had given him the spirit of nomadism, the eyesight of her race, her passion for hunting; from his father he had inherited in overwhelming measure the white man's calm and comprehensive reasoning; but whence his consuming passion for study was a mystery."

This man Bony was an extraordinary result of the two races: He

was the citadel within which warred the native Australian and the pioneering, thrusting Britisher. He could not resist the compelling urge of the wanderlust any more than he could resist studying a philosophical treatise, a revealing autobiography, or a ponderous history. He was a modern product of the limitless bush, perhaps a little superior to the general run of men in that in him were combined most of the virtues of both races and extraordinarily few of the vices. ( *Sands of Windee*, 1-2)

In almost every book Upfield makes his point absolutely clear. In Bony the two races—the primitive and the civilized, the past and the present—struggle. Caught in the crossfire Bony might suffer. He could be victimized. But instead he generally looks upon himself as the beneficiary. Bony sometimes suffers personally from condescension and insults from people, especially until they get to know him. He could be more immediately successful than he is if he did not suffer some of the physical characteristics of his mixed blood. But Bony seldom speaks with any bitterness of his mixed parentage or of that of his wife, who is also half-caste. Instead, he mentions dozens of times the advantages accruing to him as a result of the union of two different races: he has the warm-hearted intuition of his mother and the hard-headed reasoning ability of his father. In other words, he has the best of both races. This is an attitude stated numerous times by the American author Herman Melville, who felt that mixed blood—presumably the more mixed the better—made people more heroic.

Bony and Marie are obviously dark in color, as the half-castes in Australia are, and he is frequently called "Nigger," as all other slightly darker people have always been called by so-called "pure" whites. Just how dark Bony is remains something of a mystery. In the beginning of the series, he is mentioned as being quite shiny black, later he is "reddish," and he seems to get lighter as the series of books involving him develops through the years. Upfield was somewhat equivocal about color of half-castes in another of his early books, *A Royal Abduction*. In this book, Upfield pictures the half-caste, named Peter Cuff, as "a tall, slim young man with a reddish, black complexion." Upfield may have figured that Cuff was too young to have matured into his final blackness.

On another level, Bony's wife Marie is apparently tender-hearted, loving and ever pliable, as he is, though she seems to lack the cool reasoning capability that Bony possesses. Apparently this attribute was not a part of her father's personality, if it was her father who was white; Upfield never makes this clear. The couple have three sons, who are superior in their own rights; why they have no daughter Bony never makes clear. It may have been because Upfield seems to have been more comfortable with males than with females. Judging from his treatment of female children in his books, Upfield seems to have been something like the American nineteenth century author Nathaniel Hawthorne in not really understanding little girls. Nevertheless, Bony often sighs in his letters to his wife that he wishes they had a daughter. Bony and his three sons are college graduates and all have already succeeded or will.

There is no occasion for Bony to mention their color, and he never does. But apparently Aboriginal genes are recessive, and children of half-castes emphasize the white genes instead of the aboriginal ones. Therefore the sons should have been light. They would have been only quarter aboriginals, with their two half-caste parents. But even half-caste infants often are born very light. In fact, half-caste babies because they were often so light caused curiosity and consternation to their Australian black mothers.

From the vantage point of being half-way between the two races, Bony can read with clear eyes both races and the three civilizations they all three inhabit and create. He struggles against all three—nature, man and superstition—and can rise to the occasion.

Upfield makes a great point of Bony's heroic attributes which result from his mixed parentage. It is of course silly to assume that all Australia half-castes were by definition heroic. Some, like the renegade Rex in *Bushranger of the Skies*, probably became scoundrels, perhaps overly accomplished scoundrels, because of their mixed blood and heritage and resulting environment, as some mixed-bloods have through the history of folklore and mythology, and as Upfield explicitly states on at least one occasion. But there were undoubtedly as many heroes per capita among the half-castes as among the so-called pure bloods. There are records of at least two other half-castes in Australian literature who turned out to be heroic. For example, Mary Durack finds it sufficiently noteworthy to repeat an anecdote about an Australian half-caste stockman named Sam Issacs who at the wreck of a steamer named *Georgette* on the Darling River made himself a hero by riding "to and from through the surf until all [passengers] were safely ashore" ( *To Be Heirs Forever*, 250). And of course Tracker Leon Wood, the model for Upfield's Bony, was a real-life half-caste hero and was unexcelled as a tracker and apparently as gentleman and human being as well.

But though in many ways similar, Upfield's fiction differs sharply from that of Cooper and Melville. Whereas theirs is epical and therefore concerned with a nation and a people, Upfield's is crime fiction, therefore concerned with crime and punishment, though it is enacted against a background of civilization vs. pre-civilization, and takes on a character entirely its own. It would have to. The differences between Australia and America are more real than the similarities. The physical and technological degree of development of the country at the time Upfield was writing was sharply different from that in the United States during Cooper's and Melville's times. The development of the people, at least on a superficial level, was also noticeably different.

Nearly all detective fiction develops through heroes and heroines as protagonists. Generally these heroes combat crime to protect society, to set society aright after the intrusion of a convulsion of law-breaking that has knocked it askew. Such people are social heroes. Heroes of the so-called Golden Age of British Detective stories are concerned almost exclusively with putting back together the pieces of society that have been dislocated by the crime, in other words, solving the puzzle. Upfield's heroes are much more like those of the American so-called hard-boiled variety, when the hero, no matter how hard-boiled he seems in action and talk, is really soft-hearted and humanitarian at his core. He is more determined with doing good, though often acting as his own judge and jury in evaluating the crime and punishment needed, than in merely solving the crime.

Upfield's books, to be sure, concern crimes that involve frontier offenses. Often as much against nature as against man, and frontier retribution. Throughout his works there is the conflict between primitiveness and civilization, with the constant tilting of the plane of justice that such forces entail.

Conventionally, heroes have certain characteristics which mark them to others and to themselves as being extraordinary. For example, there is something unusual about their birth (some extraordinary event)—the birth is shrouded in mystery, the hero has unusual physical or mental characteristics. Also he or she is endowed with obvious traits of character that reveal this unusualness. Detective heroes in general have maintained these characteristics to one degree or another. A. Conan Doyle's Sherlock Holmes is unusual in appearance, habits and intellectual ability. Agatha Christie's Hercule Poirot is distinguished by being a comical looking little Belgian with an unusually large head with "little grey cells."

American detective heroes are generally more than their British counterparts, and they are obviously marked as extraordinary. Rex Stout's Nero Wolfe, for example, in addition to his gargantuan size and excessive sloth is obsessed with his love for orchids. Ross Macdonald's Lew Archer is a melancholy person concerned with searching for his father. John D. MacDonald's Travis McGee lives on his houseboat *The Busted Flush* and fights for the common man.

In Australia, several traditions mix and persist. Peter Corris' hero Cliff Hardy's only heroic characteristic seems to be a penchant for survival in the crime-ridden streets of the cities. But Australian academic Hosanna Brown's development of the American female part-black detective character Frank Le Roux who works among the Aboriginals carries on Upfield's tradition though without his insight and strength of development. Although an American of mixed blood, she is the equivalent of the aboriginal half-caste.

Upfield's hero, Bony, is more of the old-fashioned type, which marks him to himself and to the people he works with as being unusual, with the classic birth which is mysterious and remarkable.

The sexual union of white and aboriginal parents gave Bony some rather unusual characteristics. He, according to his own account, "was never handsome." He was exceptionally thin and his "bones stood out," thus in one book the cause of his name (*The New Shoe*, 150). But this unprepossessing child grew into a man of most prepossessing appearance and action. He stands about 5 ft. 10 inches tall, is in his early to middle forties (sometimes forty-four, sometimes, apparently, older), is in the fittest physical condition and well able to stand the severest physical, climatic and geographical conditions. Free of unnecessary flesh he is "as hard as nails." Though buffeted physically at times by other people, Bony is able to overcome all adversaries in the end. Usually, all general descriptions of Bony point out this differences.

Bony has a

dark brown face on which Aboriginal race moulding was absent. His face was neither round nor long. The nose was straight, the mouth flexible. The brows were not unlike a veranda to shadow the unusual blue eyes and, although the black hair was now greying at the temples, it was virile and well kept.

The description of his color is constantly modified, Bony growing lighter in color through the books. But the main point is that Bony in his difference from other people stands out; he is different. Like all heroes he is different from the people whom he is going to help. Upfield made a definite point in picturing Bony this way. But though Upfield heroized Bony, he was not altogether settled on the social and cultural conditions which culminated in such a person as he was. In Bony, of course, there is far more than his heroic stature. The story of the half-cast detective is the story of a continent and the mixture of two peoples.

What was Upfield's feeling about the white people who sired half-castes like Bony? Generally he condemned them for their invasion of the edenic world of the Aboriginals and for the rape of the people and the country that followed. But Upfield had one exception. In *Sinister Stones* (173) when speaking of the original

Australian settlers, that is the first surge of British who came to Australia, Upfield's praise was high:

> They were true men and woman who came out of Ireland and Scotland and England to conquer a new world with little except tireless energy and unfaltering courage. They were generous to their own and rebels against Caesar. What they won, they held or, losing, won again. They gave to their children their all—their possessions and their spiritual attributes—and left an example of independence today either ignored or scorned by those designing to lean on the state from the cradle to the grave.

In this evaluation of the British Upfield was probably admiring their independence and rebelliousness—after all it paralleled his own—and freedom from inclination toward a socialistic state more than he was approving their racial characteristics. For in no other instance was he so kind to them and to what they had brought with them and had done to the country they invaded.

Taking the entirely different point of view, in *Murder Must Wait* (125) Upfield condemned both the spirit of the British and their actions once they had arrived in Australia. After the Whites came, he says, there was no longer "law and laughter" among the Aborigines.

> The first white man to set foot in Australia brought with him the Serpent from the Garden of Eden, when no longer was there in all the land law and laughter...only the slow progress of segregation into compounds and settlements of ever dwindling remnants of a race.

The serpent from the British Garden of Eden destroyed the Australian Eden it was introduced to. Before the British came, little more than century before Upfield was writing,

the camps of the inhabitants dotted the river-side, and smoke rose high into this still air. With but little trouble, game and fish were to be had to keep stomachs full and maintain the laughter of women and children. In those far-away days, morality was of iron. Laws, customs, beliefs, in which fear played no small part in gaining compliance, ruled benignly a people who, satisfied with little, wanted for nothing.

But all these edenic aspects of life "vanished before the human offal tossed out by England." Speaking of one family in particular but by extension of all the British who pushed into Australia, Upfield remarked ( *Venom House*, 94) that

Clearing pastures, breeding stock, fighting fire and floods had done them no good. They had lived by brutality and suffered from hate. Power had withered them. Greed had rotted them. The mighty white man, armed with his guns and riding swift horses, never laughed, never knew happiness.

The havoc these maurauders wrought was catastrophic to the Aboriginals and was done with no regard to decency. Upfield wrote:

The bodies of Australian aborigines had rotted to dry dust in the hot sands of the deserts: had slowly perished in creeks and waterholes: had swelled with the effect of the white man's poison: and festered with the effects of the white man's bullets. (69-70)

And they had been abused while alive in nearly every way possible:

They had been flogged at Sydney, hanged at Brisbane, loaded with chains at Adelaide and at Perth: had sunk into the ferntree gullies of Tasmania. The aborigines had been debased, outraged, jibed at and made the butt of both coarse and refined wit. They had been drawn into the shadow of a civilization which, compared with theirs, was a riot of lunacy.   (69-70)

The half-castes, to the degree to which they take after their white forebears, can be hellish also. Rex, the half-breed son of McPherson, in *Bushranger of the Skies* suffers from such an alliance, and no one knows how long it takes to breed sadism out of a race.

What did Upfield think of the Aboriginals from whom Bony, and other half-castes descended? His feeling with the possible exception of a few stereotypic statements scattered throughout the books, was generally praise and approval. Upfield has one of his characters comment in *The Mountains Have a Secret* (132) on their attributes: "Good Australian bushmen are not ordinary guys...Australian Aborigines are super-extraordinary guys." In *Bushranger of the Skies*, (28) McPherson, the owner of the cattle station and father of Rex the half-caste, calls one of his blacks "outstanding among an unusual race," and on the same occasion

he affirms that "The Blacks are a damn sight wiser" than the whites
are.

In *The Will of the Tribe* (121) Upfield's attitude is unqualified:

> The Aboriginal culture is like a well to the bottom of which no white
> man has ever descended to the water of complete knowledge and, because of
> the ever-expanding influence of an alien white race, no white man ever will.
> Confusion has been created by the white man himself to add to the certainty
> of frustration and defeats in his latter day efforts to investigate.

In *The Sands of Windee*, Upfield's second Bony book, he devotes
a full page to Bony's evaluation of the Aborigine:

> There is a very great number of people who regard the Australian Aboriginal
> as standing on the lowest rung of the human ladder. Because they have found
> no traces of a previous aboriginal civilization, no settlements, no buildings,
> nor industry, they say that he has always been a man of very low type. Yet,
> for all that, he has possessed for many centuries that which the white race
> is constantly striving to obtain, and which its striving brings no nearer. The
> blessed possession I refer to is Contented Happiness, the only human possession
> worth having...(sic)

At time Upfield is sarcastic and ironic in pointing out the
advantages the Aborigines have over the whites:

> The despised black man, ignorant, without wisdom, is contentedly happy.
> He desires nothing but life's essentials. In his profound ignorance and unwisdom
> he ruthlessly practises birth control. He makes sure that the very occasional
> mental degenerate and the physical weakling will not reproduce their like,
> and he keeps the population down well below a point which the country's
> natural food supply will support by the same method of birth control.

Upfield's final evaluation begins with rolling drums:

> The blackfellow thus is the world's greatest statesman. Every race, every
> nation, has something to learn from him. True, he has none of the white
> man's monuments to boast of or to point to as evidence of a supreme culture.
> Such monuments he would regard as millstones about his single ethereal
> monument of happiness.

Upfield's concluding comments are an apotheosis:

Because the blackfellow is so lacking in that boastfulness which is the white man's prerogative, the white man looks on him with contempt. Yet the blackfellow possessed culture when the white man ate raw flesh because he did not know how to make a fire. He did not inscribe his culture on tablets, nor did he force it on the general community. His secrets are well kept, and his powers well restrained.

Apparently Upfield was unfamiliar with the advanced research now being done by anthropologists in the drawings and paintings that at least some of the tribes left on overhanging rocks and in caves, especially in the northern states of Australia, which demonstrate an advanced state of drawing and painting.

Unfortunately, as far as Upfield was concerned, the Aboriginals had come a long distance out of their own way of life and into that of their conquerors. In *Murder Must Wait* (102) Upfield has a white Superintendent of Education at an Aboriginal school talk about the hurt done the primitives by his own white race:

I found that these people had come a very long journey from the tribal discipline enjoyed by their ancestors. They had become too closely associated with white civilisation, and because our civilisation will not or cannot assimilate them, for I refuse to believe the Australian aborigine cannot himself be assimilated, they were fallen into a condition of racial chaos.

The Superintendent's criticism of his country-people's ways was harsh:

We came into this country and conquered with guns and poison. What a basis for national pride today! From the aborigine we took his land and the food the land provided. Worse, we took his spirit and trod it into the dust, leaving him with nothing excepting the pitiful voice crying "Gibbit tucker." When plain murder was no longer tolerated, we tossed the starving aborigine a hunk of meat and a pound of flour and told to get the hell out of here. A wonderful Christian nation, are we not?

Without placing the Aborigine on a pedestal, such whites have tried to assist the Aboriginal in regaining his former independence and self-sufficiency.

In another novel, *The Bone is Pointed*, a white character points out the strengths of the Aboriginals and the weakness of the whites. The Aboriginals are strong because they never had the curse of

Adam laid on them. They do not relish torture. They don't know poverty because they don't know riches. They do not understand the need to work when nature provides them with their simple needs. "The strong succour the weak, and the aged always get first helping of the food."

Thus these people have known "real civilization for countless ages. They were conversing intelligently long before other races—the white and the yellow and even other black races—learned to speak at all." They "practised Christian socialism centuries before Christ was born." They evolved a complicated although workable social structure that has few flaws. They don't breed lunatics or weaklings. They picked up filth and disease from the White man, not having known it before.

The civilization that the Whites brought falls over them like a heavy shadow. "Civilization came to shoot them down, to poison them like wild dogs" and then to rationalize this bestial behavior by depicting the victims as half-wits, as naked savages, to put them on reserves and compounds. Civilization took away their natural food and "feeds them on poison in tins labelled food." (119)

Bony continues to brood on the phrase "The Shadow of Civilization!" and says: "It was full time that the Creator of Man wiped out altogether this monster called civilization and began again with the aborigines as a nucleus." (121)

Civilization with its rules and reorganizations causes genocide. If officialdom began working on the Aboriginals, that would mean "their swift de-tribilization and inevitable extinction. No matter how kindly officialdom might deal with them, once they are interred with it it is the beginning of the end." (228)

Again and again through the books this is Upfield's message. The Aboriginals were superior people before the Europeans came, were superior to the Europeans, but now must suffer the agony of being defeated by larger numbers and more powerful weapons.

Yet despite his near-total approval of the Aboriginals, always Bony remained ambivalent about his mixed parentage, and Upfield spoke through Bony and other individuals in his books to show that he too was not quite certain of where he stood. Despite the fact that the child of a mixed liaison turned out so exemplary in the person of Bony, Upfield, speaking through the voice of Bony himself, says at one point that he is against mixed-marriages, and Upfield shows in several books the tragic and ambiguous results of having whites and aboriginals try mixed marriages.

But despite everything Bony, in *The Bone is Pointed* (32-3) delineates the advantages of the black civilization. Take for example Bony himself. In bush townships Bony is a

grown man. Out there in the bush I am an emperor. The bush is me; I am the bush; we are one.

At times Bony feels

a great pride in being the son of an aboriginal woman, because in many things it is the aboriginal who is the highly developed civilized being and the white man who is the savage.

In *Wings Over the Diamantina*, (114) while two whites are discussing the potential of the half-castes, the pilot of an airplane points out the advantages of the black's civilization over his. He says that he would take up the Aboriginal's life style if he could—enjoying all the festivals, not working, going on walkabouts and digging up a yam or catching a fish when he wanted to eat." In *The Bone is Pointed* (116) Grandfather Gordon, the sire of a white race that is doing all it can to assist the Aboriginals, "clearly saw that civilization was a curse laid on man, not a blessing." In *Murder Must Wait* (167) Bony praises the Aboriginals as being of "a race remarkable for its morality, its freedom from greed" and had been so degraded and "ruined" by the white civilization that its people would now steal the tribal relics and sell them for a few plugs of tobacco.

Half-castes, like people with the characteristics of both races, according to Bony in *Swagman* (16) were "invariably intelligent, and it was their white fathers who were degraded and not their black mothers, members of what was originally one of the most moral races that ever walked this earth." The Aboriginals were capable of competing successfully with the Whites if they were just given a fair chance.

Though Bony may be fair-minded and give each race—the White and the Aboriginal—its fair rating, he constantly defends the Aborigines. In *The Bone is Pointed*, for instance, Bony says:

> Don't for one moment think that I despise my mother's race. At a very early age I was offered a choice. I could choose to be an aboriginal or a white man. I chose to become the latter, and have become the latter with distinction in all but blood.

In this nation of two races there arises always the question of sexual and cultural assimilation of the weaker by the stronger. Many people think it is the only salvation for the Aboriginals, that of being taken into the white culture and thereby losing its identity. Many people, however, Bony included, are glad that the assimilation is only partially complete. In *The Bachelors of Broken Hill* (189), Upfield comments that

> despite the black man's partial assimilation by white civilisation, he remains his own man. He sees more to be drawn from the future than the present.

In *Bony and the Mouse* (63) Upfield has Melody Sam, one of his truly great white Australians, comment on the efforts of the whites to detribalize the Aborigines:

> They call 'em savages, they call 'em this and that, but they're the only decent people living in the world today.... The sloppy fools down in the cities want to have 'em brought in and made to live in houses and go to work, and eat pork and beef off china plates, and all that. I don't hold with forcing them people into our own dirty, murderous, sinful state we call civilization.

In *The Bone is Pointed* (72) Upfield talks about Nero, a black who "had been saved from becoming de-tribalized." And later in that same book, Bony pays what must be the ultimate compliment to the Aborigines when he says that amongst the "allegedly primitive peoples," he has

> for the first time, no, the second, in my career... [been] opposed by aborigines, worthy opponents, opponents who never made the stupid mistakes fatally made by the so-clever, so highly civilized white man.

In assimilation, as Bony observes in *The Widows of Broome* (193-4) when the Aboriginal race begins to die, the remnant

here clothed in rags and gaudy finery presented the dreadful tragedy of a once rigidly moral, supremely free people being devoured by an alien and stupid civilisation.

Civilization, against which Upfield inveighs scores of times in his books,

sags in the middle. The Aboriginal leaves his state and walks down hill, and he might, . . . walk up again to the white state. But the end of the road is always lower than the Aborigine.

Bony laments over the "degradation of being assimilated into the white civilisation."

These then are the attitudes of Upfield and Bony about the earlier and present-day conflicts of the two races. Yet these are the two races from which Bony, an acknowledged superman, descended. They comprise the traits and characteristics he inherited from both races that make him superior. In one way or another, to one extent or another, Upfield mentions Bony's birth and development in nearly every book. In some, either because he thought it not necessary or through sheer fatigue he fails to mention the origins of the Detective-Inspector at all.

As is so often the case in the novelistic development of character, Upfield's Bony was based on a real person, a half-caste Upfield had known as a wanderer working the various fields of Australia. This man's name was Tracker Leon Wood, surely an unforgettable character for one in Upfield's frame of mind and character.

Tracker Leon, according to Upfield's memory, speaking through his biography by Jessica Hawke, was a "strange" and memorable character. He was about thirty when Upfield first met him, of medium height, lean and tough of body, with brown skin and eyes that were penetrating blue. On his chest and back he had the cicatrices of the fully initiated aboriginal—an unusual circumstance for the half-caste, as Tracker Leon was. Tracker Leon was widely read and informed, and spoke with a wisdom about nature and tracking that no one could match. He was conservative by nature and somewhat stilted in speech, as Bony was to develop in his books.

The first time Upfield met Tracker Leon he worked with him for five months at a cattle station on the Darling River. Hawkes' dates for the two meetings are somewhat confusing. But Upfield met Tracker Leon a second time after a long separation and after his return from England. Upfield had finished a version of his first novel, *The Barrakee Mystery,* a mystery novel starring a white detective. On this second encounter with Tracker Leon, Upfield exchanged several books with the famous tracker, one of which was Abbot's *Life of Napoleon Bonaparte.* With a stroke of inspiration, as Tracker Leon departed with his borrowed books, Upfield realized that he should change his white detective to one based on Tracker Leon and he should be named Napoleon Bonaparte. It would not be an unusual name in Australia where Aboriginals had all kinds of Classical, biblical and literary names— Nero, Pontius Pilate, Sir Galahad, for example. And a detective based on Tracker Leon would be entirely new and novel and would further Upfield's desire to be as Australian as possible in his books.

So Upfield discarded the second version of his first novel and rewrote it with Tracker Leon recreated as the Detective-Inspector Napoleon Bonaparte, and in so doing created one of the three or four outstanding operatives of all crime fiction.

Tracker Leon's real origins seem to have been those that Upfield altered only slightly for his detective. In what seems to be the true account, Tracker Leon was a half-caste born in North Queensland, possibly the son of the owner of the cattle station on which Upfield worked when he first met Tracker Leon. Tracker Leon had been found with his dead mother under a sandalwood tree, his mother, apparently, having been killed by her people for breaking the law against copulation with the whites. The child had been taken to a nearby mission, where the matron adopted him as her own. At school he had shown intellectual promise and had been sent to High School, and later was on the force of the Queensland Police Department as a gifted tracker.

Bony gives virtually the same account of his own origin in Upfield's books, sometimes with less detail and sometimes with slightly different ones. Although it differs little from that given for Tracker Leon, it should be quoted in its entirety, from the version given in *The Battling Prophet* (99):

> I was found beneath a sandalwood tree, found in the arms of my mother, who had been clubbed to death for breaking a law. Subsequently, the matron of the Mission Station to which I was taken and reared found me eating the pages of Abbott's *Life of Napoleon Bonaparte*. The matron possessed a peculiar sense of humour. The result—my name. Despite the humour, she was a great woman. Aware of the burden of birth I would always have to carry, she built for me the foundations of my career. My entry to the Queensland Police Department came about after I had won my M. S. at Brisbane University, and my progress in the Department has been due to the fortunate fact that the Commissioner abhors failure in anyone....

This account needs to be supplemented with another important aspect of the events which shaped his life given in *Wings Above the Diamantina*, (53) and sometimes touched upon in other books.

After Bony's graduation from Brisbane University with his Master of Science degree,

> then occurred a grave disappointment in love that sent him back to the bush. For a year he ran wild among the natives of his mother's tribe, and during that year he learned as much bushcraft as he would have done had he never been back to school and to the city.

After this broken heart Bony came back to civilization, married a very understanding and wonderful wife, a half-caste like himself, and subsequently had two or three boys, depending on the story being read, who becoming successes, one in the footsteps of his father, the others in entirely different vocations.

In most books, Upfield does not mention how Bony rose to power in the police force except to say that it was by his exceptional genius. At other times, Bony gives in some detail the full background of his birth, his being found, the details of his life immediately after his schooling, how he had an unfortunate love affair and returned to the bush for a year in order to heal a broken heart, and other details before he went into police work. No matter what the sections included or excluded, Bony, it is clear from his comments and from Upfield's details, was an unusual person, born to achieve great results in a world somewhat alien and mad, and that his accomplishments were directly the result of his parentage, which gave him the best qualities of both races. Common to all descriptions of his birth and youth is the fact that he was discovered "under a sandalwood tree," as though there is some magic to that particular kind of tree, although no authority on the flora and fauna of Australian Aboriginal life notes that quality.

Upfield make several efforts throughout his books to explain his detective-inspector's name. In all directions his efforts are somewhat droll and a little fanciful. In one instance he says that the Matron who found him under the sandalwood tree later found him devouring Abbot's *Life of Napoleon Bonaparte* and thus thought it appropriate to name him after the general. In another case, Bony said that as a child he was skinny, and therefore was named "Bony." In many books he did not bother to explain the name. In the first book that followed his determination to name his detective-Inspector Napoleon Bonaparte, always to be called by the D-I's friends, the readers of the books, and all others, "Bony," Upfield carried on the charade about justifying the name Napoleon Bonaparte with a cloying hero-worship that formed a bond between Bony and the lady of the book. Thereafter in later books, although Bony occasionally made remarks about how much he admired the general after whom he had been named for his insistence on law and order, his respect for time, and even his promise of a true democracy in the world, the hero worship, thankfully, was kept at a minimum.

In some ways Bony in addition to being a super-human is also a "godlike" human being, as he should be in a series of books about heroes that achieve cosmic proportions. He prefers crimes that are somewhat old. Time, as he says in a dozen different ways, is an ally. Crimes must be solved slowly, in rhythm with nature. Further, Bony does not like to witness violence; and Upfield does not portray much crime in action. Most of his is done offstage or was committed in the past.

Bony is not a severe god. Generally he does not particularly care whether criminals are punished for their actions. Like Sherlock Holmes before him, Bony likes to solve crimes because they provide him with mental exercise. But he differs from Sherlock Holmes in the degree that he takes the disposition of justice into his own hands. Holmes frequently acts as jury and judge; only once does Bony act as judge and dismiss the criminal, wishing her a happy future. In one book, on the other hand, like a god Bony is vengeful and determined that he exact capital punishment for the offence committed.

As "god," Bony is heroic. He quite freely admits that once he has accepted a mission to solve a crime there is no crime that he cannot solve. He is the best tracker in Australia, best at reading the Book of the Bush, as he calls the natural world around him, and best at solving mysteries. He is a Bush "god." He will not accept an assignment in the city because that is not where his strength lies; as he says in *The Battling Prophet* (145) his talents would be wasted there. Upfield, in this characteristic of Bony, was only following common practice in Australia. Aborigines have not been used in urban areas of Australia as trackers because they invariably become bewildered in the world of concrete and close buildings— their forte lies in the wind-swept open spaces. There they are incomparable. Their eyes are so sharp and fast that they can in fact track people through the bush from a helicopter, and are increasingly being called upon to demonstrate their skill from above the trees in helicopters. Though Bony freely admits his superiority and infallibility, the characters in the books, and most readers of these books are not offended by his seeming arrogance, for Bony always makes his claims matter-of-factly, with seeming modesty, and with a smiling and ingratiating manner. Once, in fact, though in a somewhat different context, Bony admits, "I'm no hero" (*Bony and the White Savage*, 154). But he of course, *is* a hero.

The force that drives Bony is his zeal for perfection and for solving crimes is pride. There are needs for his pride. Physically, of course, he looks like his ancestry. He is somewhat underheight for a white. He is dark and he has the curse on him of being half-caste. As Upfield says in *The Widows of Frome* (97) "his aboriginal half was much stronger than the white ancestry in his make-up. But he was as open to victimization as a full blood," a charge which Rex, the half-caste heir to a cattle station in *Bushrangers of the Skies* was to confirm through his determination to conquer the white world or destroy it. Unlike Rex's hatred, Bony's rod and staff against the world is Pride, generally capitalized in his usage. This pride comes to Bony through dignity, and only through dignity can he always solve his cases. As Upfield says in *The Mountains Have a Secret* Bony's failure in any case would dethrone Pride, and nothing would be left to prop him up. As Bony admits in *The Widows of Broome*, he could not fail: If he were to fail he would be ruined:

My career will be ended, for my pride will have been destroyed. If I fail in this case the pride which drove me on and up to the summits of many Everests of such achievement will vanish, and all the influences so powerfully and continuously exerted on me by my maternal ancestors will inevitably draw me back to the bush, to become as so many others like me, a nomad, a pariah.

Little wonder that Bony is the vainest of men: his accomplishments are great; his reliance on those accomplishments monumental.

The world in which Upfield works is different from that of other detective writers. It is different from America in being a society that is generally less violent though just as down-to-earth and realistic. Upfield is more richly and more directly concerned with the physical and natural background of the country he is writing about than other detective fiction authors who write about other countries: any of the English; George Simenon about France; Wahloo and Sjowall and their stories about Sweden; H.F.R. Keating and his rich stories about India; Robert Van Gulik and his tales about Judge Dee in Classical China; and Elspeth Huxley and her proving studies of crime in Africa. Those people are more concerned in the conventional way with people and social justice. In other words, theirs are books about *social* crime. Upfield's are different; they are stories about affronts to nature, both physical and human.

Upfield does not write about the affronts to nature always sure of where he and Bony stand. Bony, Upfield is sure, does not wear his mixed race indifferently. Always aware of it, he is generally aided by his mixed blood, since it is the strength, or at least one side of it, by which he achieves his accomplishments. Without his mixed heritage he would not be the strong and superior individual he is.

But Upfield, for his part, is as unsure of his praise for the white race as Bony is. Sometimes Upfield editorializes within the content of the novels with extreme irony and bitterness on the shortcomings of the whites as a race and as a group of people who conquered and settled Australia. At best these people have only a thin veneer of civilization and superiority over the Aboriginals, a veneer that can easily be penetrated, releasing the primitive forces of a civilization much older and much superior to that of the White settlers of Australia. Bony, for his part, is always feeling the warring surges battling in his body for primacy. At its extreme, generally against which Bony battles successfully, the call of the wild reveals a Bony that is red in tooth and claw.

In *The Mountains Have a Secret* (93-4) Upfield reveals the return, though temporarily, of Bony into the Aboriginal state.

> The highly civilised Inspector Bonaparte was retreating before the incoming primitive Hunter. The dapper, suave, and almost pedantic producer of modern education and social intercourse, which is but a veneer laid upon the ego of modern man, was now being melted away from this often tragic figure, in whom ever warred the influence of two races.

It was a question of time:

> Hitherto, Bonaparte had not wholly surrendered himself to his mother's racial instincts, the great weapon of pride winning for himself the battle. He would not wholly surrender himself on this occasion, but he did give himself in part because of the conditions which would govern his life for the next days or weeks, and because of the probable forces with which he would have to content.

Driven to great extremes, Bony is unable to avoid surrendering himself fully and completely to the aboriginal instincts. Release of himself to the aboriginal state takes several forms. One is to surrender to the attraction of the Aboriginal tribes to nakedness. In their natural state, they believed in complete nakedness, to the freedom and comfort and naturalness of such a state. In extreme circumstances Bony reverts to the nakedness of complete primitivism also. In *The Mystery of Swordfish Reef*, (244-5) while being somewhat out of his element of security by being in a boat on the ocean Bony is driven to an extreme. He releases himself from his prison below decks, removes his clothes and greases himself with oil, then viciously attacks the man who had put him in the compromised position below decks and savagely subdues him. It was only then that Bony "recalled to his educational attainments, his professional rank, and his pride in his father's race. He was overwhelmed by a flood of shame that had nothing to do with his nakedness," which was bad enough, but with his loss of control and his reversion to the savage state, Bony's pride in accomplishment and success in his mission "had been spoiled by [his] own extraordinary exhibition of loss of personal control." This loss proved that despite his many other accomplishments, Bony is still "a savage." It is as Upfield has been saying all along: the Aboriginal is never far from and is ultimately inseparable from his original state.

Bony is a savage in other ways also. In *Bushranger of the Skies*, (4) when from his church-like seat among the cabbage trees Bony sees the man in the plane bomb the inhabitants of the car, he reverts to his natural self. He reveals his white teeth in "what was almost an animal snarl of fury." And a little later when he starts to fight with the Aborigines sent by the murdering pilot to make sure that the passengers in the car are dead, Bony

glowed with exquisite fire, for circumstances had temporarily removed the chains of civilized restraints from a nature in which hereditary influences constantly stirred.

Generally, this primitive stirring increased Bony's strength and made him a roaring savage. Sometimes, however, it could be debilitating, turning the otherwise strong Bony into a flesh form unable to stand without the support of internal power. In *The Bone is Pointed*, for example, Bony is attacked by his supernatural fear of the efficacy of voodoo of the bone pointing and becomes spiritually and physically a coil of inertia unable to fight against the apparent inevitable. In *The Mountains Have a Secret* (114) this primitive fear is made very clear in a description of Bony's terror of the dead:

One of Bony's burdens, and not the least, was fear of the dead, fear which, during his career of crime investigations, had often leaped from the subconscious to gibber at him, reminding him of the ancient race from which he would never wholly escape.

Somewhat later (124) the affliction is described at greater length:

Without conscious volition Bony's feet turned away from the horror. His body became as iron to the magnet of the pure night, so that with his hands he was obliged, without being conscious of it, to grasp projections of the rocky corner that he might continue to watch. A thousand demons came to tug him away. The electrical impulses which had been playing up and down his neck became needles of ice lodged into the base of his skull. Instincts became sentient beings that warred about him and for him. The fear of the dead was like an octopus wrapping its tentacles about his brain, compressing it into a pin-head of matter in the centre of a vast and otherwise empty skull.

In this reversion to the savage state Bony became an upright shaft of aboriginal fury. He had to capitulate to a stronger urge than he was able to master at the moment, though he always managed to cerebrate about it and through this cerebration to overcome it. But he was unique among Aboriginals, at least in the opinions of some whites. In *Wings Over the Diamantina*, (114) for example, two whites, both sympathetic to Aboriginal society and to the plight of the half-castes in particular, are discussing the future of the people who have to straddle two civilizations. One white asks how many half-castes could reach Bony's accomplishments, and the other responds that many could if they wanted to, but they don't want to. Unable to overcome the inertia they are afflicted with or they do not find the white civilization attractive enough:

The bush generally gets 'em in the end. You take a black or a half-caste and you put him in college or teach him a trade, but the time surely comes when he leaves it all to bolt back to the bush. They can't long resist the urge to go on walkabout.

Perhaps this sentiment represents Upfield's. It is the kind of statement which nowadays prompt Aborigines to ban his books. But he is not content to let the matter rest there. In several instances in later books, he writes of people, especially young ladies, *lubras* in the Aboriginal tongue, who leave their tribes and spend time with and in white families. But, so strong is Upfield's feeling about the wrongs that the whites have done to the Aboriginals and so deep his disgust at the veneer of civilization that he so deeply hates, he allows the women to "escape" the white civilization and go back to their original state, despite the fact that Bony constantly harps on the realization that the white's lifestyle is the life for him. Upfield's position, which must have been deep-felt, was obviously not a comfortable stance for him. But his fate was to swing back and forth between the races.

Bony looks upon himself as a biological bridge between the two races. In *The Will of the Tribe* (68) there is a poignant situation where two Aborigines, a young man and a young woman, are trying to be assimilated into a white household. Tessa, the woman, has adopted nearly all the lifestyle of the whites; the young man, called Capt., has adopted fewer. In talking to Tessa of her situation and potential, Bony discusses his own situation and hers:

> You know, there have been situations in my career when I've found myself acting as a kind of bridge spanning the gulf between the Aboriginal and the white mind. If you realise your ambition you might well build a far stronger bridge, because you are thinking as a white woman...I am only half black, and yet I, too, have felt the pull towards my mother's race.

In another novel, *Sinister Stones* (84), Bony elaborates on the bridge metaphor.

> It takes years of association and study to reach even the middle of the bridge spanning the gulf between them and us. Be patient. A thousand years are as nothing in this timeless land, and when the last aboriginal sinks down to die, despite the veneer imposed on him by our civilisation, he will be the same man as were his forebears ten thousand years ago.

The bridge between the two races, especially himself, is fortunate and unique. In *The Bachelors of Broken Hill* (15) Bony comments on his position:

> I am unique because I stand midway between the white and black races, having all the virtues of the white race and very few vices of the black race. I have mastered the art of taking pains, and I was born with the gift of observation. I never hurry in my hunt for a murderer, but I never delay my approach.

Using Time as an ally, indeed as an indispensable part of his detecting paraphernalia, as Bony says time after time, was another result of his inheritance from his mother, among with his keen tracking sense. As Upfield says in *Bony and the Mouse,*

> Much of the cat's psychology had been bequeathed to Inspector Bonaparte by his aboriginal mother, a member of a race which down the ladder of the centuries has had to cultivate feline patience if it were to survive. (116)

But the result of the mixture of the races created both a bridge between the races and an individual superman. In a kind of seeming swagger that is still not at all offensive, in *Murder Must Wait* (175), Bony says flat-out, "I am the Bridge built by a white man and a black woman to span the gulf dividing two races" and even more interestingly in *Bony and the Black Virgin,* (79) he asserts, "Kipling was wrong... The East and the West meet in me."

The bridge was extended through a TV series produced by the Australian producer/actor John McCallum and his company, Fauna Productions. Joe Kovess, an Australian authority on Upfield, who is now writing a biography on Upfield, recounts the circumstances and fate of the film.

The "Boney" series was Fauna Production's first all-color TV series. Finding an actor to play Bony was not easy. An extensive search was made to find a Aboriginal to play the part, but none was found. Then a compromise was sought in an Australian white for the role. Finally the search was completed in England, when a British actor, James Laurenson, was chosen. He apparently was a happy choice. Though he was white and British he fitted into the role precisely. Once, for example, in Alice Springs when

Laurenson was made up for the role, he and McCallum went to a bakery to buy bread for the actors, and the aboriginal girl behind the counter asked Laurenson to make his mark as receipt for the purchase! Again, when they were miles out in the desert, a full-blood Aborigine approached Laurenson and asked him what tribe he was from! A director could hardly have more spontaneous and more convincing proof of seeming authenticity!

Financing the series was a large problem. American investors would not put their money in because, at least as Kovess interprets the action, they did not like the idea of a black man playing the lead. We can only hope that other considerations, such as hour-long scheduling in those days, were paramount. Anyway, the budget for the series came to a million and a half dollars, financed by Channel 7 Network of Australia, Global Television in London and ZDF Television, Germany. Locations used were Alice Springs, Central Australia, Flinders Ranges, South Australia, the coast of the New South Wales north of Newcastle and central New South Wales.

The series was first aired in Australia in July 1972 and was last seen in November 1981. The series enjoyed great success in both England and Germany. It was not successfully marketed in the U. S. The reason may have been simply a misreading of the market by American broadcasters. According to McCallum in his book *Life with Googie*:

Whenever we showed an audition print to distributors (in the U.S.) they asked: 'Where are his guns?' They cannot understand an outback series without guns.

With the great interest in Australia and pioneer lifestyle current in the United States in the 1980s it is obviously time for another effort to have the series aired here.

Laurenson won the "Logie," the top Australian television award, for the Best Individual Acting Performance of the Year for 1972 in *Boney Meets the Daybreak Killer* ( *Bony and the Mouse/ Journey to the Hangman*), with a script written by the Australian writer, Frank Hardy, who also received the "Logie" for the Best Script-Writer. During the 1970s the Boney series was the only

Australian production to be awarded the number one rating in a foreign country (Scotland).

The TV series spelled Bony's name *Boney*. In a letter to Joe Kovess, McCallum explained:

We titled the Boney TV series 'Boney' because a) the public would have pronounced it 'Bonny' if it was spelt Bony, and b) because Upfield intended to spell it 'Boney' but a misprint in his first book where it was spelled Bony throughout forced him to stay with the spelling of Bony.

The series is still not available in the U.S. McCallum's agent in New York has a copy of the series but will not lend it out, and individuals cannot bring copies in from Australia without paying an exorbitant import fee.

Upfield's effort at bridge-building—at least hands across the sea—in this medium seems destined for further frustration. And the bridge in Australia seems not to have been sufficiently strong to carry the Australian traffic from one side to the other. In today's Australia the two societies do not meet in harmony all the time. The degree to which the chasm has been spanned depends somewhat on the person asked—Aboriginal or white, liberal or conservative. Upfield's place in the history of the rapprochment may not have been finally established in the conflict between the whites and the Aboriginals. Some Australian academics, such as novelists Peter Coriss and Hosanna Brown, feel that very little has been achieved. The Aboriginals have their own Parliament now, to be sure, but it is only a "shadow" parliament without power and effect, and Aboriginals still face the condescension and discrimination of the whites. They are still strangers in their own land.

Anthropologists, on the contrary, report that the prejudice against Australian Aboriginals is dying out and that Aborigines and white Australians increasingly are joining groups to proudly call themselves "Australian." Still, much truth lies in each extreme position, or where truth does lie, seems at this time moot. No doubt anthropologists have for their own purposes insisted that Aboriginals, who represent Australian history back 35,000-45,000 years, constitute a national treasure in anthropology and cultural history at least. But most people who live under the gun are not content to be anthropological and historical treasures.

Upfield, though he is the center of the storm did not willfully stir it up. Open-minded and thoughtful readers of Upfield's books understand that he always treated the Aboriginals with extreme sensitivity and sympathy. The books had to reflect reality as the author saw it, otherwise they would do more harm than good. To fight back the prejudice of his reading public, to declare Bony the bridge between the two races and to demonstrate causes and effects of the prejudices were goals that Upfield sought—and achieved. His success was considerable. He is today gaining in readership in Australia, in the United States, which awarded him his first reading public, and in Britain.

Upfield sometimes described the aborigines as somewhat fallen from their former glory—a fate that James Fenimore Cooper noted in the American Indians in his Upstate New York country, and numerous Anglo-Saxon authors have noted for the American Aboriginal race in general—but he never failed to point out the heroic nature of their past and present, with the implication of a heroic future. The direction his heart pointed was never in doubt. How can one fault an author who reveals his philosophy in calling the aborigines "a race remarkable for its morality, its justice, its freedom from greed," or who asserts that he knows "an aboriginal head man who might have skipped five thousand years to come down to this age"?

But reality and realism sometimes are not understood and accepted. Upfield's fate seems to have been crueler than perhaps even he, in his most cynical moments, could have anticipated. Upfield has not fared well among the Australian Aboriginals he did so much for, and their present-day sympathizers

Joe Kovess, a well-informed Australian deeply interested in Upfield's career, in a letter to Philip Asdell, reported that in a conversation with a member of the Department of Aboriginal Studies at Monash University, Melbourne, he was informed that Upfield had been declared off-limits to Aboriginal readers ( *Bony Bulletin* ).

All of Upfield's novels were withdrawn from school libraries about 10 years ago. While he presented Aboriginals in a favorable light at a time when they were considered to be inferior to whites, Upfield is now considered to have been guilty of stereotyping mental traits when he says that Bony has 'inherited the white man's ability to reason more clearly and more quickly than Aboriginals' and that 'once an Aboriginal is thoroughly aroused he is a terrible person.' Hence the bad points outweighed the good points, so Bony had to go.

Upfield's is not a name to be found in the liberal Australian literature about the Aboriginals, though his works have for years been used in the United States in some colleges and universities in classes in anthropology. Prof. Ernest Hooten of Harvard once called Upfield "a shrewd anthropological observer as well as a skilled novelist."

Upfield's fate in Australia is the price that art and anthropology must pay to the raw nerves of an awakened and outraged people. But the act of condemning and censoring Upfield for not writing with a vision of the future seems shortsighted and unwise, as well as anachronistic. His books were not science fiction, not visionary, not utopian. They were realistic and accurate depictions of the Australia of his day—of the people, the ways of life, of attitudes and mores.

Unfortunately Upfield's fate with some people in Australia parallels that of Mark Twain with his *Adventures of Huckleberry Finn* in the United States. Mark Twain's story of a heroic black and a heroic white-trash boy in antebellum America was subjected from the beginning to censorship and misunderstanding. At first the book was denied space on library shelves because the subject matter was mean, trashy and unworthy of being written about. Lately it has been in a continuous fight with many American blacks and liberal whites over the way it depicts Jim, the black man, as being illiterate and having to live in a white world where he was stereotyped. Some readers of this book, which American novelist Ernest Hemingway once called the fount and source of all American literature, will not take it for what it was and is. Perhaps that is the course of the great and seminal books. Maybe that is the fate of Upfield's books also. His and Mark Twain's works must wait for time to catch up with them. But meanwhile some readers— those who boycott the books—suffer from having these works censored out of existence, thus blotting out a part of their heritage and literary rights. One can only hope that the abused peoples in both countries will come to understand that their feelings, quite well understood, are doing them a disservice. Art cannot be condemned for not doing what it never intended to do. There must be a better way to address old wrongs than to erase them out of history. The common wisdom these days is that one must know history or will be condemned to relive it. That observation is sound, but stops short of the full observation. The axiom should be that one must *understand* history or be condemned to be tyrannized by it. A people's past can be a chain to hold them back or a catapult to shoot them forward. In order to know where one is going, it is imperative to know where one has been and the forces that drive forward. Such wisdom does not flourish in the world of half-information. The whole story is necessary.

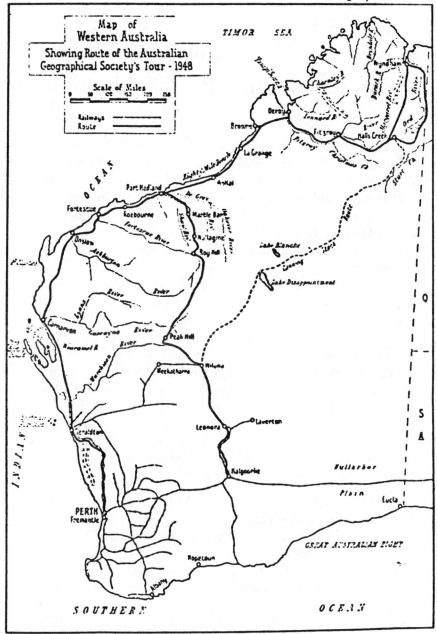

The tour was led by Upfield

# Chapter 2
# Physical Setting, Plot, Evaluation

Upfield's books, although ostensibly crime fiction, are really about mankind on the land, about strife between individuals and the battle between mankind—both whites and Aboriginals, male and female—and nature. They are crime novels in settings of violence. They describe the tension that results from the imposition of mankind on the land, and they include graphic descriptions of the flora and fauna, the landscapes and geology, the meteorology, the symbols of nature and the people and the way they live, talk, eat and act in the presence of a strong nature. One learns a lot about Australia the country from reading Upfield's novels. His books are, in fact, a basic course in Australiana.

Upfield, of course, took his backgrounding seriously. He felt the importance of giving a complete and graphic setting before starting the story. As he said in an article which appeared in the *Bermagui Big Game Anglers' Club Annual Magazine* for 1938-39 (and reprinted in *The Bony Bulletin*, No. 20, Feb. 1987):

> A background brilliantly drawn cannot be achieved by an author unless and until he has become soaked, like blotting paper in ink, in the background before which he intends that his characters shall play.

Once this background had been sketched and oiled, then Upfield felt ready to activate his characters.

Animals are, of course, important in Australian life and in Upfield's novels. He mentions at least twenty-four types, including the dog, the horse, cow, kangaroo, rabbit and sheep. According to Philip Asdell, who counted them, there are forty-one types of birds, including Upfield's favorite, the crow, and chickens, eagles, galahs and cockatoos. There are seventeen types of insects, including

48

the fly, ant, blowfly and mosquito. Reptiles appear in seven books, with the lizard in five, the iguana in three, and the goanna in two. There are sixteen types of fish. The frog, an amphibian, appears in five books.

But of far greater importance in Upfield's books are the landscapes and the weather. It cannot be overemphasized how important the land and the weather are in Upfield's works. Physical conditions are integral; sometimes they are in virtual control. Geographically Upfield covers every area of the Australian continent except the tropical areas just around Darwin, the whole of the Northern Territory and Tasmania. There are five novels based in the deserts of Western Australia, one situated north of Perth, one south of Perth and two in the edge of the Nullarbor Plain at the corner of the state of Western Australia where it meets South Australia. There are five novels placed in South Australia, two in Queensland, and sixteen in New South Wales, mostly in the interior. Of these, two are on the Murray River, three are on or near the Darling River. The location of one is not known. At the very beginning of most of his novels, Upfield describes the geographical setting and points out its starkness and force which are going to influence or control the events of the novel. Generally it is a grim locale, one to test the very strongest representative of mankind.

Often the actual sites from which Upfield's fictional locations are derived can be established. Philip T. Asdell, editor of the *Bony Bulletin*, has located most of them. Where he has established the location or tentatively identified it, we will follow his discussion in this coverage of the geographical locale, and will include his maps because the Australian outback is largely unknown to people outside Australia and because the setting of the stories is indispensable to the development and full impact of the stories.

Theoretically Bony's head office is in Brisbane. He lives, as he says in *The Barrakee Mystery* with his wife and three sons "on a ten-acre block of 'tea-tree' scrub" in Banyo, seven miles away from the heart of Brisbane. In the books Bony occasionally returns to the city to get new orders and infrequently pays visits to Sydney, Perth and other cities, generally being called there officially or going to spend vacations. He attended the University of Brisbane, getting an undergraduate and a Masters degree there, and throughout the books his three sons—he and his wife have no daughter—are attending the same university or have just graduated from it. His wife apparently did not go to college. She—called Laura in *The Barrakee Mystery* but Marie thereafter—is a half-caste like Bony, and he never mentions whether she is happy in her urban setting or would prefer to be back in the bush. Bony nearly always operates in the bush or in small towns. In two novels he works just outside Melbourne.

But like the settings of the novels, Bony's beat is the bush, the outback, because he is at home there and is assured of success while working there. In this development, as in nearly all of his books, Upfield is following reality. Aborigines are still used in the outback today for tracking, as they have been throughout the history of the Europeans' settlement in Australia, because they are unexcelled in the outback in tracking. In the city their skills would not be effective.

The Aboriginals' skill in tracking constitutes the very core of Upfield's detection in the novels, or at least *his* skill which resulted from his being half-caste. Bony says in a dozen places how skillful Aboriginals are in their inborn and natural ability. Though Upfield is technically accurate in describing their skill as natural, it is in fact not so much natural as taught. This skill, as discussed in A. W. Reed's *An Illustrated Encyclopedia of Aboriginal Life*, as reported by Philip Asdell in *The Bony Bulletin* (No. 15), is the accumulation of years of training of the young Aboriginals by their elders. They are deeply and systematically instructed in all aspects of tracking until it becomes second nature.

Australia contains some of the oldest land on earth. Therefore it has had an uncommonly long time to be eroded by water, sand and wind. Situating his novels in locales throughout Australia, Upfield is able to take advantage of the unsurpassed great variety in landscape and weather that the continent affords, and to pit his people in and against strikingly differing geographical, geological and meteorological landscapes. He makes weather, landscape and geology key players in his dramas. They are introduced almost immediately in each novel. Then having drawn in great detail the physical setting for the events to follow, almost without exception Upfield always asks immediately after beginning to investigate the crime what the weather conditions were at the time of the event: was it raining, windy, had it rained since the event? The whole physical activity of tracking turns to a certain degree on answers to these questions. The settings and plots need to be outlined.

*The House of Cain.* Published: Hutchinson, 1926; Dorrance, 1929; released, Dennis McMillan, 1983.

The locale of most of the action of this novel is Quinyambie Station, some 200 miles north of Broken Hill in the northwest corner of New South Wales, the same general locale Upfield was to use in his last novel, *The Lake Frome Monster.*

In this first novel Upfield published, Upfield has not quite sorted out the role that nature is going to play in his works. He has not made up his mind whether the outback Australian landscape and meteorology are going to be adversarial terrors that man has to break in order to survive or mere physical phenomena which might be brought round to being assets or at least can be overcome. As Upfield has a giant outbacker named Squeezem Harry say, in his devil-may-care *carpe diem* attitude: "Here's joy today, and to hell with to-morrow," whose motto, according to Upfield,

perhaps, that of ninety-nine bushmen out of every hundred; for the bush is a kind mother, and who live within her bosom are kind people. (89)

But the physical Australia in this book is not the kind mother Upfield declares her to be. She is almost too much to cope with.

The novel begins in Melbourne. Martin Sherwood, a noted newspaper man, is about to marry his love, Austilene Thorpe. But a notorious blackmailer is found murdered in her hotel room. Martin goes blind with a brain fever caused by Austilene being jailed for the murder. Austilene is rescued from jail by someone but does not surface and return to her lover and society even though a dying man confesses to having done the murder. Monty, Martin's brother, learns that Austilene has been taken to a luxurious sanctuary for murderers, called "The House of Cain" because it is supposedly

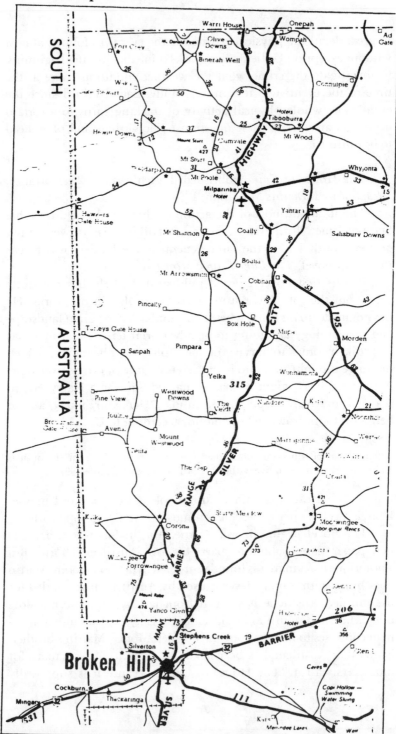

Setting of *The House of Cain, The Sands of Windee, Winds of Evil,* and *The Lake Frome Monster*

a refuge for persons who have killed their "brothers." It is financed
and run by a man named Anchor, a millionaire who has poisoned
three wives, and for his own purposes likes to have freed and
pardoned murderers around him.

The scene switches to the South Australian Border Fence on
Quinyambie Station, north of Lake Frome, in the northwest corner
of New South Wales, apparently west of the present town of
Tibooburra which is on the Silver City highway. Upfield makes
it clear that he is talking about the northwest corner of New South
Wales, some 200 miles north of Broken Hill; Broken Hill was the
city that convinced Upfield in 1910 that he loved Australia. He
worked in this area in 1927, a year or so after *The House of Cain*
was published, and may have known it earlier.

The weather in the outback is palpable, as Martin, though
blind, and Monty set out to rescue Austilene. They find their travels
"a veritable nightmare of prolonged, disjointed fatigue."

In "Silver City," the place they use as a jumping-off point
for their rescue mission, the shade temperature rises to 106 degrees
at three in the afternoon. At Quinyambie Station, in February, the
mercury soars to 118 degrees in the shade, when shade can be found.
The sun "blistered red-raw" a person's hands and neck. The flies
hummed so loud that "hearing was a hardship and speaking a
labour." A sand-storm that raged for eighteen hours made it
"impossible to eat or smoke, or indeed to sleep." The ground was
so hot that camels, with their rubbery padded feet refused "to move
from the shade of a tree." (93-94) Little wonder that Upfield felt
he had met a physical adversary that it would be difficult to
overcome.

The House of Cain consists of a large rambling structure,
painted light brown, surrounded by numerous smaller houses or
cottages. All are covered with corrugated iron roofs, and all are
surrounded by a six-foot partly-netted fence.

Anchor, the murderer who runs this refuge, falls in love with
Austilene and forces her to stay with him. To protect Martin, whom
she still loves, she dissembles her love when he and Monty get
in touch with her and let it be known that they are coming to
rescue her. Despite her pleas for the two to leave her and to save

themselves, Monty, through his heroic physique and irrepressible spirits and skills, wins Austilene's release, and she and Martin, who miraculously regains his eyesight, are reunited. Monty himself gets married. And presumably all live happily ever after.

This work is surely by no means an embarrassing plot. The idea of using the Australian outback as the locale for a novel of reclusive criminals forecasts Upfield's later interest. The landscape and meteorology are well developed. The intensity of the Australian outback, to be much more powerfully developed later, is nearly overwhelming here. The effect of the weather on the people is well developed.

But the character development of this first novel is weaker than it will be subsequently. The lead characters are too much of themselves. Martin Sherwood is unlike any person who has ever lived. Austilene floats through the air at least six inches above ground. Monty, Martin's rescuing brother, is a caricature of the hero. He is "power, cleanness, dependability, all compacted in one human form." (17) He is generally referred to as "the big man." There is too much of him too close to the reader. He is too jaunty, too happy, too resourceful—too everything. The reader comes to hope that he will be punched in the face. But he isn't. The wicked characters are generally too wicked—their evil drips too much about them.

Stylistically the novel is overdone, as this passage about Austilene, which shows also Upfield's early weakness at picturing women, reveals:

> She stood, a beautiful and gracious woman, in her becoming dressing-gown, which accentuated the soft curves of her figure and cried her femininity at him. Over each shoulder hung a rope of hair, glinting as antique copper in the light. Through narrowed eyelids Anchor regarded her. Had his spotted soul not already belonged to Satan, he would willingly have sold it for the love of such a woman.

Despite the weaknesses of the style and of characterization, however, the book demonstrates a power that Upfield was to develop almost immediately and which was to mature into some of the strongest crime novels available.

*The Barrakee Mystery*. Published: Hutchinson, 1928; released, Heinemann, 1969. Issued in America as *The Lure of the Bush*, Doubleday, 1965.

This was Upfield's first novel but he had difficulty finishing it and when he finally completed it he had already published *The House of Cain*. Dissatisfied with the first draft of *The Barrakee Mystery*, Upfield set it aside, then rewrote it with a white detective as the protagonist. Having laid this version aside, Upfield had his second meeting with Tracker Leon Wood, the half-caste with whom he had worked earlier, and rewrote the novel a third time with the white detective changed to Detective-Inspector Napoleon Bonaparte, a half-caste based very closely on Tracker Leon.

The landscape is the land around the Darling River, west New South Wales, during the time of the year, March, when it is low and slow-moving but just before an impending flood. Philip Asdell, as he searches out the exact locations and models for Upfield's plots, says that Upfield's information gives us a precise location for *The Barrakee Mystery* which is 60 miles upstream from Wilcannia, a few miles southwest of the real town of Tilpa. This area was first discovered by Charles Sturt in 1829. Asdell insists that Upfield's description of the Darling River and surrounding landscape is accurate, as indeed it should be, since this country was familiar to Upfield. It was along this route, and through Wilcannia, that Upfield had traveled in 1910 when he made his first trip from Adelaide to Momba Station, when at Broken Hill, he fell in love with Australia. Tilpa, Asdell reminds us,

was the scene of the famous incident when Upfield was arrested for having no visible means of support (his wealth of 80 pounds was hidden in the tires of his pedal-less bicycle) and put to work painting the police station.

That was the incident he later used in good stead in *Death of a Swagman*. It was along the Darling that Upfield once sold his bike and went on a sailing trip with another wanderer named "Paroo Ted," and also along the Darling that he first met Angus and his wife Mary, both of whom, but Mary especially, influenced him to give up his wandering and turn to writing.

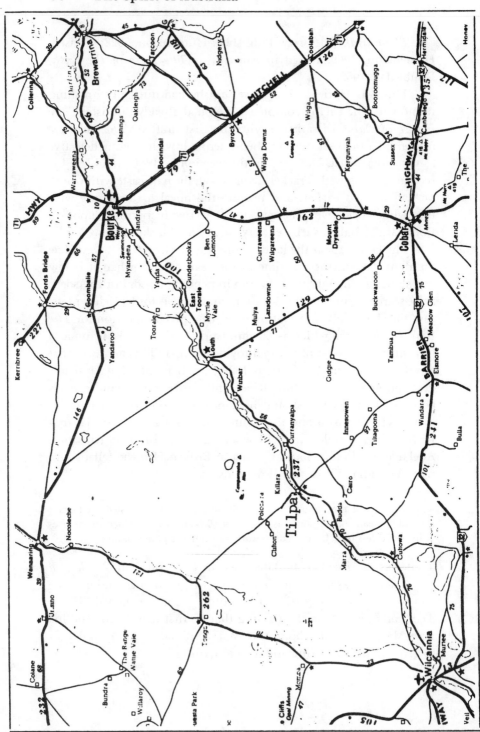

It is near the Darling River that King Henry, one of the pivotal figures in the drama, is killed, and nature in the form of a bolt of lighting and a rain that washes away all tracks approves the pact of silence among the people who committed or witnessed the deed. The river, in a leit-motif, provides the setting where the momentous events occur, and like a kind of *deus ex machina* it is the threat of floodstage that hangs over the story and which serves as the instrument which resolves the tension and solves the mystery.

To attempt to solve the mystery, Bony gets himself a job painting boats so that he can unobtrusively examine the goings-on of the whites and Aboriginals on the station. Despite the heavy rain that fell during the night of the murder, Bony finds a footprint at the scene of the crime. He identifies a boomerang scar on a tree, and reveals a great deal of boomerang physics and lore. As a matter of fact, Upfield had recognized when he was planning on writing detective novels about Australia that such things as the boomerang provided new and fascinating lore for the Australian who did not know the outback, and the non-Australian in general. Hawke (167) recorded what must have been his thoughts:

> Did a boomerang in flight contact a tree trunk, and did the weapon have a number of identifications on the sharp edge, denoting the tribe of the thrower, then the mark or scar on the trunk would reveal the weapon that had caused it, and also reveal the tribe of the man who had thrown it.

Upfield, through Bony, uses his knowledge very effectively in this his first Bony novel.

As he gets more and more involved in the family affairs of the rich of the station, Bony realizes how much a child had meant to John Thornton's wife, a gracious, delicate woman who agreed with Bony that the French general Napoleon Bonaparte had been a great general and a great man. Bony learns also just how much an assumed marriage between this couple's nineteen-year-old son Ralph and their orphaned niece Katherine means to the older couple. It is therefore all the more heart-breaking when as the story develops Ralph takes other matrimonial turns, and a far more intricate background of the whole drama is revealed.

Although this book was written before the *House of Cain* was published, it is a far superior novel. The subject matter is more natural to Upfield, the setting is more nearly the metier that he was comfortable in and about which he could write from experience. Though the plotting is loose, as is that of most of his books, the story hangs together because of the locale, the use of Bony the detective, and Upfield's extraordinary use of landscape and weather. As usual, there is an immense upheaval of nature which in effect opens the mystery and solves the plot. Though Upfield was not altogether happy with the development of the book, and revised rather extensively for re-issue in America, he had located the kind of plot and development, and the setting, that was to serve him well through the years. This book, though not as strong as the Bony books that follow it, marks the path that he was to follow successfully thereafter. It is more than a happy forecast of things to come; it is a part of that future accomplishment.

*The Beach of Atonement.* Published: Hutchinson, 1930.
Locale: Dongerra, just south of Geraldton, Western Australia.

I have been unable to locate and read this book. Therefore all I can give in the way of a plot summary comes from Betty Donaldson:

> Dudley murders his wife's lover and in escaping, more from himself than from his crime, he travels to an isolated strip of coast where he lives in such loneliness he nearly goes mad. Two women befriend him—one a widow who sets herself to work the land her husband left her, and who gives Arnold Dudley a job, and the other a younger woman who falls in love with him. Arnold gets a chance to atone for his crime when a ship is wrecked on the coast. He dies trying to save the life of a passenger.

In this second of five non-Bony novels, Upfield seems to have developed a story similar to the one later told by Mary Durack, and recounted later in this study, about a half-caste who lost his life saving passengers from a doomed vessel, though Upfield here apparently does not associate the character with Aboriginals at all. It may have been a widespread story.

*The Sands of Windee.* Published: Alder, 1931; Hutchinson, 1931; reissued Angus, 1958. British Book Center, 1959, 1968; reissued, Angus & Robertson, 1980.

This second novel in the Bony series is situated at Windee Station in western New South Wales. From the description of the activities of Bony and from other directions, Philip Asdell deduces that Windee Station

is a few miles west of The Silver City Highway (which runs north from Broken Hill to the Queensland border) and that the fictional 'Mount Lion' is probably the same as or is very close to the real town of Milparinka" (see map).

Bony is sent to the sheep station to investigate the disappearance of a man named Luke Marks, who Bony knows has been murdered when he sees in a photograph of the locale of the disappearance of Marks a blackfeller's sign on a tree that said: "Beware of spirits! A white man has been killed here."

In order to investigate the crime, Detective-Inspector Bonaparte comes to the area in the garb of a bush trapper and takes a job on the sheep farm of wealthy Jeffrey Stanton. Bony is interested in the fact that the aboriginal Moongalliti and his son Lubdi had been unable to read the tracks made by Marks and his killer. The blackfellers' sign on the tree and the under-efficiency of the peerless blacks in reading signs convinced Bony that Marks had been murdered. The only question is finding the body.

There are two remarkable episodes of autobiography tied in with Upfield's development of this story. One has to do with the strange disappearance of the body—or the fact that it cannot be found. For this fact, Upfield had called on an episode that occurred to him when he was writing the book.

One night when Upfield was talking with a fellow-worker named George Ritchie about his next book, Upfield said that he would give a quid for a "simple and perfect method of wholly destroying a human body with aids to be found at any homestead." Ritchie responded that it would be easy. He recounted his method:

Supposing I wanted to do you in. I'd kick you into the bush a bit and when you were nice and handy to plenty of dry wood, I'd shoot you dead and burn your body. When the ashes were cold I'd go through the lot with a sieve, getting out every burnt bone and all metal things like buttons and boot sprigs. The metal I'd put into a bottle of sulphuric acid, and at every homestead they keep sulphuric for tin-smithing, and your burnt bones I'd put through a prospector's dolly-pot, and toss out the dust for the wind to scatter. There'd be none of you left.

The perfect murder seemed almost completely outlined. Except that  burned animal bones will not burn to fine dust that can be carried away by the wind. But Richie was not inhibited by this fact of nature. He had the solution to that problem:

Easy, Arthur me lad, easy. On the fire-site you burn a couple of kangaroo carcasses. We always burn carcasses about a camp or a homestead to keep the flies down. Burning a carcass would also shunt suspicion of why the fire was lit in the first place. Getting away with murder is as easy as falling off a log if only you use your brain. Try it some time and see (Hawke, 199-200).

Upfield incorporated this method to dispose of Mark's body, but had Bony nevertheless solve the mystery. A strange footnote to this interesting anecdote is its aftermath. Now does indeed art imitate life. Ritchie later used this very method to dispose of some corpses of bodies that he had murdered for small gain! He too was caught.

A second, somewhat smaller though entirely crucial, portion of this book evolved from one of Upfield's experiences.

While cooking at Wheeler's Well, Upfield had noticed once that ants, especially large ants, bring up tiny pebbles from their nests to be heated in the sun and then take them back down to maintain warmth for their eggs. In one particular instance he noticed that one of the stones brought up from a hole was a fragment of glass. The idea was born, as Hawkes later diagrammed it, probably from the anecdote outlined by Upfield:

Glass! It might well have been a ruby or a sapphire from a girl's ring, proving that a girl wearing a ring had stood close by at some time or other. See the ring, minus the gem, on the finger of a girl, and there was proof that she was the girl who had stood or passed by the nest. (167)

Indeed, how little grains of sand grow into mountains of plot-solution. Upfield expanded the occurrence into a full-fledged method of reading character and story development. He developed the whole plot with vivid and effective events and symbols.

At Windee Station Bony had worked as a horse-breaker, an art Upfield had actually learned from a man named One-Spot Dick. Bony had broken several, gentled others, and had as his finest example of horseflesh a gelding named Grey Cloud. In the final dramatic hours of Bony's chase after the guilty persons, across the countryside, he rides this great gelding. The surrounding grasslands are set ablaze and as Bony tries to escape the blaze, he realizes that in fact he is caught in the midst of an overwhelming inferno. In his descriptions of the fire, Upfield rises to some of his most compelling prose.

In a chapter properly named "Dante's Undreamed Inferno," Upfield shows how thousands of acres of knee-high grass have been destroyed, how the trees and twigs were exploding with the heat from the grass-fire, and how the flame and smoke turned the scene into a "lurid horror." He calls forth his most intense vocabulary to describe the scene:

> A hundred million torches, from the great pillars of flame consuming the pine-trees, down to the tiny last flares of dead and fallen branches, turned the steadily rising smoke into lurid horror. From this inferno came an incessant fusilade of reports in all degrees of volume and many qualities of tone. Uprising through the crimson pall, universe after universe of stars rushed into oblivion, as though the gods, stooping to gather handfuls of worlds flung them up in the delirium of their power. Thousands upon thousands, two hundred thousand acres of scrub and wheat-like grass, were disintegrating, turning into those upward-rushing, vanishing universes and the vast low-hanging crimson cloud. (189)

In the midst of this inferno, Bony is overcome with heat and smoke. In developing this scene, Upfield rises to the climax in an ingenious chain of creation soaring from the surrounding burning lands to the pinnacle. First Bony must stop and rest; he does not see how he can go on or where he might go. As he lies on the ground, Grey Cloud looks at his former rider and views him as a "two-legged god" lying inert on the ground. Being of superior instinct

and knowing that they must get moving, the horse whinnies time
after time until Bony mounts him again. Trying to guide the horse,
Bony's power fails, then he resorts to the wild man's power of
intuiting an escape route from the fire. Again he fails. Forced to
stop again, Bony finally completely removes the symbol of his
humanness and resorts to only what can be judged a use of primeval
kindness, brotherhood and survival. He has very little water and
must conserve it. Yet he feels he must share it with another creature,
his horse. He takes off his shirt, digs a hole in the ground, stuffs
his shirt in the hole and pours on it half of his remaining water
supply. Grey Cloud drinks it immediately. The act is his salvation.
Somewhat refreshed, the two are drawn into an Ark-like situation
of crazed animals. Kangeroos, foxes, dogs and rabbits all dash about
furiously, maddened by the nearness of the fire. In the midst of
this Dantesque Garden of Eden,

Snakes writhed and struck in impotent fury; iguanas glared down malevolently
from the topmost branches of the trees, hate and anger incarnate in reptilian
beauty.

In this maelstrom of animal life gone crazy, Bony abandons himself
and the reins to the superior intuition of Grey Cloud, who sniffs
the safe passage through the flames and leads the other animals
from their blazing ark into the coolness of safety. The whole event
is a marvelous symbol of how the man-trained animal, the horse
Grey Cloud, once given his head is able to lead man and all other
animals to safety. Upfield is making his point clear: it is man,
whom the horse had recognized as "god" returned to nature, who
has enough sense to trust the animal that he has trained, who thus
saves his life. The symbol of the triumph of man and horse is
the gentle rising of the ground and the sound of pebbles being
struck by hoofs. (200) Finally, given his head, Grey Cloud leads
to a man-made supply of water. Upfield's message seems to be that
man and animal—man and nature—must work together for their
salvation.

In describing this fire, Upfield was calling upon his personal
experience. He knew how the Australian forests explode in a fire
and how the eucalyptus trees avoid being killed by these fires, which

the aboriginals used to set sometimes, by having their sap running inside the center of the tree-trunk instead of in the bark, as is the case with North American trees. Upfield also knew how these trees propagate themselves through their seeds which explode only from the heat of forest fires and thus start again afresh after a fire. The worst fire that Upfield remembered in later life as having witnessed was one in 1939 (some nine years after *The Sands of Windee* had been published) in Victoria when, as he wrote,

Toward the end of a prolonged heat wave with shade temperatures over 110 degrees the Warburton Ranges for seventy miles exploded.

A still gaseous heat "formed a gas canopy over the forest for 40 x 60 miles," and the area literally exploded, burning from the top down. The fire that Upfield had created out of his own imagination a decade earlier was almost as destructive.

One other remarkable parallel in this story was an episode in Upfield's life in the person of the priest Ryan, prominent in the development of this plot. Upfield had known a Father Ryan who was famous, at least locally, as a geologist and helpful in discovering many pockets of opals. But though useful to man as a geologist he was perhaps more helpful to the spirit by working to clean up the foul habits of his people. His device was to fine the drinkers something like three-pence per foul word or oath. Sometimes his fines amounted to a sovereign. The money he collected he used to buy new boots and clothes for the drunks who had spent all their money and their jobs on drinking. This was good Samaritanism supported by the people.

In this story Bony does not officially solve the mystery, though he knows the explanation and gives it to his Chief Commissioner, Colonel Spendor. In using the device of the totally-destroyed body, Upfield early demonstrates his interest in developing plots and devices unique to Australia, and particularly to the Australian outback. Upfield's development of Bony as detective is achieving more maturity. The total impact of this second Bony book is much greater than that of the first in the series had been.

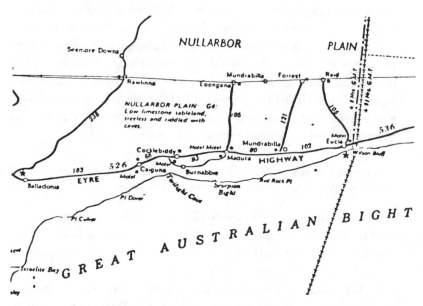

Setting of *A Royal Abduction* and *Man of Two Tribes*

*A Royal Abduction.* Published: Hutchinson, 1932; reissued, Dennis McMillan, 1986.

In this work Upfield makes his first use of caves, a use he was to repeat some four times, and specifically his first development of a story situated, at least in part, in the mammoth caverns under the Nullarbor Plains, a locale he was to use later. His cavescape in this novel is magnificent.

Specifically the caverns he uses in this book are near Eucla on the Nullabor Plains on the Great Australian Bight on the border dividing Western Australia from Southern Australia.

An Australian crook named Lawrence, for his own purposes, plans to kidnap Princess Natalie of Rolandia. He enlists the aid of an American millionaire gangster, Van Horton, and his beautiful daughter, Helen. The plan is that Van Horton and Helen, since they do not need money, will "rescue" the Princess and in so doing ingratiate themselves with her and thus ensure their upward social mobility in the future. The abduction is carried off letter-perfect, and the Princess and her entourage are safely hidden in the great caves at Eucla, which Upfield describes at great length and with various kinds of sexual symbolism.

Her quarters, as described by Upfield, are indeed a Princess' quarters. They are large rooms; the Princess' is hung with blue velvet "hangings" that caught and reflected the light "as the surface of a mountain lake reflects a clear evening sky." The main cavern is some fifty yards across, with a central peak or arch "some forty feet above," from which is suspended "The Sword of Damocles," "a glittering needle-pointed stalactite," which reflects the electric light "in every tint and shade of the spectrum." Upfield's praising description is both lyrical and sexual:

It was as a peacock preening its feathers, for once oblivious of the hen birds are represented in duller colours by crystallized lumps of rock set in the limestone walls that sent back gleams of brown and slate blue from their irregular polished surfaces. (122)

These geologic surroundings, contrary to Upfield's usual attitude, constitute a womb, a haven, a maze of safety for both the kidnapped and the kidnappers. But, as in any haven of safety, human nature causes discord, and violence and death erupt. When Upfield returns to these caverns, in *The Will of The Tribe*, he will use them without all the rich resonant connotations of sex here so lavishly employed.

With a large number of people imprisoned in the caves, and several people in on the conspiracy to hold them prisoners, plans naturally get complicated, and development of the plot unsure. Lawrence's plans are frustrated, and with the help of the democratizing influence brought about by people living together in the caves, the survivors see life in a different light after release from their imprisonment.

This second non-Bony novel is far superior to the first, *The House of Cain*. In this novel Upfield has much finer character development, his people are far more life-like. Upfield's symbolism, especially that of a sexual nature is maturing. His use of the landscape and cavescape of the region is Upfield's most accomplished to date. He is, however, somewhat hamstrung by his rather weak delineation of women. More important, his notion of what common experiences, down-to-earth lifestyles, and love of the common man can do to the privileged in democratizing them is a little far-fetched. But such characterization, though at times perhaps reaching proportions of caricature, comes only at the very end of the book. The earlier portions are strong and well-executed.

*Gripped by Drought.* Published; Hutchinson, 1932.

Betty Donaldson reported that despite all her efforts she could not get a copy of this book to read. I have had the same trouble. Donaldson, however, did receive some word on the book from Mr. Gerald Austin of the Hutchinson Publishing Group, Ltd., in England who called up his "precious file copy from our library at Tiptree," and quoted some material from and about the book. The first two paragraphs below are part of Mr. Upfield's introduction, the third is from the advertisement at the front of the book:

There is no greater Australian drama than a three-years' drought, and such a drought, associated with drought in the human heart, is the theme of this plain tale for plain people.

The course of this fictitious drought is based on the course of a real drought. I have followed the weather records over an actual three-year drought period, and no city critic can say that such a drought is impossible. Similarly, I have followed actual wool prices over the same period. And, finally, the succession of mental phases which the 'new-chum' in the bush proper must live through, or else desert to a city, is real and based on personal experience.

*Gripped by Drought* is a powerful story of a man's battle not only with the elements of nature which threatened the ruin of his huge Australia sheep-farm, but also with a loveless and unhappy marriage. For Frank Mayre, master of well-nigh a million acre sheep station, life assumed its most dreary aspect. No rain for his farm, a wife who involved him in a orgy of spending and entertainment, and with disaster just round the corner, there seemed little prospect of happiness. Yet in the darkest hour of all, after many unexpected and sometimes thrilling situations, the darkest hour of the drought gave way to rain and Mayre's tribulations became of the past.

Although it might be tempting to assume that some of Upfield's personal troubles in marriage may have intruded into this plot and development, not having read the book, I would be reluctant to make any comments about development or style.

*Wings Above the Diamantina.* Published: Angus, 1936; Hamilton, 1937, as *Winged Mystery.* Issued in America as *Wings Above the Claypan:* Doubleday, 1943.

In *Wings Above the Diamantina,* Upfield's seventh novel, nature of a different kind plays a dramatic role. In the Coolibah Cattle Station on the Diamantina River in Queensland, John Nettleford and his daughter Elizabeth find in the middle of waterless Emu Lake a downed bright red monoplane with an unconscious girl in the front seat. There are no tracks around the plane showing that someone left, and no reason for the girl who appears to be unconscious to be in the plane. The two take her out of the plane, not paying as much attention to the whole physical set-up as they might, remove the unconscious girl to their home and call the doctor to see what he can do to solve the mystery. Soon it becomes clear to the reader that this drama is being played out on a "supernatural" scale. Although airplanes are regularly a part of the life of people in the Australian cattle stations, here the symbol takes on a deeper meaning. The girl is found unconscious in an airplane; the white doctor called to her attend her rides to his task in his own airplane.

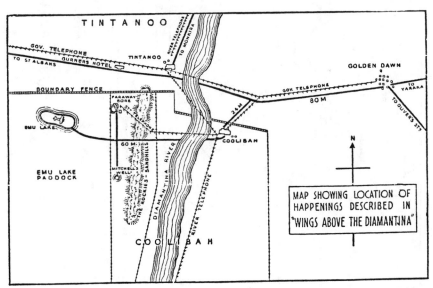

Area for the setting of *Wings Above the Diamantina* and *The Bone is Pointed*

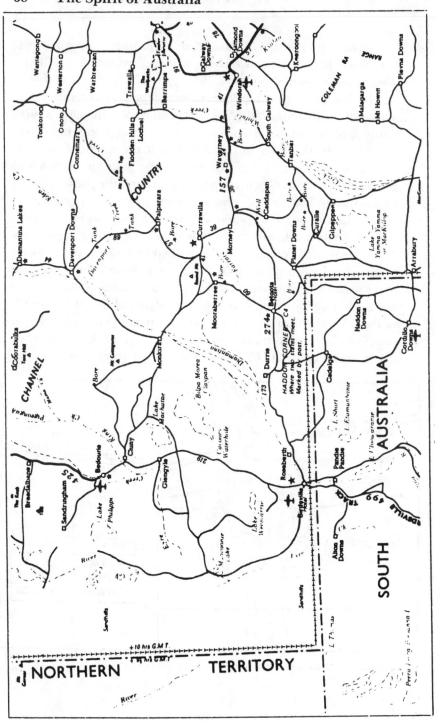

Setting of *Wings Above the Diamantina*

He is unable to cure the girl, and as a final gesture Bony has the government send an airplane, "an emu that flies," to seek the aid of old medicine man Illawalli. Illawalli has to convince the white doctor and the other whites against their will to allow him to practice his magic on the girl. But, finally, since there is no hope, they permit his ministrations. Illawalli, recognizing that the girl has been poisoned with the same drug that natives use to dope fish, provides the antidote and administering it with soothing but compelling conversation literally talks the girl back into consciousness and life.

Nature is frequently used by authors as antagonist to human beings in their quests. But in Upfield nature is used to deepen and intensify the struggle and to shade his own philosophy. In this book it is used twice for such purposes.

In the first instance, one of Australia's remarkable sand phenomena is used, in two ways. In the first instance, Bony and his helpers are tracking the person who blew up the plane that had been used to try to murder Muriel Markham, who now lies unconscious in the home of Nettlefords. They have come upon an important clue. At that moment a giant sandstorm that has descended upon them unbeknownst forces them to abandon the hunt.

But the sandstorm intervenes in another even more dramatic way. The reliable pilot Captain Loveacre is flying a Mr. Cartwright, an insurance agent, out to investigate the downed red monoplane that Markham had been flying in. As Loveacre and Cartwright take off from the town of Golden Dawn, they are confronted by the sandstorm, a sandstorm without wind, which had been stirred up near the eastern border of Western Australia. Now it was a worthy adversary. From the top,

the sand cloud now presented an inspiring sight. It has the face of a moving cliff four thousand feet high. The sunlight slanting sharply upon it brought into sharp relief bulging escarpments and inward sucking caverns. It was as though this enormous thing were living, that, as it advanced across the world, it were actually breathing. (104)

This cloud of sand, which is caused by wind creating updrafts on the powderlike sand, is 60 miles wide. It can only be likened to the vast tons of soil blown into the sky in the American Southwest during the Dustbowl days, where, like this phenomenon in Australia, the sun shown through blood-red, and the dust, like the sand, as it settled down covered everything that could not shake it off.

This sandstorm so graphically described in this book had been equally graphic when Upfield had experienced it while he was with two camels out waiting to visit Lake Frome. One of the worst sand storms in years bore down upon him and his camels from the north, to be swirling in with a gentler wind from the west. Together they created havoc. On a quiet, hot day, strangely still, there seemed to be nothing amiss. The moon rose in blood. The day dawned with a strange throbbing in the atmosphere. Approaching from the northwest was a living wall of sand. In words strangely like those that Upfield had used in his novel, Hawke ( *Follow My Dust*, 142-3) relived the scene:

The face of the mass was palpitating, vast areas being gently sucked inwards, and corresponding areas gently puffed outwards. The declivities were jet black, the proturbances livid crimson. From deep inside the horror originated the pulsating beat which seemed to be born in the depth of the mud.

The camels lay down with their rumps in the face of the storm, and were covered with many inches of sand as it came to rest on them. Upfield, driven into his tent, thought that he was going to be killed. He witnessed the alternating shift of darkness and light, of storm and quiet. After the horror had passed on, he rose to find a world cloaked in sand as a landscape in more northern climates is covered in snow. To touch any object was to cause a cascade of fine red sand. The experience was enough to sober all living creatures, even camels.

Nature continued to fight against the human beings who were trying to solve the mystery of the drugged girl and to prevent her death. The second force that nature throws at the people comes in the form of a gigantic rainstorm. After the white doctors in the vicinity have failed in their efforts to cure Muriel, Bony sends

Captain Loveacre, the only pilot in the vicinity, to the north to bring in Illawalli, Bony's old friend the medicine man, to whom Bony is "father...mother...friend...son," (200) and the only person who can cure Muriel. But as the plane is only an hour from its return-destination, Bony anxiously reads the sky and sees a gigantic rainstorm rising like an "aerial ice pack," (182) flecked with lightning that will impede Loveacre's return on a direct route to the station. Bony's religious skepticism is intensified: "I once told Dr. Knowles that the almighty holds the scales evenly between good and evil." But here obviously he had tilted them, as even Dr. Knowles concedes: "'Even the elements have conspired against us." To Captain Loveacre, in his plane trying to combat the elements, the rain cloud was a "writhing, twisting wall of snow-white cloud," a "perpendicular field of imitation snow and ice." (178) The resulting downpour flooded the Darling River and made it impassable to everyone but the most herculean. Bony barely manages to survive the effort required to cross it.

In this closely-knit novel that wanders very little from the compression of a relentless search for the criminal, Nature appears to be more than indifferent to man's action. It seems more to be positively hostile, and on the side of the evil that men do. All of which helps to make this book Upfield's strongest to date. It is particularly rich in Australian lore, Upfield's use of the weather as a formidable antagonist is especially impressive. It brings in a considerable body of folk culture and Aboriginal culture. It is a *tour de force*.

*Mr. Jelly's Business.* Published: Angus, 1937; Hamilton, 1938; reissued, Angus, 1964, Angus & Robertson, 1981. Issued in America as *Murder Down Under*: Doubleday, 1943; reissued, London House-British Book Centre, 1964, as *Mr. Jelly's Business.*

This book is set in Southwestern Australia, in the wheat belt. Upfield centers his plot around the town of "Burracoppin," which is in fact a real township, as Asdell describes it, "15 miles northeast of Merredin and 175 miles east of Perth" (see map). In addition to its wheat, the district also grows pigs and sheep. In the desert

Setting of *Mr. Jelly's Business* and *The Sands of Windee*

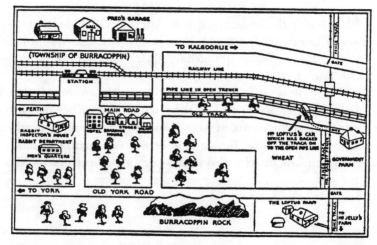

Setting of *Mr. Jelly's Business*

The dray from the rear, where Upfield wrote *The Sands of Windee*.
From *Follow My Dust*, courtesy Don Uren.

east of Burracoppin in 1887 gold was discovered at Southern Cross, and later in 1984 in Kalgoorlie, Upfield's novel centers on wheat.

A farmer named George Loftus has left Perth after a week of business and pleasure. On his way home he stops at Burracoppin at a pub and apparently gets drunk; still he insists on driving home. On his way he crashes into a ditch and disappears. Bony travels to Burracoppin and gets a job as a Rabbitoh repairing and maintaining a stretch of the longest rabbit fence in the world— 1500 miles. He discovers two mysteries in the vicinity: not only the disappearance of George Loftus but also the strange behavior of a farmer named Jelly, who regularly disappears from his home, stays a few days, and then returns to his two daughters with no explanation of where he has been. In solving one mystery, Bony solves the other.

This is a farm-land novel. Wheat symbolizes, of course, life and abundance, and this symbol plays ironically in the development of the plot of this book. Nature-grown wheat is manipulated into cloaking a man-made crime—an event which is contrary to nature, and which is revealed by nature. The working-out of the plot is natural but symbolically effective.

This book is well packed with symbolism, with Upfield's philosophy of life in Australia and with character development. One of his strongest Dickensian characters, "The Spirit of Australia," is developed here. In his early books, Upfield often drew upon experiences from his own life, as all novelists do, as sources for development in the novels. "The Spirit of Australia" comes from such an experience.

The Australian outback was always packed with "characters," people who began somewhat off level-balance or who became that way because of the kinds of life they led. Upfield met and frequently traveled for short spells with them. Once he traveled with a man named Dave the Spouter, who at one time delivered an hour-long lecture to the stars—and nobody dared interrupt him. Such characters were educational!

One especially educational character and experience was a red Irishman who wandered with Upfield for a hundred miles. A giant of a man, he always complained that nobody would fight him and he was just aching for a battle. So he and Upfield plotted to start a brawl in the next pub they entered. Upfield, being smaller, was the bait. He taunted the men of a droving outfit to attack him, fully expecting the Irish giant to then clear the place. But having been knocked four-ways to the wind, he looked around and discovered that the giant was not visible. He was outside relieving himself. But when he stepped in a moment later, he started throwing drovers against walls, out windows, through the doorway—until the place was emptied. It was a glorious fight. As Upfield remembered the fracas it taught him to foresee the conclusion before starting the beginning. But, more important, it provided him with an episode to demonstrate the Herculean spirits of one of his most powerful characters. "The Spirit of Australia" rivals the brawling capabilities of the strongest of his kind, including the Americans Davy Crockett, Mike Fink and the whole slew of frontier fighters.

In the character of Mr. Jelly, Upfield creates one of his strongest heroic personages. A close-knit "cottage mystery," this story is strong, heroic and effective. It is sentimental in dealing with Mr. Jelly's daughters, one of whom is particularly young and overly sweet, and Bony is especially foolish in his association with her. Further, the book is unusually severe in Upfield's conclusion about the fate of a murderer. In general, however, it is one of Upfield's stronger books on one side of his philosophy.

*Winds of Evil.* Published: Angus, 1937; Hamilton, 1939; reissued Angus, 1961, Angus & Robertson, 1980. Doubleday, 1944; British Book Centre, 1961.

*Winds of Evil* is another remarkable book which is so tied to nature that it is hardly a detective story but is instead a crime novel. It is an exercise in atmosphere. It begins in nature's terror, develops through its supernatural strength, and ends on its aftermath. It is a drama of human action motivated and controlled by forces greater than man.

The book begins in a sandstorm that is about to destroy everything in its wake. Bony, disguised as Joe Fisher, swagman, is struggling to get to Carie, in New South Wales. Bony at first is not offended by this weather. As he says, "to be appreciated, beauty must be felt as well as seen." (72) Upfield elaborates on this beauty, in a lyrical passage which sees beauty where others read threat:

To those having the eyes to see and the soul to feel, the great plains of inland Australia present countless facets of beauty: these same plains offer to the man with good eyesight, but a shrivelled soul, nothing other than arid desert.

Nature wears many faces, one of which is violence, when

Like a thousand devils the wind howled among the trees and plucked at their branches to tear many from the parent trunks and lay them violently on the ground

that was the face nature was currently wearing. Her blood heat was exceeding 118 degrees in the shade, had there been any shade. Upfield intensifies the force of nature with the fury of superstitions which begin to rage through Bony's blood:

Tortured by inherited superstitions, lashed by the contempt of reason, Bony maintained an incessant watch, visually searching for a monstrous figure slinking through this shrouded world of wind and noise. It was like waiting to spy upon one of those legendary half-dead people who are supposed to crawl from their coffins at sunset to roam the earth as living entities until sunrise. It was like a defiance of the bush bunhip, that horrific thing, half-dog, half-human, which, during the daylight hours lurks invisibly in the heart of a bush, behind a tree, at the foot of the mirage, and at night takes material form to stalk venturesome blacks and half-castes who roam away from their rightful camps.

Though the air was hot, Bony shivered.

Reason and inherited superstitions warred within him with nerve-racking ferocity. After all is said about reason, it flourishes best in the sunlight and drawing-rooms. A dark night with a prowling, foul murderer at hand is apt to wither this flower. (225-26)

At the beginning of the book, Bony meets a bus which stops because it is generating so much electricity in the storm the driver is afraid the bus will explode. Bony touches the radiator, and blue flames streak from his hand to the ground. Other people tell about how the electricity created in these wind-created hells cure rheumatism but cause headaches and all kinds of erratic mental behavior. The murderer in the story is an otherwise fine individual but one whose behavior is influenced by the electricity in the air, just as his parents' was. He is literally controlled by the electrical sparks in the atmosphere. Upfield says at the end of the story that "the evil in the guilty party was born during the raging sand-storm," who was "controlled by the peculiar conditions of these wind-storms." So the whole book is a sustained metaphor about static electricity and lightning. Although not as portentous, it nevertheless reminds one of Ahab in *Moby-Dick* playing around with the electricity on the mast head of the *Pequod* when he is trying to read and explain his future.

Meteorologically, in this book Upfield compresses nature into a tight ball that explodes finally in violence. Around the commotion of the static electricity he creates a fine set of characters and suspense. The characters include Mrs. Nelson, the owner of Carie, a major figure. The suspense revolves around the mischief that can be created by natural weather conditions. In no other book has Upfield taken the weather of Australia and woven it into a more compressed and effective book. His style is nowhere stronger than when writing of the power of the nature that drives people in this instance to crime:

Like a thousand devils the wind howled among the trees and plucked at their branches to tear many from the parent trunk and lay them .iolently on the ground. It threatened to throw the detective off his feet, and when it passed it left him gasping. (149)

This passage demonstrates the power of Upfield's writing throughout the book. It is strong and effective.

*The Bone is Pointed.* Published: Angus, 1937; Hamilton, 1939; reissued Angus, 1966, Angus & Robertson, 1984. Doubleday, 1947; reissued London House-British Book Centre, 1966; reissued, Garland, 1976.

Upfield's next book, *The Bone is Pointed,* is one of his two
or three most effective efforts. In it Upfield uses outback nature
as Charles Dickens somewhat earlier had used urban London, as
background and foreground for the events that transpire. This use
takes on three forms.

In the first place the book begins with a natural event which
assumes sinister overtones as it continues to strike the characters
and the reader. A woman named Mary Gordon in the Meena Station
homestead near St. Albans, Queensland, is nervously pacing the
floor on the twelfth anniversary of her husband's death from falling
from a horse. It was raining the night of his death, and now her
son is out on his horse, and she fears perhaps lying beneath it
wounded or dead. Then, as now, the rain falling on the tin roofs
of the various houses beat a kind of nerve-chilling deathknell.

Another kind of unrelenting atmosphere is the voodoo and
superstition of the aboriginals which penetrates and controls the
book. An evil white man named Jeffrey Anderson has disappeared.
Detective-Inspector Bonaparte of the Queensland Police arrives at
Opal Town to look into the disappearance. There are several
problems in the case. The disappearance is several months old.
That would not ordinarily hamper Bony's efforts, but he is
constantly shadowed by the aborigines apparently trying to prevent
his learning much about the apparent murder and determined to
keep up with the information he gathers. When it becomes apparent
that Bony will solve the mystery, the aborigines take action and
point the bone at him (that is, hex him). Bony, who stands half-
way between the white and the aboriginal cultures, struggles against
his fate, but is forced to give in. He becomes weak and ill. In a
remarkable mixture of psychology and *materia medica* Upfield, who
is always interested in abnormal psychology, has Bony cured and
the case solved. The cure is a theatrical *tour de force* that
demonstrates yet again Upfield's insistence throughout his books
that the veneer of civilization—and of abnormal psychology—is
thin. His description of the whole process is explicit:

> The act of pointing the bone was, of course, merely a theatrical show,
> having a psychological effect both on the bone-pointers and the victim. The
> power to kill lay not in the outward show but in the mental willing to death

conducted by the executioners. Bony knew that the pointing bone could be used by any male member of nearly all the Australian tribes, but its success in killing depended on the mental power of the pointers. If the victim could conquer inherited superstitions, and then if his mind were stronger than the minds of the bone-pointers, he might escape death long enough for his relations to find out who was pointing the bone and at once exact vengeance. (137)

It is remarkable that Bony who is generally heroically superior to all trials is unable to be superior to this common practice of hexing. It takes outside psychological assistance to cure him.

Finally, adding a kind of macabre sense of humor, the book is peopled by one of the most interesting Dickensian characters Upfield ever created, Bill the Better, who will wager on any topic, and will wager against his own wager. The book crackles with a Dickensian peoplescape.

With its powerful subject, Upfield's masterful handling of Bony in his activities, and the people involved, *The Bone is Pointed* becomes one of Upfield's stronger books.

*The Mystery of Swordfish Reef.* Published: Angus, 1939; reissued, Angus & Robertson, 1983. Reissued, Heinemann, 1960. Doubleday, 1943.

*The Mystery of Swordfish Reef* has an unusual bit of nature in it in that it is an unnatural setting for Bony, the sea instead of the land. Despite the fact that Upfield was in reality a fisherman with considerable experience at sea, he had Bony admit at the beginning of the novel that he was reluctant to undertake this assignment because he recognized that he might fail, since this assignment was on the sea and his strength lay in the deserts and plains of inland Australia.

The setting for this book is Bermagui, a real town some 180 miles south of Sydney on the New South Wales coast, a section which was first settled in the 1830s. Joe Kovess, an indefatigable Bony expert, conjectures that Upfield's adventure was based on a real event which happened in this vicinity, to the north of Bermagui, in October 1880. At that time Lamont Young, a Government geologist, an assistant named Max Schneider and three members of the crew of the boat they were using to inspect the goldfield, disappeared and nobody was ever heard of again. The place where

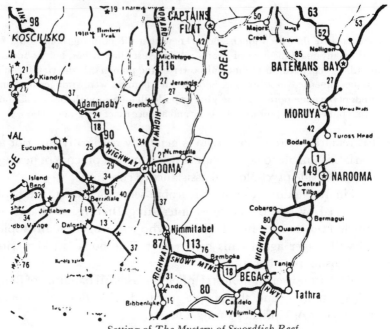

Setting of *The Mystery of Swordfish Reef*

Setting of *The Mystery of Swordfish Reef*

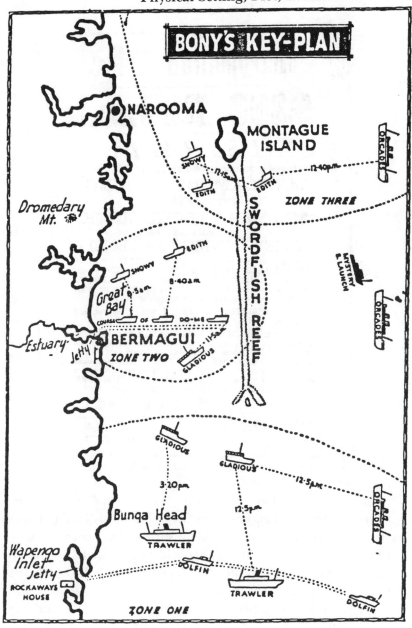

Setting of *The Mystery of Swordfish Reef*

Notice of 19th century mystery which may have inspired *The Mystery of Swordfish Reef.*

the empty boat was found is named "Mystery Bay." Interestingly, it was the American author Zane Grey who in his fishing books after 1930 celebrated Bermagui and the surrounding waters and gave it fame. One area described by Upfield as a "gradual ascent up a green slope" is now, ironically, "Zane Grey Park." Nevertheless the area was vivified by Upfield.

With the sea as his field of battle, Upfield rose to the demands of description and use of nature. He begins the book with the statement that a depression that had caused much turbulence on the seas had passed away and left the sea clear and calm. But in this idyllic setting a fishing boat, the *Do-Me*, fails to return from its fishing expedition, and the people on land, quite rightly, think that there might be foul play somewhere.

In addition, as Bony gets closer and closer to solving the crime, his physical world undergoes a sea-change and he is beaten, tied up and thrown into the hole of a fishing boat. The result of the change in the nature of setting for this book creates a Bony who is different from all those we see in the books where the solid earth is the setting. On land Bony is dignified, reserved, steady in character. On sea he is, on the contrary, too bouncy, too unreserved, too lacking in the dignity that results from his pride in himself to be natural. We have great difficulty recognizing our familiar Bony in the character who braces himself on the sea, and in one instance becomes as savage as a male tiger predating his own kind. It is as though Upfield did not quite know how to handle the new metier. This attitude is perhaps best illustrated in the concluding paragraph of the book. Bony in the latter sections of the book has reverted to the basic primitivism best represented by his maternal inheritance. In so doing he abandoned the reserve and intellectual sophistication of his father's race. Though successful in his goal, he is not sure of himself.

He is happy because he felt he had atoned for that fall from the height to which his pride and natural gifts had lifted him. But, when he turned to face the glittering sea in time to watch, far away, a beautiful fish dancing on its tail, memory of his temporary fall was expunged from his mind and his delicately shaped nostrils quivered. (256)

Clearly Upfield never got his sea-legs in this book. But, interestingly, Upfield, very much in love with the sea, thought this novel his best to date.

Bony admits that he is a kind of reverse fish-out-of-water; he is a drylander-in-water. But Upfield was in fact an experienced fisherman, and he carries out the development of the sea-material with real skill. One of his strong points in the story is his carrying out the theme of clothes as metaphor for civilization vs. primitivism. Here, when Bony is pushed back into the primitivism of his aboriginal mother, he abandons his clothes, reverts to absolute savagery and overwhelms his adversaries. In such passages, Upfield's language is as strong as it is anywhere else in his works. There is a compelling momentum in his phraseology which sweeps the reader along helter-skelter. Despite several weaknesses, this is a powerful and enjoyable book, though not among Upfield's strongest.

*Bushranger of the Skies.* Published: Angus, 1940; reissued, Angus, 1963, 1965; reissued Angus & Robertson, 1980. Issued in America as *No Footprints in the Bush*: Doubleday, 1944; reissued, London House and Maxwell-British Book Centre, 1963.

This is one of Upfield's most remarkable books. The locale is McPherson's Station, 80 miles northwest of Shaw's Lagoon, South Australia. Just as all of Upfield's books picture the intrusion of the white culture into that of the aboriginal and thrust of crime into an otherwise peaceful situation, and just as his books ordinarily picture violent nature, this book describes two kinds of aberrations in an otherwise tranquil scene. The scenes are of interrupted nature and of a destruction of race-culture.

The book begins with a remarkably effective religious setting, in a kind of Garden of Eden into which violence intrudes. That is, the setting is a cabbage-tree cathedral. Upfield liked the figure of nature presenting a church-like appearance. In a short story called "Walls of China," he uses the metaphor that standing on the depression outside the Walls of China "is not unlike standing in a cathedral doorway after the service." The scene is not dissimilar to that in this work. The cabbage-tree (apparently, Livistona australis—cabbage-palm) has been particularly useful throughout Australia's history. Being of a particular upright shape with leaves clustered at the top which have been used for both head coverings and for food, it is, therefore, a tree filled with unusual symbols. Upfield's book begins in a setting of these trees, mentioned as being extraordinary:

One of Nature's oddities was the grove of six cabbage-trees in the dense shade of which Detective-Inspector Bonaparte had made his noonday camp. They grew beside an unmade road winding like a snake's track over a range of low, treeless and semi-barren hills; and, so close were they, and so virile their foliage, that to step in among them was not unlike stepping into an ivy-colored church on a brilliant summer morning.

The unmade road looking like a snake's trail symbolizes the evil that will be enacted outside the church. And evil it is. A white man is attacked by a man in an airplane and is blown up. Bony in his "church" is bombed by the same man in the same plane. After the bombing, Bony comes out of church, retrieves a briefcase from the bombed car and then is fronted by a group of aborigines who obviously have been sent to the bombed car to see that all was destroyed.

The second unnatural happening in the book is a case of miscegenation. The owner of McPherson's Station married Tarlalin, a black, and had a son, who has turned into a monster. As Upfield says, following the line of folk wisdom for ages, half-castes turn into either fine individuals or monsters. Bony, his wife and three sons, are fine half-castes. This one is not.

This is a particularly savage and primitive book. Once Bony is outside the church of the cabbage-trees, all kinds of evil are afoot in the land. For example, Bony is forced to fight the blacks who have been sent to see about the bombed car. During the battle Bony's

blood glowed with exquisite fire, for circumstance has temporarily removed the chains of civilized restraint from a nature in which the hereditary influences constantly stirred.

Upfield's use of the airplane here is likewise unusual. Ordinarily the airplane is a machine of mercy; here it is a catapult of destruction.

There is another use of nature, or of the return of the aboriginal to nature, in this book that makes it remarkable. Sometimes Upfield uses nature, as in *Wings Over the Diamantina*, in a slow-moving inevitability. At other times he is given to such scenes of dramatic speed that they are bewildering. He can have his characters speeding toward a goal in a headlong rush that is dizzying. In this book he has this kind of motion. Once Rex, the evil half-caste son of McPherson, has destroyed the good doctor's airplane and is about to escape, a whole band of aboriginals ride their horses desperately toward the plane trying to prevent its taking off. Upfield makes quite clear that the destruction here is of a primitive nation against one who is not quite of them and is evil. The aboriginals shed their clothes as they rush toward the plane. But Upfield also demonstrates that Rex's half-caste status allows him to escape the destruction of Bony, another half-caste.

This is surely one of Upfield's strongest books. It is filled with various kinds of symbolism—of religion, of clothes vs nakedness, of action, of the fruits of love of white for aboriginal. Throughout the prose is rich, resonant, compelling. In this book are passages which are as rapid, graphic and enspiriting as in any other book. The only rival is *The Will of the Tribe*, which, to a certain extent at least, parallels some of Upfield's attitudes in this earlier book.

*Death of a Swagman.* Published: Aldor, 1946: Angus, 1947; reissued, Angus, 1962, 1964. Doubleday, 1943; reissued, British Book Centre, 1962.

The story is set in "Merino," a small township in New South Wales, a place of 80 inhabitants, close to the Walls of China, a large strip of sand twelve miles long, three quarters of a mile wide and some 125-130 feet high. These walls are located some 70 miles northeast of Mildura, Victoria (see map). Called by neomorphologists "lunettes" (that is, crescent-shaped dunes), these hills were formed some 25,000-15,000 years ago. They are not a wall at all but formations of fine sand, which Upfield found puzzling. He speculated and described these walls in a short story called "Walls of China," in which he talks about their geologic make-up:

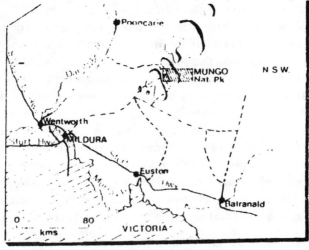

Setting of *Death of a Swagman*

ank

Tank

Burkeetts or
Golgalan Tank

Daveys Well

Dajara Tank

Nº1 Tank

Gibson's
Swamp Tank

Cane Grass
Basin

Nicholsons Tank

Cane Grass Tank

Baalkaalo Tk

Mowolma Tank

Melville's Tank

Gilbies Tank

*Leaghuk*

Mulga Well

Doortung Tank

Poo Poo
Tank

Bight Tank

Kieanco Tk

*Top
Hut*

Stockyard Tank

Tourimundow Tank

Mowomla
Tk

Junction Tank

*Mungo*

Melvilles
Middle Tank

Allans Tank

THE WALLS OF CHINA

Stewarts
Tank

Ulva Tk

Arumpo Bore

*Arumpo*

Natara Tank

Juni Tank

*BULBUGAROO
LAKE*

Ravine
Tank

Collin's Tank

P W P
Arumpo Tank

Weeyangun
Tank

*Petro*

Pimpompla
Tank

*Chibnalwood*

Bunchie
Tank

*Banoon*

Possum or
Violet Tank

*Tourlee*

Websters
Tank

Setting of *Death of a Swagman*

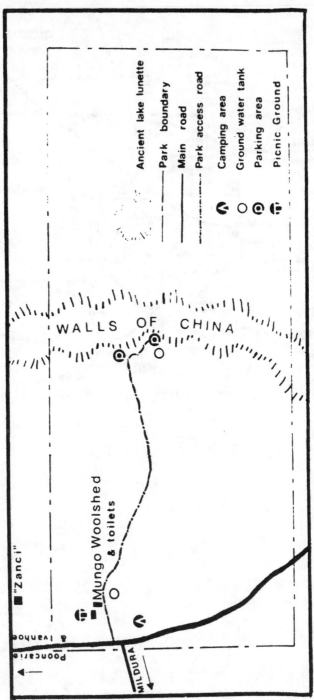

*Setting of Death of a Swagman*

The white particles composing the walls, on which nothing can gain root-hold, are smaller than those composing the western and northern red sand-dunes. To the touch the white sand is like satin; the red sand feels more like velvet. Perhaps it is that the red, wind-blown particles, being the heavier, sink into, or are engulfed by, the white particles so jealous of their beauty. Certain it is that the red sand blown against the walls in tons every year instantly vanishes.

These hills are mysterious and create illusions, as he describes in this same short story:

To observe the Walls of China beneath a cloudless sky for a lengthy period is to suffer eye strain; to observe human beings walking on them is to marvel at their mass.

Such formations, apparently always called by geologists "Walls of China," are not restricted to Australia. There is a similar set of sand dunes in the Eureka Valley, northeast of Death Valley, in California, also called "Walls of China." The dune system blows back and forth—constantly changing shape but, protected from the fiercest wind by the rock spine called the "Wall of China," they do not shift location.

In his district Detective-Inspector Bonaparte drifts, disguised, as usual, and because he is impertinent to Sergeant Marshall is locked up in the local jail. After he reveals his true identity, Bony, Marshall and the judge conspire to keep him in jail while he paints it, a common practice with law officers in the outback, and ferrets out the murderer. Bony is assisted in his work by the trenchant observations about the locals by Florence "Rose Marie" Marshall, the sergeant's 8-year old daughter. Three murders occur, and the kidnapping of Rose Marie, before the mystery is solved.

This is a thin but lively and persevering study. Nature is unusually severe and beautiful. The characters are lifelike, there is a little more humor than usual with Upfield, and the treatment of the outback people is realistic. Realistic, that is, except in the case of Rose Marie. As soon as he is thrown into jail, in an exchange based upon an episode from his childhood, Bony is released by Rose Marie upon his promise that he will not run away. The incident is sentimental and reveals Upfield's general inability to handle children as characters when he tried to make them more than background. In this instance he fails. But though she is a faint blot on the general effect of the novel, she is no more, and the book is a success. In this striking sandscape, Bony triumphs over two adversaries, an isolated region, swept by a powerful nature that is indifferent to the people living there, and over man. In other words, he triumphs over "the bush and the white man." (16)

Setting of *The Devil's Steps* and *An Author Bites the Dust*

*The Devil's Steps.* Published: Aldor 1948; reissued, Angus, 1963. Doubleday, 1946; reissued, London House and Maxwell-British Book Centre, 1965; reissued Scribner's 1982.

The geographical setting for *The Devil's Steps* and Upfield's next book, *An Author Bites the Dust*, is as close as Bony ever came to working in a big city. In *The Devil's Steps* Bony is at a place called the Wideview Chalet, which is some 30 miles out in the country from Melbourne, in the "Australian Alps," a place of great beauty to Bony until murder bloodies the picture.

Detective-Inspector Bonaparte, seconded to the Army on a secret assignment, has gone to Wideview Chalet to investigate some apparent foreign conspirators. Mr. Brumann is found dead in a ditch with his luggage missing. Constable Rice, who has been summoned, arrives simultaneously with a visitor for Mr. Brumann, and is found by him shot dead. Bony does some of his more interesting investigating in hidden passages and runways, and some of his more imaginative sleuthing. As a consequence this work is one of his most "thriller" type books. Here, and in this type book, Bony is less his usual genial self, is more grim, tense. Upfield seems to have been an intense patriot when it came to international espionage. The balance and quality of his work suffers because intensity of feeling with Upfield interferes with art.

But Bony is aided by Bisker, a marvelous Dickensian character. This "lovely case— a glorious mix up of a case," as Bony calls it, is the first of two involving Upfield's serious indictment of the Australian literati, and our first look at Clarence B. Bagshott, a portrait of himself by Upfield. In Bagshott we like what we see. In this book Upfield is less concerned with landscape and weather than he usually is. The situation, Upfield's serious attack on the Australian literati and the development of Clarence Bagshott make this work, in general, a first-class crime story.

*An Author Bites the Dust.* Published: Angus, 1948; reissued, Angus, 1967; reissued, Angus & Robertson, 1984. Doubleday, 1948; reissued, London House-British Book Centre, 1967.

In *An Author Bites the Dust* Bony is again out of his strongest element, for he is not in "the vast pastoral lands and the semi-deserts of inland Australia." Instead he is in the "Australia Alps," where he was in *The Devil's Steps*. This second novel in the same area is located slightly farther out of town than *The Devil's Steps* was and is in the fictitious town of "Yarrabo" in the valley of the real Yarra River, only a few miles short of the real town of Warburton. Thus, Asdell located both settings as "in the scenic resort area bounded, roughly, by the towns of Lilydale, Healesville and Warburton." "Yarrabo," he thinks "suspiciously close to the real Yarra Junction."

It is a proper setting for a group of Australian literati, whom Upfield despised, to be preening their feathers. In *An Author Bites the Dust*, the author of the title is the self-famous leader of Australian literature, Mervyn Blake, who died of mysterious causes in Yarrabo two months before Bony comes to investigate. Bony is sent to see what has happened. Staying with Miss Pinkerton as a visitor, Bony visits one of the literary soirees and gets to know the people well. He sniffs around talking with various persons until he comes to grasp the picture. He meets his old friend Clarence B. Bagshott again and through him learns the true nature of the literati.

This is one of Upfield's attempts to do a locked-door type British detective novel. His landscape, aside from the outside, is the country of his life-long hatred for the literary poseurs of Australia, who kept him beyond the pale throughout his literary career. A part of the scenery is his old friend Bagshott. Bony finally solves the case by proving that the one he would least like to implicate is guilty. The method of death is one of Upfield's most exotic, the use of coffin-dust, a method authenticated by Taylor's *Principles and Practice of Medical Jurisprudence*, as Upfield says in Chapter 21 of the novel.

The case of "coffin-dust" being used as a poison demonstrates how widely Upfield, like all authors of poison-literature, reached out to find the exotic and unique kinds of poison (reminds one of Agatha Christie's various discoveries of new lethal uses). John Hetherington, in his article "Arthur Upfield, Murder is his Business," reprinted in *The Bony Bulletin*, No. 4, reported that Prof. Alfred Swaine Taylor's book *Principles and Practice of Medical Jurisprudence* was in Upfield's library when he visited him at his home in Bowral. The reference to coffin-dust appeared last, apparently, in the 10th edition of the work (1935), and had been there since the 5th edition (1905). It is worthwhile to quote the entire passage:

Surely of all curious substances to be used for a poison this must be the most so, and must show the mixture of superstition in human nature, which will serve all science. The fact of an alcoholic extract proving fatal to rabbits warrants the editor nevertheless in publishing this letter, which is one written by Dr. Percy Smith to Sir Thomas Stevenson in November, 1895. The publication of it here may bring fresh material to light:—

"I was conversing with a doctor from Colombia (South America), and he told me that in his country it was a popular belief that the dust of a decomposed body gathered from an old coffin was poisonous, producing, after ingestion, diarrhea and death.

A case had happened where a husband, being jealous of his wife, procured some "coffin dust" from a grave, and administered it in soup. A fortnight afterwards the woman had diarrhea and died. The doctor was called in at the trial of the man (some three months after the death) to advise the court if coffin dust was really toxic. He, being unable to answer the question, requested three months in which to make experiments.

Accordingly he procured some dust from a coffin which had been buried about six years, the contents of which were quite friable-grey powder —and an extract into a rabbit was fatal.

He thereupon professed himself unable to decide the question, not being a toxicologist and because further experiments were necessary.

The question is, 'Can the ptomaines survive the decomposition of the body, and exist unimpaired in the residue?'

The possibility of a definite poison having been administered together with the dust is negatived by the fact that the natives thoroughly believe in the efficacy of the dust, and would not trouble to get it unless they really did so.

Philip Asdell, who did the quoting from the Taylor volume, pursued the question of toxicity of coffin dust by asking an expert in the field of poisons, Dr. John H. Dirckx of Dayton, Ohio (author of "The Compleat Poisoner," *The Thorndyke File* No. 7, Spring 1979) his opinion. Asdell quoted the letters, or portions of them, in *The Bony Bulletin*, Oct. 1 (Oct. 1983):

I don't know why 'coffin dust' would be poisonous in small quantities, especially by mouth. Ptomaines are harmless when taken by mouth. An embalmed or mummified body shouldn't go to dust; but if it did, the preservatives might prove toxic. The tiny amount of dust that could be administered in a drink seems unlikely to do anyone any harm, unless he knew what he was getting and succumbed to superstitious terrors.

In a second letter to Asdell, Dr. Dirckx added to his earlier comments:

The injected coffin dust might have killed the rabbit by way of a foreign protein reaction (though this seems far-fetched), which would not be expected to occur when coffin dust was administered orally, either to a human or to a different species. The death of the rabbit might of course have been due to the alcohol used to extract the injected material from the source. We aren't told how or how fast the rabbit died. Perhaps it had a hemorrhage or peritonitis, related to the injection. It seems self-evident that there is not, in a human body, significant amounts of toxic substances during life; hence, if coffin dust really is lethal, it is because of something that happens after death. Ptomaines, as I mentioned before, are not harmful when taken by mouth. (So-called ptomaine poisoning is due to other substances.) Whether any produce of decomposition remains actively toxic into the dust stage is a question upon which we just don't seem to have any data, except one deceased bunny.

Though in fact Upfield may have lighted upon a bit of pseudo-poisoning that does not hold its strength in the laboratory, who cares? It is a marvelous fictional device for doing away with one's enemies, and especially appropriate for causing the demise of a member of the literati snobs, Upfield's *betes noir*.

Anyone who knows Upfield's background in trying to break into the literary world of Australia will delight in this book because it reveals Upfield's revenge at its sharpest and most trenchant. But it is not a diatribe. On the contrary, this is one of Upfield's cleverer books, though a kind of locked-cottage type, involving nothing of the great outback which was Upfield's strength. Nevertheless, it is a readable and enjoyable book.

*The Widows of Broome*. Published: Heinemann, 1951; reissued, Heinemann, 1967. Doubleday, 1950; Scribner's 1985.

In *The Windows of Broome* Upfield returns to his strength, the outback of Australia. This time the setting is Broome, on the northwest of Western Australia. Upfield refers to it as a town with a population of eight hundred people that has no Main Street and no regularly scheduled life. The real Broome is located on Roebuck Bay over 1000 miles northeast of Perth. Founded in the 1880s, the town was well-known as a pearling port which was renowned by 1900 as the pearling center of the world. At its peak Broome had a population of 5000, with about 400 pearl-luggers. But plastics had brought about the decline in Broome's activities by the 1930s. Broome apparently has always had a section called "Chinatown," where some of Bony's activities in this book took place.

Broome is being terrorized by a series of murders of attractive widows. Two have already been murdered when Bony, as Mr. Knapp, psychiatrist, comes to town to investigate. On the surface the murders seem to have little in common and to be without reason. Bony, however, soon sees what they have in common and the apparent reason for the killings. He becomes more and more apprehensive as the moon works toward the full, when, in fact, a third murder is committed. By now, however, Bony has enough facts to lay a trap for the murderer, whom he exposes.

Bony pictures the town as probably deader than it actually was. His is a study in abnormal psychology, as *Wings Above the Diamantina* had been, where he investigated a man "temperamentally unstable," and *Winds of Evil* demonstrated the

SHIRE OF BROOME

FIRST TOWN IN THE KIMBERLEY

Setting of *The Widows of Broome*

convulsions that some forms of weather can cause in the human mind and nerves.

Upfield's setting for *The Widows of Broome* is a mindscape centering on the forgeries of the so-called "respectable" people. Bony reads the mind of a perverted man who because of insecurity with his past and present life is obsessed with the feel of feminine undergarments and the punishment of women who wear them.

Upfield is careful in his cluing the reader in on the causes and results of such perversion. The result is a meticulous and interesting study in abnormal psychology and detecting.

*The Mountains Have a Secret.* Published: Heinemann, 1952. Doubleday, 1948. Pan, 1983.

Bony's next adventure, *The Mountains Have a Secret*, is a return to the parts of Australian landscape that Bony works in most effectively. This time the setting is Dunkeld, near Mount Abrupt in the Grampians, Victoria.

Disguised as a sheep farmer on vacation, Bony visits the Baden Park Hotel in order to investigate the disappearance of two self-reliant Australian girls. One policeman, Detective Price, out for the same investigation, was found shot to death in his car. Jim Simpson, owner of the hotel, is a cold, arrogant man who keeps around him suspicious characters. He and his sister Cora live behind high barbed-wire fences and electrically operated gates. Presumably these measures are for the protection of their prized sheep, but Bony suspects more sinister reason. Bony is aided in his investigation by the elder invalided Simpson, to whom he doles out sips of whiskey, and Glen Shannon, a Texan, who has his own reasons for working undercover.

Upfield manages to convey the awe in which he holds the landscape he is working in. Bony first sees the Grampians as they "rose from the vast plain of golden grass...isolated rocks along the northwest horizon, rising to cut sharply into the cobalt sky."

After being briefed by Senior Constable Groves at the Dunkeld Police Station about the disappearance of the girls and the murder of Detective Price, Bony heads north, rounds Mount Abrupt on the road to Halls Gap. This novelistic geography is partially

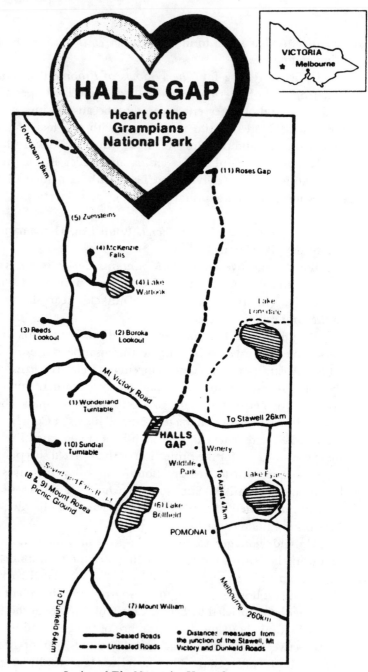

Setting of *The Mountains Have a Secret*

identifiable. Mrs. Gail Barwell of the Stawell Library reported for Asdell that the "Bade Park Hotel," where Bony conducts the first part of investigation might have been the Bellfield Hotel, but that there was no fishing lake in the vicinity of this hotel. There was, however, a fine fishing lake called Lake Murihead, but no hotel. The supposition is that Upfield may have rearranged his geography a little for the benefit of his story.

Stylistically, the landscape calls forth Upfield's most herculean descriptions. In describing the origin of the beautiful and mighty Grampians he reports that

The rocks united and upon that quarter of the plain it could be seen that a cosmic hurricane had lashed the earth and created a sea, a sea of blue-black waves poised to crash forward in graphical suds.

These awesome physical characteristics allowed the imagination full-play:

Distance presented mystery, released the imagination, stirred the memory. Beneath these curling wave crests surely dwelt the Beings of Australia's Alcheringa Era, or where perhaps await the Valkyries of the Norsemen to carry the remains of heroes into the Halls of their Valhalla.

It is with these prophetic words that Upfield sets the stage for what will be the Twilight of the Gods in a cascading *Gotterdammerung* of organ manipulation, through which there is a maddened escape by the guilty parties amid a hail of bullets.

Generally speaking this is an effective crime novel, though it gets somewhat adumbrated by being another of Upfield's studies in foreign conspiracies and entanglements. The study of Glen Shannon, the Texan, though exaggerated into a kind of foreigner's caricature of the virtuous and humorous Texan, is interesting, and reveals just how much Upfield cared for America and Americans. Caves play a large part in this book, again revealing a great interest of Upfield's in cavescapes and in the symbolism they allow him to produce. All in all, this is a high suspense drama, and a fine Upfield story.

*The New Shoe.* Published: Heinemann, 1952; reissued, Heinemann, 1968. Doubleday, 1951; reissued, Scribner's 1979; the Mystery Library, 1976.

In *The New Shoe* Upfield is again in his element. This story takes place at Split Point, 80 miles from Melbourne between Angelsea and Lorne.

The corpse of a naked man has been found in a locker of the Split Point Lighthouse. Bony comes to investigate. Since the lighthouse is inspected only on a regular schedule, Bony assumes that the murdered man is a local and that he was murdered by people who knew the schedule of inspection. The local community is in a serious agitated state of mind, which confirms Bony's suspicion that local conditions caused the murder. He unravels the events and the causes—and passes his own personal judgment.

Bony begins the book with a seascape that points up the starkness of the geography and the warmth of Bony's heart. Upfield discusses the cold sea and the approaching night, and how even the birds, fearful of impending darkness, flee the sea for the safety of the land. All escape except a wounded penguin that cannot quite make the shore. It gets colder and colder until "lethargy quieted all his fears" in death. Then Bony, warmhearted, buries the dead bird, somewhat embarrassed but feeling that he is unobserved. Then in a striking paragraph, Upfield contrasts Bony's warm heart and the nature of living life with that of the geography of the physical setting, of death and of symbolism:

Split Point is not unlike the distended claws of an angry cat's paw, forever thwarted by Eagle Rock standing safely out at sea. Bony surveyed two of these claws rising sheerly from the beach for a hundred feet or more, and then the less precipitous slope of paw rising to the base of the lighthouse.

As the scene develops, Upfield introduces two elements that will figure distinctly in the developing symbolism:

At the base of the right cliff two caves offered cold shelter, and within the rock funnel in the face of the left cliff the wind swirled grass and dead bush round and round without cease. At his low elevation, he could see all the lighthouse save its foundation upon the grassy sward, a tapering white stalk holding aloft the face of glass beneath the cardinal's hat.

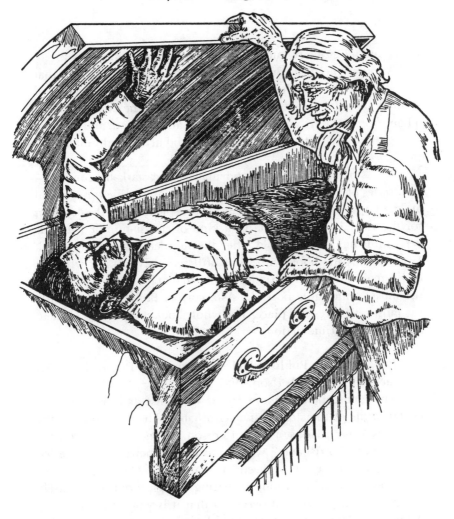

*"You wouldn't like to try her with the lid down?"*

Illustration for *The New Shoe*. Artwork by Dick Conner, Published by University Extension University of California, San Diego, 1951.

Caves and religion are integral to the development of the book.

Another piece of landscape explored at great length is that of a coffin, into which Bony crawls and the top is lowered and secured. This landscape of horror is palpable. The book is indeed a haunting and terrifying scene of nature and religion, and a fitting place for scenes of man's suspicions of and acts of inhumanity to man.

The story is enlivened—and made more stark by contrast—by a series of Dickensian characters who are unexcelled in Upfield and perhaps elsewhere as well. Despite the solemnity of the occasion for the visit, Upfield maintains a kind of corpse-humor which is very amusing. For example, after the murder has been resolved, Upfield ends the book with Bony still seriously talking with the coffin-maker about how to make the coffin that he, Bony, has ordered the most comfortable possible. As a corpse, Bony will want only the most restful resting place. The whole book is first-class Upfield and first-class crime fiction.

*Venom House*. Published: Heinemann, 1953; Doubleday, 1952. Reissued, Angus & Robertson, 1985.

The landscape of *Venom House* is intense and graphic. The actual locale of the story is indeterminable. The town nearest the fictitious Venom House is called Edison, "a one-pub town on the coast south of Brisbane," which must be somewhere on the 65-mile stretch of road between Brisbane and Coolangatta. But regardless of actual location, the setting of this story is so intensely psychological, so evil and perverted that it is worthy of an Edgar Allan Poe. Mrs. Answerth is found strangled in the moat that surrounds Venom House, a strangely isolated house. There had been a similar death, that of the local butcher, Ed Carlow, and Inspector Stanley had been unable to solve it. Bony is called in after the second death. Venom House is peopled by strange characters. Mary Answerth is a tartar of a woman, more masculine than feminine, who prides herself on the fact that there is no man, except Bony of course, and no horse she cannot tame. She has the local men intimidated. Her sister, Janet, is a smooth-talking, lisping, sweet person, educated and smooth, but clearly dangerous. Their

Setting of *Venom House.*

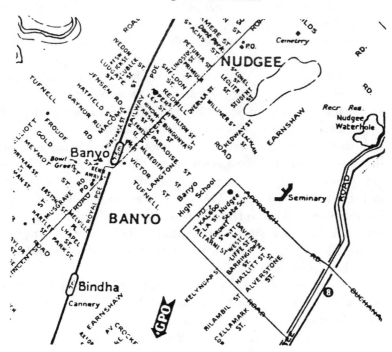

Setting of Bony's Residence

half-brother, Morris, is an adult in body and child in mind. He is kept locked in a second-story room, where he plays with a toy train and a lasso.

This is a marvelously compressed and disturbing story. It consists of several geographies. The first is of the house. Upfield contrasts the outside of the house, a thing of bewitching beauty, with the inside evil:

The tinting of the gold sank downward to claim the mist to the glassy surface. The air was cool and pleasurably breathed, and it brought the scents of luscious growth, of cattle, of gum-wood burning in a stove. A distant shadow materialised in the mist, became a featureless oblong based on nothing, and both men silently watched as the shadow solidified to a large flat-roof house. The tips of the taller of the dead trees standing in the Folly were guided by the sun, and the mist magically thinned to reveal the windows and the great arched porch to the front entrance of the distant house. (37)

Another geography is that of the three residents of the house. Again Upfield is playing amateur psychologist and studying perverted minds. Mary is too masculine, has denied her femininity, and offends the men of the town. An Amazon, she "offends my sense of what is right in a woman," as the locale constable says. (33) Janet is likewise offensive and somehow contrary to nature. Her lisp is her sign of Satan. Morris is feeble-minded as a result of the sins of his parents as well as those of his half-sisters.

Another sinscape that fires the book is real offenses done by the Answerths of preceding generations. They stole their land from the Aborigines, destroying and killing them wherever they tried to protect their holdings. The sin  of the whole Answerth tribe is symbolized in *Venom House*, and in Bony's immediate statement upon seeing it for the first time that it looks like Buckingham Palace. Thus in Upfield's mind the royalty of Australia is no different from the royalty of England in its theft.

This is one of Upfield's most compelling stories; though it does not concern the outdoor landscape of Australia, it does deal with human traits and characteristics, especially abnormal psychology, which call forth Upfield's novelistic strengths. The setting is tight—a kind of island-mystery and compresses its horror so intensely that it seeps through the pores of the readers. The strength of Upfield's accomplishment in this book is so overwhelming it makes the reader cower. The characters are well-developed, the conversation vernacular for the Australian outback, and the development compelling. This story is the nearest Upfield comes to a story that would have made Edgar Allan Poe envious. It makes us all thankful for the story—and that it is only fiction.

*Murder Must Wait.* Published: Heinemann, 1953. Doubleday, 1953. Reissued, Angus & Robertson, 1984.

The setting of this book is Mitford, on the northern bank of the Murray River, New South Wales, "wide open to the cold southerlies of winter and of the hot northerlies of summer." Up close, "a broad tree-shaded boulevard skirts the river, and Main Street is flanked by squat emporiums crammed with goods likely, and unlikely, to be needed by people who own the surroundings vineyards and who operate the canning works for ten weeks every year." (5)

Asdell places this book fairly conclusively. Upfield says that "Mitford" is on the River Murray in the State of New South Wales. It is in a fruit-growing district, with a cannery and irrigation channels found nearby. There are references to a bridge over the Murray River, paddle-steamers and local fruit and wine industries, an airport, etc. Although Upfield says that "Mitford" is half-way between Albury and Mildura, there is in fact no such town in existence; so Asdell concludes that Upfield has renamed Muldura, which otherwise fits all the criteria for identity with Upfield's "Mitford," for the site of his adventure. "Mildura" is a Aboriginal word for "red cliffs," many of which mark the Murray River in this district.

Four babies have turned up missing and Bony is called in by Inspector Yoti, who is sure that this case will prove too much for the great detective. As Bony arrives in Mitford, the police are discovering that Mrs. Rockcliff has been murdered and her baby taken from its crib. The case is difficult. To assist him Bony calls in, for the first time in the series, his "cousin," First Constable Alice McGorr, whose knowledge of women and babies is very useful. Development and explanation of the mystery turns on rather

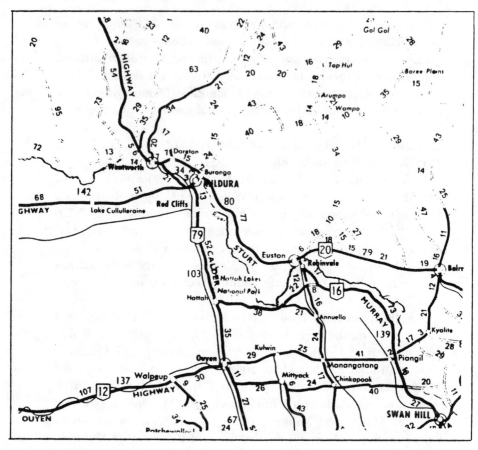

Setting of *Murder Must Wait*

extensive use of Aboriginal-lore which reaches out in two or three directions.

The landscape of the book centers on the interaction of a lot of people, including the intellects of some simple-minded academics who work among and teach the Aboriginals, a Satanic Dr. Nonning, who represents the academic at its worst, and the physical setting and activities of the Aboriginals and their legend about the birth of children. Upfield often makes oblique, and sometimes direct, references to other writers of crime fiction. In this case it is to Edgar Allan Poe's "The Purloined Letter," to help danken the atmosphere of this novel.

The concept of this story demonstrates how widely Upfield's mind ranged in his crime fiction, for his concern here is much more with the children than with the murdered woman—thus the title—for solving the disappearance of the children takes precedence over solving the murder. Solution of the kidnapping turns on Aboriginal legends and birth-lore. This is a tender story, braced by the introduction of "cousin" Alice McGorr, who is such a strong personality that the reader only wishes Upfield had used her more often.

*Death of a Lake.* Published: Heinemann, 1954; reissued, Heinemann, 1967. Doubleday, 1954. Reissued, Scribner's, 1982.

*Death of a Lake* is as intense and unremitting a story as Upfield ever wrote. It should be, for it was very close to Upfield's personality. Asdell has located "Porchester Station," which consists of 800,000 "acres and was populated by sixty thousand sheep in the care of some twenty range plugs" as being the real Albermarle Station where Upfield was first hired as a cook in the 1920s and where he began his writing career. Upfield's "Lake Otway" is probably the real Victoria Lake on the Station. Upfield's "Sandy Well" is likely the real Wheeler's Well. In a hut at Wheeler's Well Upfield was inspired to create his Bony after a visit by Upfield's friend Tracker Leon Wood.

Bony, disguised as a horse-breaker, visits the lake station to investigate the death of young Raymond Gillen, who went swimming in the lake one hot moonlit night and was never seen again. He left behind twelve-thousand-dollars, which have disappeared, that he won as a half-share of a lottery ticket, and a motor bike, still around. In the intense heat which reaches 118 degrees in the shade, the various people at the station—including Mrs. Fowler and her daughter Joan, who are sexual rivals for all the men present—sweat out the drying-up of the lake, which will surely reveal the corpse of the disappeared Gillen. One night the house at Lake Otway burns, along with the body of Mrs. Fowler. Bony, sensing arson, is able to clear up the mystery surrounding all the events pretty quickly.

The novel begins with a death-knell:"Lake Otway was dying. Soon there would be nothing but drab flats of iron-hard clay." The lake had been born in happiness and glee and now was dying in despair and apparent murder. "The Lake which had lived and danced and sung for three years and now was about to die." Death and decay, degeneration and discord permeate the book like a miasma from a giant swamp. In its death throes the lake held the attention, the conversation, the gaze of all the people at the station. It was the eye of the storm that brewed in the personalities of the people and their lives as the summer heat grew to 120 degrees in the shade and in the hearts of the people to even higher degrees. The intensity is that of the most accomplished reality and naturalism.

*Sinister Stones.* Published: Heinemann, 1955 as *Cake in the Hatbox.* Doubleday, 1954. Reissued, Scribner's, 1982.

This novel is set in Agar's Lagoon, 300 miles inland from the coast, 1500 miles north of Perth and 240 south of Wyndham. As Asdell points out, these directions are explicit enough to suggest the real township Upfield is using for his model is Hall's Creek, situated on the Great Northern Highway between Fitzroy Crossing and Wyndham.

Agar's Lagoon, so far back in the bush that transportation gets there irregularly, is symbolized by the ring of empty bottles that surround it, accumulated because the town is too far away from Perth to make recycling them economically feasible. Into this desolation Bony is forced one day when his plane develops engine

Setting of *Sinister Stones*

Setting of *The Battling Prophet*

trouble and has to set down. Bony is induced to investigate the death of Constable Martin Stenhouse, and refuses to take the accepted explanation that the murder was done by Stenhouse's tracker. Bony sees stones arranged for the reading of trained eyes, and the smoke signals indicate that there are many people talking to one another about the event. As it turns out, the tracker also has been murdered and in a way "turned into a horse." As the mystery is resolved, Bony, as he is wont to do, acts as both judge and jury, and though he must arrest the person who did the murder, he will do all he can to lighten the sentence, if there is one.

At times Upfield uses nature alone to sketch the power and desolation of the Australian land mass. At other times he uses man and man's actions to intensify the desolation. Such is the case in this book. The physical setting is nothing compared to that strewn by the human modifiers of the landscape. Agar's Lagoon is a tiny settlement of 13 houses, which symbolized the emptiness of the lives of the inhabitants. Another bit of landscape, this time of the aboriginals, is the inside of a horse's belly, a site used to hide the body of a dead aboriginal.

*Sinister Stones* is not one of Upfield's strongest books, but it is nevertheless educational, fascinating in its treatment of outback life, and reveals clearly the weakness Bony has for young women and for people in the cattle stations who have been abused by life and events. All in all, it is a creditable production.

*The Battling Prophet.* Published: Heinemann, 1956; reissued, Angus & Robertson, 1981.

The setting for this book is the South Australia/Victoria border near the town of Mount Gambier on the Cowdry River, just out of Melbourne. The place is the real town of Mt. Gambier, a city which in the mid-1980s numbered some 20,000 people, though it was considerably smaller when Upfield was there. One of the more remarkable geographical features, which plays no role in the story other than to be a point of interest, is the famous Blue Lake, which occupies one of the three volcano craters just south of the town. For eleven months of the year it is a dull gray, but during November it turns a vivid blue. As Bony passes this lake on the bus going to see his friend John Luton, the bus driver explains that the bright color results from the fact that "The Mount Gambier people emptied tons of washing blue into it." In his *Land of Australia*, Frank Clune suggests instead, that the blue is an optical illusion resulting from light dispersion and the reflection of the blue sky. Philip Asdell suggests, perhaps more correctly that there are micro-organisms present during that month which color the water.

In this story, Meteorologist Ben Wickham is famous and respected in America but is thought a quack in Australia. When he dies, his death is certified as being the result of an extended drinking spree and his body is cremated. Lifelong friend John Luton insists that Wickham was murdered, that they had been drinking vast quantities of booze for decades and he knows that the noted meteorologist did not expire from drinking booze. Bony visits his friend John Luton while on vacation but gets involved in the murder. Again he calls on his friend Constable Alice McGorr to come in and help him control the troubles and solve the problems.

Instead of landscape, this story turns on meteorology and on man's greed and envy. During "The droughtiest year for the last seventeen ' across South Australia, Victoria and high into New South Wales," people are suffering untold privation. This is a proper setting for a story of a meteorologist who can correctly predict dry and wet years, an art appreciated only be Americans. The weather prophet is killed by Communist agents because of his skill, and the impact it has on their nefarious operations. The violent reactions this murder triggers create a story that is vastly suggestive and rewarding.

This is an unusual crime story for Upfield, but, revealing the vast range of his interests, it is one of his better ones. The story is not riveting but the characters are. Constable Alice McGorr returns and is at her strongest and most profane best. She seems to demonstrate that when Upfield, who usually is very respectful of the women he places either on a pedestal or in very clean and neat dresses, creates a profane one, he wants a *profane* one. She is. And she is extraordinary, and should be appreciated as one of his major creations. She demonstrates that though she is very much a lady she is also muscle, and can toss and kick, and order, people around

with the profanest men. She is superb. John Luton, a booze head
if there ever was one, is also a fine creation. Upfield is often at
his best when writing about pubs and pubbers. This book is an
excellent example. The strength of the plot is somewhat attenuated
by the intrusion of foreign communists, who are out to wreak havoc
in Australia. Though this conspiracy is the fulcrum on which the
story balances and is something of a distraction, the book
nevertheless coheres and develops smoothly and logically. It is an
enviable production.

*Man of Two Tribes*. Published: Heinemann, 1956. Doubleday,
1956. Reissued, Angus & Robertson, 1984.

Locale: Nullarbor Plain, Western Australia and South Australia
on the Great Australian Bight.     In *Man of Two Tribes* Upfield
leans on and develops his story as much as in any other book out
of the landscape of Australia. This time the setting is on the western
edge of the Nullarbor Plain in Western Australia and South Australia
on the Great Australian Bight and the cavescape which underlies
portions of it.

Upfield's fictional town in the Plain is "Chifley," consisting
of "railway buildings, the water tank, the oil containers for the
new diesels, and the few cottages occupied by the permanent way
men and staff. Other than this, there was nothing of Chifley; no
streets, no shops, no hotel." The description fits any of the small
remote towns on the Plain along the Transcontinental railway route.
In one place, this railway stretches for 300 miles without a perceptible
curve, as Upfield describes at the beginning of his novel. The general
area and the caves are virtually the same Upfield had used some
years earlier in one of his non-Bony novels, *A Royal Abduction*.

This stringent desert, though facing the sea, is as severe a treeless
region as one will find, although after infrequent rains a few flowers
do bloom. The origin of the name of the Plain is still in debate.
Although linguists insist that the name comes from the Latin
meaning "No Tree," some Australian archeologists and
anthropologists insist that the word is aboriginal in origin. Whatever
the origin, the name is fitting, for it describes a flat limestone plain
underlain with extensive caves and tunnels which have egress to

the surface through blowholes, which occasionally sigh and groan as the heat of the plain sucks the air from the cooler regions of the caves. The caves are now being extensively investigated by archeologists, who are finding evidence through paintings and other markings that aboriginals were in these caves some 35,000 years go. They did not use the caves extensively, however, or the plains because of fear of their legendary "Ganba, the Man-Eating snake," as Upfield called it. Aboriginals did visit the caves to get flint to be used in their weapons and utility instruments.

This is Upfield's fifth use of caves in his books. In all others he uses cases as symbols of religion, sex and rebirth. In this one, the caves remain mainly just caves, cool, comfortable refuges from the heat of the plain, though still prisons.

The plot of the book has to do with prisons and release from them. Myra Thomas, though guilty of murdering her husband, is acquitted by the jury because of misplaced sympathy. Myra disappears from the train on the Nullarbor Plain and Bony begins the search to locate her. Posing as the nephew of a wild-dog tracker, Bony visits the desolate sand and saltbush of the Plain. He is captured by four wild aborigines and thrown back into aboriginal geology and a strange world of caves under the Plains, there to find several people who were guilty of murder but had been released from prison before their sentences had run out.

This is surely one of the two or three strongest of Upfield's novels. It is an eerie mixture of Aboriginal folk customs and white man's greed and lust for revenge. Something of a study of abnormal psychology, it nevertheless turns on people's very natural and nasty feelings. One of the more dramatic settings for much of the story is a throw-back to a scene used earlier though in something of a different way. The adventures of the people who follow Bony demonstrate just how tough life in Australia can be and how hardy the people can become. Stylistically, Upfield adjusts the cadence and rhythm of his prose to that of the people and the desert. For example, on the desert the people witness a terrifying phenomenon, as the winds create a snake made of giant accumulations of straw:

> The party stopped, to gaze in wonderment at what was happening. They could see neither the eastern nor the western limit of what appeared as a pale-yellow snake, alive and menacing, its body rippling in effort to digest a meal.

Here and there it bulged towards them, at places it rolled over and over, and at no place was torn asunder. Bony knew it could roll over a man and do no hurt, but it appeared to be as weighty as molten metal.

The book is a splendid combination of plot, setting and development.

*Bony Buys a Woman*. Published, Heinemann, 1957; reissued, Heinemann, 1967. Issues in America as *The Bushman Who Came Back*: Doubleday, 1957. Reissued, Pan, 1984.

In this book Upfield uses the outback cattle station in a new and powerful way. The scene is a cattle station alongside a dried-up lake that, as Upfield tells the story, periodically freshens and dries up. The lake is modeled on the real body of water Lake Eyre, which lies north of Marrie, east of Williams Creek and northeast of Coward Springs. Called by Upfield "The-Sea-That-Was," a puddle sixty miles wide and a hundred long, Lake Eyre, as Asdell points out, is the largest of many salt "lakes" that remain from having been at one time connected with the sea. If Lake Eyre were to receive water it would come from Cooper Creek and the Diamantina River. But it has filled with water only four times since its discovery in 1840 by the explorer Edwards John Eyre.

In Upfield's novel the woman owner of the station is murdered and her daughter is taken by an aboriginal, presumably the murderer, out into the nearly-dry lake's center. In pursuing Old Fren Yorky and the child out into the lake, Bony suspects that the aboriginals know more about the business than they admit. The trail into the lake-bed is at times sticky and invisible and extends for miles into the center. Once there, Bony and his suspect and prize must hurry out before the lake rises again and drowns them all. Meanwhile on the edge of the lake somebody is shooting at them from the blinding sun with a Winchester rifle. The compression of haste and anger on the lake bed is given with Upfield's usual unrelenting terror. Upfield's picture of the lakescape is both compelling and lyrical. This is the land, in which "to run was to crawl" (64) but a place of infinite beauty: "Before the sun rose, during those magic moments when the Earth is pure and without deceit." (90) But it is also a land where an old aboriginal chief, this time Chief Canute, can be promised beautiful young

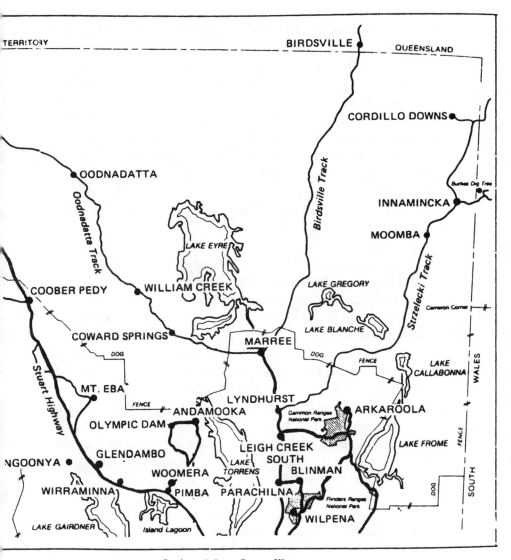

Setting of *Bony Buys a Woman*

Meena, though she is in love with Charlie, a man of her age. Bony, out of a sense of the injustice of many aboriginal December-June marriages and for his own purposes buys Meena for forty plugs of tobacco. In so doing he brings happiness to the young and creates no hatred among the old who otherwise insist on the aboriginal laws and practices.

Though the beginning of the book is somewhat sentimental, especially in Upfield's usual inability to handle the roles of young females, it becomes one of Bony's great adventures. Because of the interplay between whites and aboriginals, Upfield is able to make his various comments on the differences between the two races and the superiority of the latter. He pictures the merits of aboriginal society. And he uses weather—in this case the threatened rising of the lake—to picture man's heroic stature. The setting, the events, the pace of telling the story, the style of telling it—all combine to make this a tight, effective crime novel.

*The Bachelors of Broken Hill.* Published: Heinemann, 1958, reissued, Angus & Robertson, 1983. Doubleday, 1950.
Locale: Broken Hill, New South Wales.
In *The Bachelors of Broken Hill* Upfield switches from the outback to an urban district. The place is Broken Hill, the "third city in the state of New South Wales," and the first city Upfield saw when he came to the Australian outback in 1910. Broken Hill is nothing like the other cities in that state: "There is nothing parochial or bucolic about Broken Hill." There is no city in all Australia remotely like it, excepting perhaps the golden city of Kalgoorlie. Upfield must have especially liked it, not only because of his nostalgic association with it but because of its democratic way of life. As he said:

There is nothing of the snobocracy of Melbourne, or the dog-eat-dog taint of Sydney, in the community of Broken Hill, and there is no thoroughfare in Australia quite like Argent Street, Broken Hill's main shopping center.

Argent street was "unique." (3) Little wonder that Upfield was nostalgic about the town.

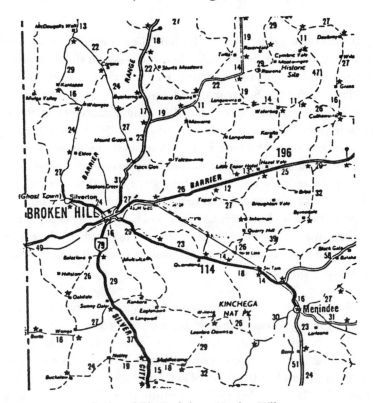

Setting of *The Bachelors of Broken Hill*

It had been the town that Upfield had seen in 1910 when he was on his way to Momba Station, his first outback job after arriving in Adelaide and leaving it for the interior. He had arrived there early one morning by train, had gone from the railway station to the Southern Cross Hotel for breakfast and to wait until 10 a.m. for the horse-drawn coach of the Cobb & Co. line that would take him to Wilcannia. Upfield was charmed by the setting, which included riding hacks along the hitching rails.

The sidewalk was of boards. Along the street bronzed men drove paired horses harnessed to buckboards. Other bronzed men leaned against the verandah posts.

Broken Hill became the "real" Australia to Upfield. In this town and its environs Bony was to solve nine of his cases.     In this case, disguised as Mr. Knapp, Bony visits Broken Hill to investigate the deaths of two elderly men who have died of cyanide. Bony visits the places where the people have died and sees that there are several unexplainable events concatenated. He fortunately bumps into cat-burglar Jimmy the Screwman and intimidates him into being a second-story man in the interest of finding a murderer. Although he is relieved of responsibility for the job, Bony perseveres and finds some people who have reason to act as strangely as they do.

This is another case in abnormal psychology, and Upfield handles the episode and the probing deftly. In this story Upfield is less intense than in some others, less the unrelenting dog after his prey. But his characters are very much alive, especially Jimmy the Screwman, and he does an above-average job of developing some of the women in the story. All in all, a splendid story, although surely not Upfield's best.

*Bony and the Black Virgin.* Published: Heinemann, 1959. Collier, 1965; reissued, Angus & Robertson, 1986.

This novel is set on a 150,000 acre sheep ranch in Mindee on the Darling River in New South Wales. There has been a three-year drought, and in this land of sand and aborigines there is great danger. The Downers live well over a hundred miles from the nearest town. Upfield knew from personal experience the joy and the danger of living for a long time in the outback. Some people were driven to the coast, others were forced as occasion allowed to try diversions offered by the hotels and bars of the nearest settlements. Most apparently loved the outback for its tolerance of independence and self-assertion. But as the people had discovered, independence could be half-brother to loneliness. Upfield restates his observation in this book. The sun "cures as smoke will cure sides of bacon." (13) In this book the curing process brings out the very worst and the very best in the people concerned with the drama.

The book begins in the town, with Eric Downer and his father John Downer leaving town after John's annual binge. Eric has had to chase his elusive father from bar to bar, finally to catch him with the aid of the Constable. As they approach home, they see that something is wrong. A man lies dead, and the farm animals are near death. Bony is called in to investigate, and he gets more and more unhappy as the finger of guilt points more and more at people he has come to like.

This element of the plot—the desolated station and the rotting death found—there grew out of an earlier Upfield experience, when he was pushing his bike through the outback. One summer in South Australia Upfield had propped his bike against the verandah post of a squatter's house only to be mobbed by three dogs that were obviously dying of thirst. Curious about the circumstances of this cruelty to the animals, Upfield investigated. He knocked on the door of the residence, finally opening it and going in, where the explanation for the deprivation became obvious. The room was filled with the odor of death, as the decaying corpse of the squatter was found lying on the bed. He had died and in so doing had become the cause of death of many sheep that had starved to death because their water had been cut off and the near death of three dogs. Upfield had to cope with a situation where there were no telephone communications to the outside world, and almost no possibility of getting water to the animals. He cursed the squatter for having been foolishly stingy in not preparing more for the business of carrying on a station by installing a telephone line. But Upfield kept the image of the devastation in his mind to be used later in this book.

When Upfield gets down to the point of interracial sexual relations, he in effect is writing on one of the topics closest to his heart. Here his picture is unusually poignant. Caught in the iron grip of separation from his kind, of loneliness, of sexual attraction, Eric Downer is a victim of life. Though sentimental and perhaps overly dramatic in its ending, this book is especially effective.

*Bony and the Mouse.* Published: Heineman, 1959; reissued, Heinemann, 1961, 1967; reissued, Pan, 1984. Issued in U.S. as *Journey to the Hangman*: Doubleday, 1959.

Few books go to greater length to establish the scene of the countryside than does *Bony and the Mouse.*It is set in Daybreak, 150 miles inland from the terminus of the branch line at Laverton in Western Australia. Although the town is fictional, Asdell is convinced that it is based on the real town of Laverton, located about 150 miles north of the Golden Mile at Kalgoorlie. "Daybreak," the scene of the action, is supposed to be another 150 miles "inward" from Laverton; but 150 miles inward from Laverton there is nothing on the maps.

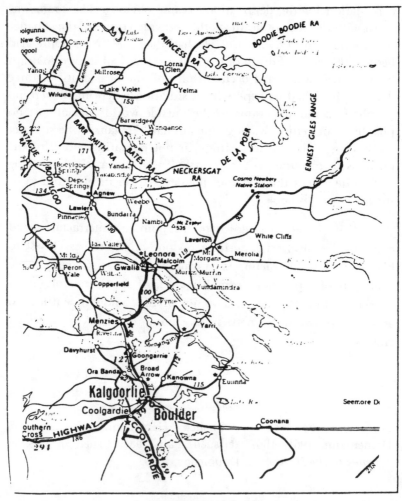

Setting of *Bony and the Mouse*

Upfield makes the setting mysterious and ominous by the way Bony enters it. He uses as his setting the mysterious surroundings of nature and the superstitious aborigine. Nature is represented by a "mulga forest the like of which is exceedingly rare in modern Australia, where steel axes have been frantically wielded for more than a century." This mulga forest is at least ten miles across, almost as far as the eye can see. It is a land of hot north wind and "scorched clouds" moving across the sky, and not one "passing over the face of the conquering sun." Upfield describes this forest in different and greater detail than he ordinarily does. It is a forest which some aborigine burned off centuries earlier in order to frighten out the game so he and his family could eat. The fire burned the trees but

the native trees dropped their seed encased within iron-hard pods which nothing but fire-heat could burst open. They exploded like small-arms after the major fire had passed by, scattering the seed wide to fall into the cooling ash.

Thus Upfield explained that phenomenon of the forest that is actually aided by the annual or occasional burn-over. The result of this particular instance was a graceful forest

Of uniform height, about twenty-five feet, they were uniformly shaped, the branch-spread dome-like, the trunks straight and metal-hard, and matching the dark green foliage massed to give shade, unusual in the interior of this continent. It is a forest ethereal and other worldly, giving forth a voice as of from nature itself. The summit of the arches swayed; the walls of the arches did not move.... Nothing else moved. (6)

Contrasted to the mysterious workings of nature and the obvious superstitious workings of the aborigines, there is an arrangement of stones.

The stones were roughly circular and flat, each about the size of a white man's soup plate. Between each was a space of about two feet. They formed two circles joined by a narrow passage, that farther from the rock-pile being much larger than the nearer one. Twenty men could have stood without contacting one another in the larger circle, ten could have done this in the smaller one, and two men could walk abreast along the connecting passage, a hundred yards long. At the far curve of the large circle, three stones were missing, so that it was possible for a man to walk into the circle, and from it along the passage to the small circle, without stepping over the outline of the design.

This is obviously an aboriginal ceremonial ground. The white quartz stones had been brought from outside the forest and were carefully maintained to keep the enclosed ground hallowed.

The seeming contrast between the two settings is not real. Actually one is ideally situated inside the heart of the other, for the spirits of the aboriginals come from the trees to whisper their taboos at the ceremonial grounds, and "in every one of those identical trees was imprisoned for eternity the spirit of a once living aborigine." (10) Thus Upfield creates the setting for the conflict of the story and gives clues, though paradoxically, as to how the plot will unfold. As is often true in Upfield's stories, there is a conflict between civilization and Aboriginal, between the axe of the whites and the spirit of the Blacks.

Daybreak is a one-pub town, owned and lorded over by Samuel Loader, otherwise known as Melody Sam. Because of his wealth and eccentric behavior, he is honored and feared. Bony comes to town disguised as Nat Turner, horse-breaker, and gets a job as yard-man at Melody Sam's pub. Here he can investigate the three murders that have shaken the town. Bony has an ally in the person of Sister Jenks. As Bony gets closer and closer to solving the crime, Australia's awesome geography and geology rise up not only as silent partners in the drama but as actual causes for the final solution.

Though lacking in some of the tightness that characterizes Upfield's strongest books, this thriller is nevertheless a powerful success. The geography and geology are stark and proper setting, the people are alive and flexing with pain and apprehension. Upfield's style is proper for the story. And here, as he so often does, he creates a major heroic character in Melody Sam who is unparalleled and unchallenged. Melody Sam is gargantuan in taste, in action, in affection and hate. He stands at least eight feet tall metaphorically.

*Bony and the Kelly Gang.* Published: Heinemann, 1960; reissued, Pan, 1983. Issued in America as *Valley of the Smugglers*: Doubleday, 1960.

*Bony and the Kelly Gang* is perhaps a self-indulgence on Upfield's part caused or encouraged by the place he was living when he wrote the book, Bowral. It is not a particularly successful book. The setting is around Bowral, 80 miles southwest of Sydney, New South Wales, where Upfield lived the last 15 years of his life. In the story a truck driver evaluates Bowral to Bony as "Smallish. Four-pub town. Three policeman. Five hundred yapping dogs." Bony's mission, as he passes through Bowral, is to get to "Cork Valley," where he will try to infiltrate the two clannish families living there to determine who murdered Eric Tarbay, an excise officer of the Customs Department whose body had been found along a road three miles outside Bowral. "Cork Valley," a fictional place, is pretty surely the real place of Kangaroo Valley, southeast of Bowral.

At the beginning of the book, Upfield makes it clear that Bony is out of his element. He is off his geography:

This was certainly not Inspector Bonaparte's country of mulga forest, rolling sand dunes and saltbrush plains, of barren residuals and ironstone ridges. This country was no less beautiful, no less mysterious, but it wasn't his own." (7)

Oliver Lodge, courtesy Philip Asdell

Setting of *Bony and the Kelly Gang*

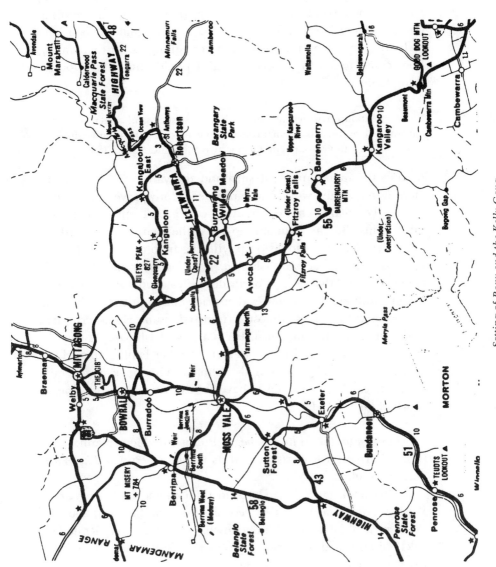

Setting of *Bony and the Kelly Gang*

It is a land of physical mountains and mountainous men. Everyman, and many of the women, seems a physical giant, roaring in stentorian tones, living a heroic life and playing a giant game. It is a land of Irish giants, who do not smile upon strangers. In their midst, Bony comes to like the people, though Upfield admits it is a foolish thing to do:

The foundation on which he had built a most successful career was being undermined by this liking of people whom he ought to regard with cold antipathy since probably among them were ruthless murderers. (88)

Among the mountains that surround the valley and among the mountain men and woman who people it, Bony proves that though physically smaller he is smarter, wilier and superior to the inhabitants. But he is unable to resist the charm of the Irish in the valley. His effort to keep up with the Irish does not call forth Upfield's greatest accomplishment. Bony, who in all other books has emphasized that he lives on Pride, with a capital P, and without it he is nothing, compromises that pride and dignity in this book. He becomes at times almost a minstrel man. He is cringing, undignified, nearly unethical. He is a stage Irishman. As such he does not do credit to himself as seen in other books. Aboriginals do not make good professional Irishmen. This book is generally not a success. Upfield seems to have been seduced by the geography in which he worked.

*Bony and the White Savage.* Published: Heinemann, 1961; reissued, Angus & Robertson, 1961. Issued in America as *The White Savage*: Doubleday, 1961.

This book takes Bony back to the extreme southwest tip of Western Australia, 150 miles west of Albany and directly south of Perth in a place called "Timbertown." The locale is Rhudder's Inlet, almost within sight of Leeuwin Lighthouse. "Rhudder's Inlet" probably is the real Hardy Inlet, within sight of a real lighthouse on Cape Leeuwin, not far from the real town of Augusta. In the story, Upfield, somewhat reminiscent of the earlier story of the Nullarbor Plain, makes great dramatic use of the craggy banks and caves of the mainland. He is in a land of cold and indifferent nature and of somewhat eerie human nature, confronting a mountain of a man who is called "a throw-back to a prehistoric monster." (19) The story is so heroic in its setting and in its people that it seems a classical legend, a fantasy: It is a land of legendary people and events out of touch with reality. Bony's task is to bring the people back to reality.

This is a remarkable book. It is a story of unadulterated evil in conflict with pure innocence, in the presence of a background which seems indifferent and is powerless. Marvin Rhudder, the monster, is evil, his accomplices are good. Marvin, thief, rapist and murderer, returns to his parents' homestead and the scenes of his growing up. Bony, as Nat Bonnar, travels to One Tree Farm to stay with Matt and Emma Jukes, as tourist and fisherman. Bony establishes that Marvin is still in the neighborhood and through following a person he thinks is implicated in the conspiracy to keep Rhudder hidden he discovers that Rhudder's evil presence has again overwhelmed the joys of his youth. In this book an outstanding symbol is a cave, a symbol that Upfield used in five books. Here it represents retention of childishness and of bursting from the womb into a world of reality. In this book Upfield's language is classical but vernacular; it raises the mundane onto another plane. His understanding of naivete and its reaction to evil is perceptive. This is one of Upfield's superior efforts and accomplishments.

*The Will of the Tribe.* Published: Heinemann, 1962; reissued, Angus & Robertson, 1983. Doubleday, 1962.

*The Will of the Tribe* is almost a novel about the supernatural. It is centered near the real town of Hall's Creek, in the same vicinity Upfield used for the *Sinister Stones.* The action takes place near or in Wolfe Creek Meteorite Crater, which Upfield renames Meteorite Crater, and two nearby cattle-stations, "Beaudesert" and "Deep Creek," some 70 miles south of Hall's Creek. The Hall's Creek that was visited by Upfield in 1948 when he was leading the Australian Geographical Society Expedition no longer exists. A new town of the same name was begun on a more convenient site in 1952. Wolf Creek Crater is accessible by highway some 90 miles from Hall's Creek. The diameter of the crater is about a mile, its greatest depth is about 100 feet, and in spots the rim rises 100 feet above the plain. Presumably the crater was first discovered by Mr. N. B. Sauve, a geologist, who saw it from a plane on June 21, 1947. It remains today a striking and unusual geologic formation, evidence of a dramatic collision of astronomical objects with the earth in the distant past.

Upfield disguises his scenery. He makes the crater two miles wide, situates it two hundred miles south of Wyndham on the northern edge of the great inland desert of Western Australia. Though aborigines swear that the Stranger from the Sky (the meteor) came hundreds of years ago, Upfield himself had lead the National Geographic Society expedition in 1948 which established that the meteor had fallen in 1905. Whenever it fell, it created a tiered crater that dried out and cracked from the heat, and which exercised a superstitious hold over the aboriginals of the area.

A white man is found in the center of the declivity, obviously murdered. The superstitious hold of the people exercises a great power on the people involved in the story. In the atmosphere of this superstitious setting there is carried out another bit of human landscape in the persons of the kindly Brentner family who are trying to educate Tessa, a young aboriginal girl, and make her into a school-teacher-bridge between her people and the whites. The human landscape is scarred, however, by Captain, an aboriginal young man who is determined that Tessa not leave the tribe. Upfield and Bony watch the action on the human plain and witness its outcome—in success or failure, depending on your point of view.

This is undoubtedly Upfield's strongest book, for a number of reasons: 1) Bony is at his best in his detective work; 2) Upfield is at his best in studying the social and cultural situations of the white and the aboriginals; 3) though the physical setting is less intense than in some other works, it is strong here; 4) Upfield's symbolism—especially in the use of the metaphor of clothes vs. nakedness—is extraordinarily complex. There is no doubt that this particular book is a masterpiece in every way.

*Madman's Bend*. Published: Heinemann, 1963; reissued, Pan, 1984.

Upfield is never stronger than when he has the powers of nature compressed and driving Bony into immediate and heroic actions. Such is the case in *Madman's Bend*. The scene is a homestead on the Darling River, near White Bend, New South Wales. Asdell locates this landscape about halfway between the real township of Tilpa and the other real township of Louth. This area is particularly important to and familiar to Upfield, since it was through here that he first traveled in the Australian outback in 1910 when he was going from Adelaide to his first job in Momba Station, having to go through Broken Hill and Tilpa to reach his destination.

A brutal husband disappears, and immediate suspicion falls on the step-daughter, Jill Madden. The husband, William Lush, is a sadistic drunkard who beats his wife. As the story opens, his wife has been seriously beaten by her husband. As Lush tries to get into the house again, presumably to beat his wife more, Jill, determined to protect her mother from further assault, fires through the door at Lush, and assumes that since he disappears she has killed him. Bony works under the assumption that Jill did not kill her step-father but nobody can find the body. The extensive search is hampered by a terrifying flood on the Darling River, a flood so intense that it almost destroys everything.

This novel is one of Upfield's major accomplishments. Jill's anguish—her ambivalence—is well-documented. Bony's determined search no matter where guilt falls is fascinating. Again, the most dramatic actor in the drama is Mother Nature, who here raises floods that almost overwhelm everybody and everything. The true test of Bony the hero is proved in his ability to overcome the great physical obstacles placed in his path. This book is Upfield at his best.

*The Lake Frome Monster*. Published: Heinemann, 1966; reissued, Pan, 1966.

This novel was left unfinished at Upfield's death. In the physical setting Upfield gives only the haziest of references. He suggests that "Quinambee Station" has been losing cattle to rustlers suspected of coming from "Yandama Station," lying "North of Quinambie" and running "right up to the corner." Asdell has located a "Quinyambee Bore" on a track 80 miles southwest of Milparinka. A real Yandama Station lies north of the bore, some 35 miles due west of Milparinka, near a track which goes due west through Mount Poole and on to Lake Frome in South Australia. Upfield was definitely in this area in 1927 when he was patrolling the dingo-proof fence along the border with a team of camels.

This is a part of Australia where the living is not easy:

> The section of country through which Maidstone had to pass had some features which make it quite unique, not only in Australia but possibly in the world. Quinambie Station was on the eastern side of the dog-proof fence which followed the South Australia border from Queensland to the Murray River—a distance of about 375 miles. Between the homestead and this Fence was an artesian bore known locally as Bore Nine and almost immediately on the other side of the Fence lay its counterpart, Bore Ten. Some 50 miles farther west was Lake Frome homestead, and beyond it lay Lake Frome itself, some 15 miles away.

Thus Philip Asdell locates the setting. Lake Frome homestead contained about 60 square miles. In addition the physical geography is complicated by the presence of a mad camel that aboriginals called The Lake Frome Monster. Camels run wild by the tens of thousands in Australia, as the folklore goes, and constitute a nuisance and a hazard throughout the outback. Upfield develops the plot around only one wild camel. He knew his grounds. He had had experience with rogue camels. Once in 1927 he was attacked by one and escaped only by climbing a tree. He also knew how camels became "monsters." Fawke recounts Upfield's story of a camel-driver who singled out one camel as object of hatred and abuse with his whip. After the man had left this particular job he turned up three years later on another station as fence-rider, where the abused camel was, and still remembered the abusive drover, who, however, did not remember the camel. The camel exacted his revenge—killing and scalping the man and breaking virtually every bone in his body.

Because the book was in fact written by three individuals, Upfield, J.L. Price and Mrs. Dorothy Strange, it is somewhat hazardous to speculate on precisely what is Upfield's and what the other two, using Upfield's notes left for the purpose, created out of whole cloth.

Maidstone is found murdered near Bore 10. The aborigine trackers are unable to discover any evidence. Bony sets out to discover the killer. He manages to subdue the mad camel, he hears strange sounds at night—in an eerie world that in itself sounds mad.

Because the book was in fact written by three sets of hands, it does not have the coherent ring of the usual Upfield novel. But it has all the ingredients. There are sand storms galore, there are mad camels, there is personal and professional deprivation, there are rabbits by the millions. In this typical Upfield country, there is the boredom of loneliness, there is the sheer weight of the Australian outback; it is vintage Upfield.

As such it is interesting in its own light as well as in being the final statement Upfield made on his favorite subject: Australia.

*Breakaway House.* Published: 1987, Angus & Robertson.

The manuscript for this novel was recently found among Upfield's papers. The locale for the non-Bony story is on the Murchison Breakaways, north of Perth, northwest of the real town of Mt. Magnet, some 80 miles inland from the sea. Although the date of composition is not given, internal evidence seems to indicate the early 1930s, soon after *The House of Cain* and *The Barrakee Mystery*. For a full discussion of the book see Chapter 12.

# Chapter 3
# Knowledge and Use of Literature

Upfield seems to have felt all his literary life that he was an outsider in the world of literature, at least as that world was interpreted by the Australian literary establishment. Perhaps the feeling was underpinned by his realization that he had not received the full benefit of education in England, had not been "certified" by the academic establishment, had been expelled from England by his father and because he had not really cared for the conventional literature he studied while in school. Regardless of cause, his rancor against the literary establishment constituted a cancer that grew in his psyche throughout his years in Australia.

Yet he should have felt comfortable in his knowledge of literature. His experience: in at least one kind, the popular type, was extensive. His familiarity came to him naturally. He was a born story-teller and as a child on various occasions when his brothers were sick abed, Arthur had entertained them with stories in the manner of Scheherazade of the *Thousand and One Nights* when she told stories *ad seriatim* from night to night in order to prolong her life. Young Arthur was a master at stretching his stories from session to session. He had developed a kind of physical or artifactual literature by memorizing the physical details of a particularly gruesome murder, for example, and then trying out these physical details with his siblings in their large house in Gosport. Later, in Australia, in one of his books, *Will of the Tribe*, Upfield used this daily tale as a device to prevent strife in a small community. Dr. Havant, in the story, while he and other murderers are entombed in a cave beneath the Nullarbor Plain, strings his stories out to provide entertainment for the killers so that they will not resort to violence.

Upfield's creative instincts had served him in bad stead in school in England. He would often prefer to create literature to learning what others had created. When in high school, when fourteen and fifteen years of age, he wrote his first novel, 120,000 words about a fantastic voyage to Mars. Later, when Upfield was older and was supposed to pass three exams to become fully qualified in an auctioneer's institute, his mind centered on writing novels. The first exam was an entrance exam, the second was to get him the Associateship, the third to earn the rights as Fellow.

Upfield failed the first exam because he had spent too much time writing his second hundred-thousand-word novel, this one on the theme of a Yellow Peril successful invasion of Europe. Next year, when he tried the exam again, Upfield failed for the second time because he had written a sequel about the Yellow Peril; this time it was flung back from the European shores.

In addition to these early efforts to break into the world of literature, young Upfield got many more boosts in learning about popular literature. He was afflicted with acute bronchitis and spent a lot of time in bed with his sickness. During these days and weeks, his father supplied him with piles of novels and with one of the great time-passers of the age, the *Illustrated London News*. Upfield also read and was bewitched by Alfred Harmsworth's publications—*Answers, The Boys' Friend, Boys' Own* and *Chums*. Later he borrowed from the newly-created free library the adventures of Fenn, Henty, Maryat, and still later the science fiction novels of H. G. Wells and Jules Verne. In addition to the novels he had written as a youngster, during Upfield's many years in Australia he kept up his practice of writing by sending home to his mother in England a long letter every week.

Upfield also remembered well what he read and what he read about. He tried to keep in touch with the world of literature by reading London newspapers. So there is no doubt that he knew what was going on in the world of literature. Through his works there are kinds of evidence that he was widely read both in popular fiction of his time, that of Australia and of England and of the United States, as well as numerous books which Australians would have classified as more "serious" than the usual run of popular books. He was surely sufficiently knowledgeable about the Australian literati to know that those people did not accept popular literature as anything but trash. But he despised them, so their opinions should have carried no weight with him, and in fact might have only strengthened his respect for the kinds of literature they rejected. In Chapter II of *Follow My Dust*, Hawke tells of Upfield's attending a few meetings of the "local literati" in Melbourne in the 1930s. But they rejected him. They were literary snobs. The rejection inflamed and embittered Upfield as it has embittered authors throughout history. From the first, apparently, Upfield knew that he would not be accepted into the world of Australian letters; he knew that his lack of university training and background in the outback would scar him for life. Herman Melville's college had been the hull of a whaling vessel; Upfield's had been a pedal-less bicycle that he pushed from one odd job to another. But from the first efforts, Upfield had known that he was going to write, if he wrote at all, about Australia. As Hawke recounted Upfield's determination:

To Upfield there was only one people worth tuppence, and one country worth tuppence, and as he had begun in the days of Wheeler's Well, so he determined to carry on—to tell the people outside Australia of the New Heaven within which they could throw off their economic chains and all the inhibitions born of the mania to 'keep up with the Joneses'. (225)

Australia never had a fiercer partisan than this made-over Englishman.

Upfield knew the road to success in Australian letters, but he did not care to travel on it:

To be a success in Australia, you must work somewhere else, for Australians are constitutionally unable to appreciate their own creative works unless the authors are living abroad or dead. At present, I'm not interested in the former condition and I'm not really in a hurry to achieve the latter one.

He said this as he recorded his feelings in Pamela Ruskin's short essay on Upfield's life ( *Bony Bulletin*, 6).

Upfield gives a splendid and devastating picture of the Australian literary people in the first chapter of *An Author Bites the Dust,* one on his two books which treat the literary scene. One Mervyn Blake, the featured speaker at the bi-monthly meeting of the Australian Society of Creative Writers, is a pompous ass and lecher, who is always eager to use anybody he can for his own advancement. "One must use people, especially influential people," he says. He pontificates that unfortunately modern publishers must "pander" to the demands of the modern and "comparatively uneducated herd," who demand "sensationalism slickly put across." He understands that publishers must give these people "their pound of flesh." One member at this meeting of the literati protests that "It's the pictures painted by the words that count, not the words that paint the pictures. The story must be paramount...." Blake calls the man an ass and says: "We were discussing the novel and novelists, and you bring forward the atrocious efforts of a "whodunit' writer." Upfield has thrown his profession into the ring and found it rejected. Blake insists that it is literature with a capital L that is worth being considered.

Upfield's point of view about his notion of proper writing is represented by the man at the meeting who thought that the story is paramount. Upfield thought that a good story is of the greater importance than and superior to style: "Better a good story with plenty of errors than a piece of prose perfectly done and having no story. That, however, is no excuse for careless or bad writing." he once commented ( *Bony Bulletin,* 5). Despite thinking that the story is more important than the style and even if he knew that he was a superb story teller, Upfield throughout his career felt that he was not an effective writer, not a "good" writer, and he constantly tried to improve his style. Admittedly his style is at times florid and somewhat old-fashioned, yet his stories generally flow with great speed and effectiveness, at times, indeed, with breathlessness seldom matched by other writers.

Though Upfield's pen crackles with the electricity of hate for the literati, he was very much sensitive to the critics of his books, especially the foreign ones such as S. American,    Italian, Danish, Dutch, Japanese, Canadian, German, British and the American, in whose countries he always sold well, and took notice of their comments. He would receive from forty to 100 reviews for each book published, and he studied them carefully to see what he could learn from the observations. His willingness to hear the critics, perhaps an over-sensitivity, is revealed by the fact that if three or more objected to some particular point he would avoid that point in the next book. If three or more should stress some particular aspect of the book, say its background, Upfield would "take note of that also for future use." Upfield felt that through the years the critics in general had been kind to him. And he prided himself on his detail in his stories and on his Australian idiom—as indeed he should have.

Despite negative comments about the way he wrote his stories, Upfield was dogmatic about the kind of story he wanted to write. He felt that he had tried both kinds of stories that he might write— sex and crime—and knew which one he could write more effectively. As he said once to John Hetherington in an interview about his life's work ( *Bony Bulletin*, 4):

There are only two subjects to write about—crime and sex. A good clean murder, no matter how badly written, is better than a sordid seduction, no matter how well written. That's my view and I don't imagine I'll ever change it.

There is no question that he wrote the crime novel more effectively than the sex-seduction type, which he tried in some of his early novels and found uncongenial. There is also no doubt that Upfield was something of an old-fashioned moralist. He found sections of *Follow My Dust*, somewhat "bawdy." By bawdy he must have meant something of an invasion of privacy, for that book is in fact so mild it would bore a minister in the privacy of his study. Upfield said once that he hoped he was not a prig, and he probably was not. But old-fashioned he certainly was.

It seems difficult at times to understand Upfield's real attitude toward popular fiction he was familiar with. He seems to have developed and maintained a healthy respect for some of the "classics" which he apparently had not liked as a student years before. In some of his fiction Upfield seems to derogate the popular fiction of the day and those people who read it. He calls the popular books

"Blood-and-gutzers" and "blood and thunders," as they were commonly known. But in general he shows the greatest respect for such fiction.

Early on in the series, Upfield has Bony admit that his wife Marie, whom he admires and loves deeply, though only a half-caste and therefore no grand lady "likes to read the best books," and among them are dozens of crime mysteries which she reads consistently. Bony obviously knows all about the popular fiction and admits that he finds the books "the very breath of life" ( *The Widows of Broome*, 102) He once admitted that he uses detective fiction as a model for his very accomplished art of disguise: "In the old-time story-books great detectives are ever the masters of fictitious background." In other words, he has learned from detective fiction to cover his tracks and bolster his background so that no one can penetrate his disguises and expose him.

Bony thinks that popular fiction is the backbone of culture, especially Australian culture, because it has no pretentions. He recognizes popular entertainment, fiction as well as the movies, as a way to keep people out of crime. For example, in *The Widows of Broome*, a study similar in its delving into the psychology of crime and criminals to the earlier *The Beach of Atonement*, Upfield explains the criminal as "a man who had never wasted his time at the cinema and never read fiction less than a century old," and that was his problem. In *Venom House*, an excellent study in abnormal psychology equivalent to Poe's *Fall of the House of Usher*, though there are many English classics on the shelves of the library, there is not a mystery book there. Again, Upfield is giving a clear indication that where there is no popular fiction there is likely to be ignorance and evil. At times Upfield is more positive about the good results of popular fiction. In *Bony and the White Savage*, a powerful book that alternates between reality and mythology, Emma, one of the leading characters, reads popular fiction because she cannot afford 'real' books. But there is no condescension in Upfield's treatment of these thrillers. He says that Emma has read hundreds of them and is a very sensible and deep-thinking woman. Upfield obliquely praises the owners of bookstores who supply these kinds of books. For example, Emma tells Bony where and how she obtains her book titles:

> Oh, all sorts.... Blood-and-gutzers, you know. Can't afford real books with proper printing and proper covers to 'em. You see, when I go across to Albany I calls in at a bookshop and buys up our stock for the year. This time I bought Wuthering Heights and a couple of Edgar Wallace's and a beaut looking job called Ivanhoe. The woman who runs the bookshop knows we don't go nap on the sexy stuff, and I got to rely on her what I bring home. Ivanhoe is better than Wuthering Heights. (76)

They were also supplied such titles as *Kidnapped, Peyton Place, Boon on the Sand*. Two of the favorites in the family were the Bible and *Uncle Tom's Cabin*. (12)

At times, also, for reasons of advancing his plots, Upfield makes use of references to other non-fiction, and non-popular books. Sometimes the references are oblique and glancing. At other times they are extended enough to make a point, to develop a character or to advance the plot. Generally the references are extensive enough to indicate the author knew what he was talking about, not just name-dropping.

Such references to other works of popular literature abound. In Upfield's second published book, *The Barrakee Mystery*, Ralph, the half-caste son of the station owner, has "well-nigh assumed personalities like those of Dr. Jekyll and Mr. Hyde." On several occasions Upfield refers to Joel Chandler Harris's stories of Brer Rabbit, always with some kind of thought or action appropriate to the character of the famous rabbit. For example, once when Bony is hiding from his enemies, Upfield notes, "Like Br'er Rabbit, Bony remained snug in his little bower," although he did not have Brer Rabbit's obvious reasons for caution (*The Mountains Have a Secret*, 101).

Upfield shows his knowledge of other kinds of literature in various other references, to classics as well as contemporary literature. He uses the cliche "and so to bed, as the immortal Pepys used to put it" (*Sands of Windee*, 58). In this same book Father Ryan, a good man who serves as a kind of foil to Bony, has been reading a book by Nietzsche in which he says a lot about human progress being an illusion, and that mankind advances and retreats alternately in historical cycles.

In the same novel Bony has been consulting Mendel's "Treatise on heredity in flowers." When Bony, a non-believer in Christianity, goes to visit Father Ryan, he takes Marcus Aurelius and Virgil with him to help counter Father Ryan's religious arguments. In other words, Bony takes with him literary cannon to help him defend his position. Once, in another book ( *Mr. Jelly's Business*, 62), Bony walks across a field which provides difficult walking, and he likens his difficult passage to the morasses of philosophy, saying:

No one desiring a quiet stroll to contemplate philosophy of Spinoza or the profound problems discussed by Haeckel would have undertaken that pathless journey.

There is absolutely no evidence that Upfield ever read the American author Herman Melville, but this tinkering with physical travel and philosophical journeying through the mind is an exact parallel to the activities of the American novelist. In other books, Upfield shows that he remembers Coleridge's "Rime of the Ancient Mariner" (perhaps from his school days) and *Alice in Wonderland* ( *Bony and the Mouse*, 86) as well as the American poet Henry Wadsworth Longfellow.

And Upfield absolutely delights in the anecdote promulgated by the 18th century American preacher-author Mason Locke "Parson" Weems' *Life and Memorable Actions of George Washington* (5th ed. 1906) in which Washington confessed to his father that he could not tell a lie, it was he who had cut down the cherry tree. Upfield uses this anecdote to ingratiate himself with others, to get persons to reveal their nature by correcting him in his misquotation, and at times for sheer fun.

There are numerous other references to literary works. Upfield refers to *My First Ten Thousand Years* and wonders how a particularly obnoxious character reacted to the adventures of the Wandering Jew. He thinks that taste in literature reveals clearly and emphatically the character of the reader; it can be used as an excellent guide. Upfield finds that an unpleasant character, or one whom he suspects of a crime,  has on her shelves a complete set of Bishop Turlock-Elwick's *Notes on the Book of Revelations*, two beautifully bound volumes of *The Decameron*, Jane Austen's works, and Somerset Maugham, who represents the moderns. And Bony finds his special favorite, *Paradise Lost*. But the person's character is apparently deficient in one respect: there is "not an inch" devoted to mystery fiction.

Of all kinds of books, it is clear that two obviously had had a profound influence on Upfield, the Bible and Shakespeare. Though Bony is a religious non-believer, Upfield has him in several places refer to the Bible, and once he says that he particularly approves of the philosophy of the Old Testament, that is of an eye for an eye. And Upfield constantly makes references to Biblical characters such as Joseph, Ishmael, Samson ("betrayed by a woman") and others.

But far more profound was the influence of Shakespeare on Upfield the author. Shakespeare's pervasiveness in 19th and 20th century Australia was clearly just as deep and wide as it was in the United States in the 19th century. In the United States during the frontier days two books, the Bible and Shakespeare, were committed to memory by many people. So too in Australia, at least with Shakespeare. For example, Upfield has Bony say that he once had known of a drover who over a two-month period "had recited wordly-perfectly, every Shakespearean play." And, incidentally, Bony knew of another who would repeat long passages of the opening chapters of Balzac's *Wild Ass's Skin* ( *Death of a Swagman*, 40). Drovers and other loners in Australia obviously had to use every tactic to frighten off loneliness, and, as many a person relegated to solitary confinement can attest, recitation by rote of all one knows is an effective technique to ward off madness.

Upfield's knowledge of Shakespeare was both deep and wide. It surely was long. In his English schooldays, Upfield and his classmates had found English literature in general and Scott, Lamb and Shakespeare in particular the greatest bores probably because the students had to stand and read aloud the works of these authors, with no effort to tell what they meant or what they were worth. In other words, the works without any humanity attached to them. But, as is often the case in what one learns, some of the material stuck in young Arthur's mind. Though he never used Sir Walter Scott, other than a comment on the superiority of *Ivanhoe* over *Wuthering Heights,* and Charles Lamb as references in his works, he frequently quoted from Shakespeare in ways that enriched and advanced the plots of his books.

Sometimes the references to Shakespeare's works are oblique and are used to test the knowledge of the person who is listening. When Bony incorrectly cites Parson Weems' recounting of the anecdote about George Washington being unable to tell a lie, attributing it to Shakespeare, Bony is corrected by his auditor (*Mystery of Barrakee Reef,* 21). Once Bony delightedly says "A king once shouted, 'My kingdom for a horse!' You hear me shout: 'My kingdom for a cup of tea!'." Mr. Dickenson, one of Upfield's major Dickensian characters, says to Bony "It was, I think, Shakespeare who wrote: 'O, what may man within him hide, though angel on the outward side'." (*Widows of Broome,* 129)

But Upfield's knowledge and use of Shakespeare runs much more deeply than the mere quotation. In one book (*Death of a Swagman,* 40) Bony tells a person,

You should read "The Rape of Lucrece," a poem written by Shakespeare. Old Shakespeare was a good criminologist. He describes the growth of an idea of the crime in the criminal's mind before the crime was committed. Often the crime of murder is the effect of thought extended over a lengthy period.

In fact Shakespeare provides a kind of leit motif that this particular story turns on.

Another author of extreme importance to Upfield was Rudyard Kipling in the philosophy expressed in his poem "The Ballad of East and West" (1889) in which he says that the two parts of the world can never meet. "Never the Twain shall meet." This philosophy is in fact the antithesis of Upfield's message through Bony, and one that Bony reiterates at least once in every book, sometimes several times. Upfield felt that Bony the half-caste who was at home in both white and aboriginal cultures was the bridge between the two cultures. Both had met. "Kipling was wrong. You are, too. The East and the West meet in me." ( *Bony and the Black Virgin,* 79) and found their commonality and peace in him. Thus he personally refuted the observations of the imperialistic Kipling. But it was not easy for the two to lie down together like lion and lamb. Upfield shows just how difficult this feat is in the person of the very much loved Aboriginal Tessa in *The Will of the Tribe*. She is taken up and genuinely loved and raised by the Brentner family, is going to be sent off to college in order to prepare to become a school teacher so that she could teach the Aboriginals the ways of the whites, and thus bring them over from their aboriginal ways. But in her case the bridge broke. She never could leave her tribe, but she was in fact full-blooded Aboriginal, and Bony points out that it is virtually impossible to train the bush out of a full-blooded Aboriginal. In a few other instances he tried to demonstrate that the half-caste might be the bridge. But in one case, that of Rex in *Bushranger of the Skies*, though he looked more like a White than Bony did, Rex reverted to the wiles of his mother's race, and though he used many White practices (deceit, raw power, guile) and wanted to take over power in the White world, Rex essentially could not free himself from the shackles of the Aboriginals.

But of all literary people, contemporary or predecessors, Upfield obviously owes his greatest debt to Charles Dickens, or at least is most similar to Dickens. In many ways, Upfield, with no diminution of his own creative powers as an author might with compliments to both authors be called the Australian Dickens, so similar are they in many ways and especially in the development of unforgettable characters.

Upfield's background in Dickens was everyday and profound. He grew up in a Dickens-like society, in which Dickens' works and imitations were plentiful and the very air seemed heavy with Dickensiana. In this society he had himself been tagged with a Dickens-like name—Arkum Willum. His Uncle Charles looked like Mr. Pickwick. Once on a trip to see Nelson's flagship, the *Victory*, moored off the Gosport shore, Upfield's Uncle Charles and he were ferried over by a Dickens-like wherryman, aged eighty-one and as tough as the wherry he commanded. Upfield fell in love with Dickens' house. In many ways Upfield's world was a Dickens world. Upfield once assured his biographer, Jessica Hawke, that his relatives were all Dickens' characters and that the rest of English society was almost the same. He assured her

that within forty miles of Gosport, that is, away from the coast, many of the people in the villages spoke what was almost a foreign language, and that to see them going to church and chapel on Sundays was to observe every character ever portrayed by Charles Dickens. (p. 29)

Clearly these characters so deeply impregnated Upfield's mind and life that he could not forget or ignore them in his works. Like Gosport, Upfield's Australia is peopled by these strange curiosities of the past.

Upfield uses spot and casual references to color his world Dickens-red. In one book he has a cat named Mr. Pickwick ( *Bony and the Kelly Gang*). Upfield calls one person his "artful Dodger" ( *Madman's Bend*, 129). On another occasion ( *Death of a Swagman*, 171), Bony says, "'I may be wrong...but I think it was gentleman named Sam Weller who used to say: "cut the cackle and get to the hosses ." '"

But Dickens' strongest influence was in the development of numerous characters, who in many ways are cut from the Dickens cloth, and in a few instances rival or outclass Dickens' characters. In one book (*The Widows of Broome*, 156) Upfield admits his debt to Dickens, by describing a parallel figure Bony is working with for the ultimate solution of a crime:

Seen on his feet and without his chauffeur-cum-sea-captain uniform, Luke Briggs would have delighted Charles Dickens. He was quite bald. His face was the colour of teak and marvellously wrinkled. About five feet eight inches in height and weighing in the vicinity for a hundred and thirty pounds, he could be taken for a Cockney chimney-sweep or a race-course tout. To guess his age, one could range from sixty to a hundred, and ten be out at either end. For his evening stroll, he wore rubber-soled canvas shoes, grey Harris tweed trousers and a coat much too long for him. The coat made him look like a soldier crab inhabiting a conch shell, but it was worn for a purpose—the inside pockets were capable of taking a dozen bottles.

In his cast of characters Upfield develops a whole menagerie of characters which, properly recognized, will do for Australian literature what Dickens' cast of characters did for English Victorian literature. Many of his characters are shady and beyond the law. Many are helpful to Bony and some are heroic and challenge the finest characters of the heroic in any literary descriptions. All are recognizable by Dickensian names. Of course the tradition of attaching outlandish names to people is that of the frontier. It was an American custom, and it was an Australian custom. It went with the territory. But in addition it was a strong literary custom, a la Charles Dickens. And when a strong creator of characters ties in the frontier custom of the outlandish heroic generic name with the skill of a Dickens or an Upfield in developing a character to fit the name, the result is a strong and fascinating literary tradition.

At times Upfield needed only one stroke of the pen to create a Dickensian profile. The novel *Mr. Jelly's Business* has at least two such characters. Mr. Jelly, the namesake of the book, is cigar-shaped. As Upfield describes him:

> If you possess imagination sufficient to magnify a cigar to the size of a six-foot man you will obtain a pictorial impression of Mr. Jelly. His head was small with a pointed crown, and his feet were small. From his head downward and from his feet upwards Mr. Jelly's circumference gradually increased till the middle was reached. He was between fifty and sixty years of age, bald save for a ring of grey hair which rested upon his ears like a halo much too small for him. His complexion was brick red, not alcoholic red, but the red of sunrays and strong winds. (20)

In the same book there is a tornado of a woman, Mrs. Wallace, the only person in Burracoppin, especially in the pub, who could handle the ferocious "Spirit of Australia" when he was on a rampage. In comparison to the "Spirit" Mrs. Wallace was shorter but "wider and deeper." She was "a trimmer," and trims the Spirit's spirit by throwing him out of her pub.

Upfield sketches in other characters, both major and minor, with a broad and wavy though distinct pen. One of his earliest triumphs is Frederick Blair. Blair is a terror, looks and acts the part. He is a small wiry man, less than five feet six inches tall, with a goatee beard jutting from his chin, a blistered complexion, but with the spring and suppleness of youth.

...To the people of Wilcannia he was known as the fierce little man whom it required the combined energies of the entire police force to put into the lock-up. This occurred every time Blair visited Wilcannia, which was every quarter. ( *The Mystery of Swordfish Reef*, 37-8).

In addition to being insolent to the police, threatening to beat them up, Blair loved fighting and sought it out whenever he could.

To ask why Frederick Blair so loved fighting is to ask why a dog loves to chase and kill a cat. The love of fighting may have been inherited, for Blair's grandfather had been a notorious blackbirder, almost officially designated a pirate. The little man lived some three hundred years too late. Even in Bully Hayes's time he would have secured world-wide fame; because, not only was he a natural fighter, but he also was a natural leader ( *Mystery*, 263).

In addition to gouging and pulling, using every bone-breaking hold possible, Blair loved use of the unorthodox method of fighting: Once

finding that his head was lower than the big man's face (his opponent's) so that he could not knock it out of shape with the back of his head, Blair devoted a few seconds to tattooing tender shins with the heels of his boots.

There is little wonder that such a fighter almost always wins his rounds.

There are many Dickens-like characters whose names resonate with Dickensian truth and which reveal their character and characteristics: Loony Pete and Needle Kent, Dead Man Harry who goes around saying "I'm dead;" his custodian the man who takes care of him is, of course, Mick the Warder; Mick the Tickler, who is a mobster who executes people with his "tickler." Dot and Dash are inseparable pals who are given punctuation mark names— inseparable pals—Dot is a short American, Dash a tall Englishman. Hangdog Smith is a murderer who is inclined to hang his victims. Jimmy the Screwsman is a second-story thief; a German who came to a community and was named Hun is called 'Un. Aboriginal men have such names as Nero, Plato, King Henry, Pontius Pilate and other classical monikers. A tracker is named Shuteye.

Many of Upfield's characters are so unique that they must be described in his own words, or must be allowed to speak for themselves.

One is Robin Foster, a "Neanderthal," who works for the Answerth's in *Venom House*. His language is a porcupine of oaths: " 'All bloody right...But I bloody well tell you I bloody well know nothing.' " ( *Venom House*, 78-9) Bisker, in *Devil's Steps*, though he speaks less profanely of vengeance, is a cacophony of profane language. Awakened as is usual at 5:30 every morning, he bursts into his litany:

'A man oughter be sunk a million miles below the bottom of the deepest well on earth,' he said, in his heart duty wrestling with the desire to strike. 'Q, what a limbless fool I am! Curse the drink. You dirty swine...it's you that stops me saving enough money to get me outer this frost-bitten, rain-drowned, lousy hole of a joint, get me back to where there's a thousand tons of good, dry wood to the acre, and where a man can lie abed all day if he wants to. Oh, blast!' He then calls his employer: 'If that old cow sezs two words to me this morning, I'll up and slap 'er down.'

Upfield's description of this character is no less picturesque than the language. He

revealed naked, bandy legs below the hem of a cotton shirt over a flannel undervest. He stepped into trousers which appeared to be wide open to accept his legs and small and round pauch, pulled on a pair of old socks and then stepped into heavy boots he did not trouble to lace. A thick cloth coat and a battered felt hat completed the ensemble, but to this had to be added the working kit comprising one pipe, a plug of jet-black tobacco, a clasp-knife, a tin containing wax matches, and a cork-screw.

Others, though of totally different kinds, are unforgettable people. Sam the Blackmailer is a case in point. He was a superlative cook but extremely temperamental and ready to quit if anybody complained of his cooking. He got his name because once when he asked for his pay from his employer whose rich wife lived in the city, he was told that there was no money with which to pay him. Sam merely hinted that if the cash was not forthcoming in thirty minutes he would write to the wife concerning her husband's peccadillos with a local lubra. The husband was innocent, but the money was paid quickly. ( *Death of a Swagman*, 67-8)

Another case in point is Bill the Better, in *The Bone is Pointed*, who needs to be described in Upfield's own words.

> He was a shrimp of a man, this Bill the Better. Scanty hair failed to cover his cranium that would have delighted Cesare Lombroso who, it will be remembered, determined criminals by their heads. A long nose appeared to divide the gingery moustache which he constantly pulled down by the ends and watery blue eyes invariably contained an expression of great hope of a brighter future.

Bill would bet on anything, even against himself. He will bet on who is going to die first.

> I'm game to bet you a level fiver you die first outer us two. We can put the money in an envelope wot can be kept in the office safe and handed to the winner. (19)

Melody Sam, of *Bony and the Mouse*, is a triumph in character development. As we have seen earlier he is called "an antique, a character, a history, a ruddy legend." But he is far more. He virtually owns everything and everybody in the town of Daybreak. Although a fine individual, like everybody else in the Australian outback he must have his bouts with liquor. When he does, he goes down in the cellar of his pub, where he keeps his booze, and takes with him some explosives. While there for a couple of weeks, eating nothing and drinking nothing but booze, he holds the town in mortal terror because his orders are that nobody try to come down and interrupt his bout or he will light his explosives and blow himself and the pub up.

A much gentler but equally effective character is Mr. Dickenson, in *The Winds of Broome*. He is a character triumph. Again, Upfield's description should be used:

> He was tall and thin, and his beaked nose appeared always as though frost-bitten. His hair was white and abundant and was carefully brushed back from a noble forehead. The pointed white Vandyke beard greatly added to the air of distinction, but the general effect was ruined by his disgracefully old and soiled clothes.

Mr. Dickenson is continually embarrassed by having his money from the government run out each month four days before the new check arrives, and he is thereby deprived of four days of booze. Mr. Dickenson's philosophy about drinking is simple and safe: "Always stick to spirits, and never take more than two drinks unless you can see it came out of a bottle." He is a shrewd observer of human behavior and a philosopher of human nature: "The saints, I have noticed, become amateur sinners...when it is dark. Give me the hearty sinners."

"The Spirit of Orstralia" is another giant among the many characters Upfield developed. As we have seen earlier, Upfield's description of this Mr. Garth, called by his neighbors "The Spirit of Australia," is explosive.

The Spirit of Australia! If any man was rightly nicknamed, this man was. Age rested on him as a crown of jewels, not as fetters of lead. More than eighty years old! It was incredible—till one peered deeply and saw that tremendous experiences had been the battlements which defied the onslaughts of Time.

What is he in the eyes of his neighbors? One characterizes him.

'E's a cocky ten miles out....'E drives sixteen 'orses in the old-fashioned way of two abreast, carting in ten ton of wheat every other day, when his sons get goin' proper with the harvester machines. (32)

In the barroom one night, this 80-year old giant of the past is offended when somebody splashes beer on him:

The Spirit of Australia, impatient as is the youth of the country, deemed the easiest way of finding the offender was to manhandle everyone within doors. Man after man was gripped with vicelike hands, lifted off his feet, and rushed to one of the doors, from which point he was propelled for ten or twelve feet onto the gritty roadway. (34)

This kind of action prevailed when he was in one of his darker moods. But the Spirit's moods changed easily, and he changed instantly from rough destruction to beatific smile.

Among his triumphs of character creation, Upfield is of course not excelled in the development of Clarence B. Bagshott, a popular author of bestselling fiction. Bagshott, who is obviously a takeoff on Upfield himself, is a character representing a point of view that Upfield had had stewing in his mind over the years. Bagshott is a projection of the kind of person Upfield thought or wished he was.

We first see Bagshott as a character in *The Devil's Footsteps*, where Upfield develops the story of murder in a luxury mountain chalet outside Melbourne, where two murders are committed. One of the prime suspects because of the size of his boots is an enigmatic and somewhat mysterious figure who lives in the neighborhood and writes novels. His name is Clarence B. Bagshott. Bagshott is famous for his unusual character and actions and for the way he researches and writes his novels. After considerable enterprise and imaginative action, Bony gets to meet the infamous author and discovers that his feet are not cloven nor his tail pointed. He is in fact "disappointingly ordinary." But his head is unusual, indicating a phrenological proclivity toward his way of life: "his brow was low and narrow, but the back of his head was exceptionally wide. His eyes were constantly alert." And when he smiled he "seemed human enough."

The snobs in the chalet, who represent the grandest flourishes in Australian literature, think Bagshott's writings "trash." As the leading voice of Australian "literature" points out:

Educated people don't read Bagshott's stuff.... No one knows him outside the readers of newspaper serials. Our glorious Australian literature has had too many obstacles to surmount in order to become established without having Bagshott's tripe added to them. They call his books Australian, and people unfortunately read them and judge Australian literature by them. (155)

But Bagshott is more than the sum of all his critics, a rare Dickensian character. He talks loud, drinks hard, likes fishing; he is larger and gustier than life. Once he is cleared of suspicion of murder, Bony and Bagshott wind up on a fishing and pubbing spree that will keep both from their work for several days.

Bagshott reappears in Upfield's second shot at the Australian literati, *An Author Bites the Dust*. In this book, Mervyn Blake, self-proclaimed famous author and critic, is found dead in his home west of Melbourne after he has just returned from a literary soiree in the city. Again the air is perfumed with snobbishness and pretense. All people there condescend to the authors of bestselling popular fiction. Blake, the greatest pretender and snob of the lot, is murdered. Bony is called in to solve the mystery. Bagshott reappears as Bony's former friend and as someone who is familiar with all the people in the little episode. Again, Bagshott is more fully developed within the outline given in the earlier novel, and is all fire and gusto. He explains that he has just "five weeks, three days and—let me see—, yes, and nine hours to go before starting off for Bermagui and the swordies." That is, he is about to engage in one of his favorite physical activities. But he takes time out to explain the difference between his vocation of writing bestselling novels and that of the people who produce literature. He defines the two:

In this country literature is a piece of writing executed in schoolmasterly fashion and yet so lacking in entertainment values that the general public won't buy it. Commerical fiction—and this is a term employed by the highbrows—is imaginative writing that easily satisfied publishers and editors because the public will buy it. (73)

Again, speaking through his alter ego, Upfield has had his say against the people who will not admit him into their closed literary circle and who represent the negative, the false, side of Australian literary endeavor. He has used as a spokesman one of the guttier and gustier individuals that he created.

Several woman in Upfield's books could have stepped right out of Dickens' world and pages, or could have walked right *into* them and felt perfectly at home. We will look closely at them in the chapter in this book called "The Role of Women."

Upfield's greatest creation in characters is of course Bony himself, surely one of the most nearly unique detectives in all literature. As we have seen in the section of this book called "Upfield's Philosophy," Bony, though completely lacking in what anyone might call Dickensian characteristics, has just enough eccentricities to be unique. He is Upfield's embodiment of sanity and humanism in a world that is tense with pressures that pull people apart or push them together to grind them into erratic behavior. Though perhaps not as verbally flashy as others in this field, and although restricted in some ways by the geographical setting he operates in, Bony nevertheless stands as a giant in the literature of mystery and detection. In his field he has not been excelled.

# Chapter 4
## Literary Style

Throughout his writing career, Upfield felt that he was not a smooth and polished author. But he was not greatly concerned about his style of writing. As his literary alter ego Clarence B. Bagshott in the two novels *The Devil's Steps* and *An Author Bites the Dust* insisted, the story is of greater importance than the style in which it is presented. Being a natural storyteller, as he admitted in a letter to his friend Louise Mueller in Wisconsin, in his books Upfield was "careless in writing and impatient with the work once the typing has been done." With the attitude of a man of action, he felt that publishers should provide people "to smooth away an author's silly mistakes." Besides, he always felt that the mechanics of presentation were less important than the event itself: "Better a good story with plenty of errors than a piece of prose perfectly done and having no story," he insisted.

Despite his early school successes at writing, which he may have engaged in partly to avoid boredom, Upfield did not easily turn to writing as a adult. In fact the story of the urging required, the timing of the urging, though by no means unique in the annals of literature, is rather poignant and needs to be retold, for the literary world owes a debt of gratitude to a perceptive woman who apparently pushed Upfield into literature.

In 1924, when Upfield was 36 years old, fourteen years after he had first come to Australia, he was still wandering in the bush, earning his living in various ways. Upfield was now becoming discontented and somewhat concerned about his future. Luckily at this point he met for the second time two sensitive people who could help him. In his earlier years, one mid-February day, Upfield, heading for nowhere in particular, had approached the cattle station of a couple named Mary and Angus; their last names are not given by Upfield in his reminiscences. Maybe he forgot it! Or, more likely, he wanted to heroize them by giving them only first names. Upfield lay down in a shed to sleep, was awakened by Angus and offered breakfast. This couple had lost a son about Upfield's age in World War I, at Gallipolli, where Upfield had also fought. The couple were sympathetic to Upfield's wanderings, offered him a job helping to build two 400 thousand gallon water tanks. After this job was finished Upfield stayed on five weeks longer because the couple was congenial.

In the spring of 1924 Upfield came again to the small station owned by his friends Mary and Angus. This time economic times were tough, and Upfield, though he might not have recognized it completely, was about burned out in the bush. He asked if he could stay on the station for while, even at no pay. In answer to questions, Upfield admitted that the open sky had got at him. He confessed:

I've come too close to a kind of precipice and something is warning me about it.... It's the sky I want to get away from. I want to sit at a table with a white cloth, and talk and listen.

During the days that followed, Mary gently questioned Upfield about the three novels he had written as a kid and which had been discarded and forgotten. She urged him to write about his Australian experiences: "Why don't you write about your experiences in Australia?" she asked him. She even suggested that some people get paid enough for their writing to allow them to settle down, though Upfield surely must have known this. Though it is difficult to imagine that to one of Upfield's fierce independent spirit an appeal to God, to country and to family would be effective, Mary turned her big guns on him and her little sermonette worked, or helped to work on a person whose way of life was beginning to crumble:

It is sinful to toss back to the Eternal the talents He has given. Try to understand that life is so very short, and roaming here and there, year after year, is just plain silly. And think of the hopes your father and mother had of you. You told us you never miss writing to them once a week. The next time you write, ask them to tell you candidly if they are or are not disappointed in you. And then sit on a sandhill and look at yourself in the mirror of a mirage.

The time, the country, fatigue, weariness and the sermonette seem to have come to the right person at the right time. By now, Upfield, having tried many of the possibilities of life that Australia offered, realized that his mid-life crisis was upon him. In its obituary of Upfield the New York *Times* quoted him as saying:

I realized that I was getting nowhere, and that my creative talent was writing, through which I might reach a standard of life more fitting to the growing years and responsibilities.

Though always a wanderer in spirit, Upfield was a pragmatist and realized that there is more to life than irresponsibility.

Despite that fact that Upfield had already had two articles published in the London *Daily Mail* and two short stories in *Novel Magazine*, the writing he began to turn out did not come easily and was not without its flaws. Again, coincidence drove him to authorship. Hired by a certain James L. Hole of Albemarle to cook for some twenty men at his station, Upfield found that he had time on his hands, time to put his hand to writing. He took it up seriously. Upfield stayed on this job for three years. While there he laid out the plots for three short stories and worked on them continuously, rethinking and rewriting them. Enjoying the pleasures of creating characters and stories, Upfield's imagination became filled with the lure of all would-be authors: To write significant stories. Why not write a detective story with a setting in Australia that would turn out to be the Great Australian novel? Upfield recognized that nobody knew more about the flora and fauna, the landscape, the life of Australia than he? There was so much new about Australia that anyone staying there for a week or two could find enough new material for a novel. And he had been there years—he was or could become the premier novelist about the Australian outback.

His desire to write about the Australian outback became almost an obsession. To Upfield there was only one people and one country worth writing about. Australia was to him the Garden of Eden, and Australians, though not always Edenites before the fall, were the premier of people. Theirs was the land where people could throw off the chains of economic necessity and the hurry of meeting the clock, and there they could enjoy living.

His first novel began developing a plot that centered on the fact that some half-caste children are born white and change color years afterwards, sometimes by the age of ten, sometimes, as Upfield was to say in later novels, as late as age thirty. In the early draft of this book, a white detective is brought in to investigate the death of an Aborigine. It seemed like an effective plot. But it was not strong enough to suit Upfield. As luck would have it, about this time Upfield's old friend Tracker Leon Wood came again on the scene. And after a talk with him, Upfield recognized that he had in that half-caste the exact model he needed for his detective. Upfield then rewrote his novel for the third time, with Tracker Leon as the half-caste detective named Napoleon Bonaparte. The novel was named *The Barrakee Mystery* and though later Upfield would see some mistakes in it and would in fact rewrite it partially for a new edition, the book contained pretty much the seed for all of Upfield's subsequent novels. It was an effort of which he could be proud.

But Upfield's literary career thereafter was not an immediate bed of roses. He had a novel finished but it was unpublished. By now he was reading the Times *Literary Supplement* rather regularly, seeing in the pages the fate of literary people in the hands of critics. He was especially nonplused when he saw a review of a book on Tasmania by an Australian whom Upfield greatly admired reviewed in the columns entitled "Also Rans." In his perusal of the *Supplement*, Upfield came across the advertisement of a literary agent named George Frankland who offered advice on quality, mechanics of getting published and other needed information on manuscripts. Upfield sent his manuscript to Frankland at his Buckinghamshire address. Frankland treated the manuscript with sharp criticism but much respect. He bewailed the repetition he found in the manuscript, but generally approved of the construction. He especially praised the unique use of the boomerang as a murder weapon.

But *The Barrakee Mystery* did not become Upfield's first published novel. He was still searching for his preferred field to write in. Once, in Adelaide he had visited and talked with a bookseller named Jeremy Long, who advised him that sex is the ingredient that drives books toward the bestseller list. Very much hungering for that bestseller list, Upfield gathered a pile of bestselling novels, read them, and found, as Long had said, that sex sells. Accepting the faulty advice Long offered, and his own too-hasty observations, Upfield wrote a weak novel about a subject that he knew nothing about and was not comfortable with—sex. Though it was his first published novel, *The House of Caine* was a literary mistake, one that perhaps he should never have attempted. It involved a silly newspaper man and a fatuous ladyfriend, a brother who is so heroic and preposterous that he is unbelievable, and a rich and eccentric murderer who at his place in the desert gathers together for his purpose other murderers who have been released from prison. Though it is centered in outback Australia, this plot is not with the Australian society that Upfield knew. It was a resounding literary failure. Artistically the strongest part of the book was the Australian outback    Upfield knew well and about which he was to write tellingly. But he could not write about sex.

It may have been Upfield's growing up with so many older people and grandmothers and aunts, but his sexual drive seems to have been sublimated. He was married during his five-year stay in England after World War I and had a son named Arthur James Upfield. He apparently lived with his wife and son off and on in Australia. But when his wife would not give him a divorce, Upfield seems to have left her and their son and, sometime later, to have taken up with and lived with a lady named Jessica Uren.

In the Australian bush Upfield apparently did not need to lead a regular married life. Hawke said "Throughout this period of wandering from job to job, Upfield was troubled less by sex than by other demands." (149) Of course his wanderings through Australia tended to discourage marriage. The macho attitude among the outback wanderers dictated that men use but despise women. Upfield made this clear in his earliest book. A giant character named Squeezem Harry outlines the attitude in *The House of Cain*:

Directly a man gets tangled with a woman, it's good night. He becomes an also-ran, a back-number, a has-been. To his fellow-men he's never more of any account. "I'd sooner take strychnine than a wife. Strychnine's quicker, and less painful." "Marriage is a funny thing. I've known blokes wot used to go on the drunk every year regular, until they got married. Then they changed." (90-91)

But, as Upfield recounts in several books, there were swagman who abandoned their lonely ways and got married. Upfield could have faced down the Wandering Millie, the Australian wander-lust, at any time and turned to a more sedentary life. But Upfield seemed more interested in working something out of his system than in getting married. He would take his sex only occasionally and in its proper sequence.

Once, after a long stay in the outback, Upfield went to town and bought the services of a whore, for a pound, for an hour. When she took him to her room, he sat down on the bed and started talking to her. When she asked if he was "not going to have her," Upfield said he would much rather talk than have sex. She consented, apparently talked well in response to Upfield or just listened well. He arranged to take her to the races the next day, then to dinner that night and talked with her more and more. Apparently when he was talked out, he had sex with her. This occasionally bought sex is still the habit of outback cattlemen. Sometimes they stay isolated from women for as long as six months at a time. When they can they go to town and still release their pent-up loneliness, sexual and racial tension through extended drinking, fighting and sexual bouts. Such is the practice of isolated men.

Upfield had had a somewhat similar tempting experience when he was a rent-collector in Gosport, England, when one of his tenants, a cute little lady had asked him if he would like to take the rent out in trade. He refused. The importance of this rather common youthful brush with sex is underlined by the fact that he recounted it to his biographer at least 40 years after it happened.

Another similar incident which Upfield recounted to his biographer occurred when he first got to Australia, it will bear repeating. In his third job in Adelaide, Upfield was serving as fourth cook at the city's finest hotel. Also working there was a voluptuous, teasing waitress, who delighted in rubbing up against the men trying to excite them. Probably most men appreciated the attention. But apparently Upfield did not. While in the cold storage room choosing vegetables for dinner, Upfield selected a large and long parsnip and skewered it on a string and dropped it from his waist between his legs. Hawke's coy, Victorian paragraph in *Follow My Dust*, (44) of the ensuing events is both amusing and revealing:

> Dinner was in full swing when the teaser came again. Her leg met the parsnip, then her hand wandered. Her head jerked. She stared unseeingly at the fourth cook arranging her tray of sweets, and, opening her mouth to scream, fell backward in a dead fain⸴

Men and women were both more sexually innocent and more impressionable in those days and in that country than they are now.

Trying to find the backbone to the novel that would become *The Barrakee Mystery* and would allow its fruitful development, Upfield fortunately bumped into his friend Tracker Leon Wood again, talked with him for hours, and exchanged some books with him. As Tracker Leon left Upfield again, Upfield realized not only what a commendable and unusual character Tracker Leon was but—in a moment of great importance to himself and to literature in general—what an amazing model he would make for a detective. The inspiration was the equivalent of the scales falling from his eyes and Upfield's seeing the obvious. Tracker Leon was everything Upfield needed. As Jessica Hawke recounted the experience:

> The advantages were instantly apparent. No white could track like an aborigine or as expertly as a half-caste, and no white man in all the world could read the Book of the Bush as knowledgeably as Tracker Leon.

So Napoleon Bonaparte, after some days, was born, a half-caste investigator, like Tracker Leon, "who possessed the acumen of the aborigines plus the reasoning ability of the educated white."

Although the rewritten *The Barrakee Mystery* was published as his second book, literary and financial success did not come to Upfield. He blamed his failure on the literary establishment in Australia the members of which, as is usual in aspiring literary communities where the people are not sure of their own accomplishments and insist on following the models developed in other countries, felt that detective fiction about a half-caste was not admissible into the canon of worthy literature. This exclusion apparently embittered Upfield, who kept his anger boiling for years until he vented it in two novels, *The Devil's Steps* and *An Author Bites the Dust*, two cutting and slashing profiles of the Australian literati.

After *The Barrakee Mystery*, not sure of the direction    his writing would take in the future, Upfield published *The Beach of Atonement*, a study of loneliness and abnormal psychology. After that Upfield took his fourth book, *The Sands of Windee*, back to Bony as his hero. Then he was at sea again in purpose. According to his biographer, Upfield wrote 90,000 words of a thriller, working for fourteen days and nights, and then, dissatisfied with what he had written, he burned it. But he kept on writing novels, with each one becoming more sure of his skill and desires. In 1931 Upfield moved to Perth and turned to supporting himself in journalism. But this venture was not a success. Upfield was not cut out to be a journalist, nor was he appreciated by his peers. In 1933 Upfield moved on to Melbourne, where after trying his hand again as a journalist, he finally settled down to be a full-time novelist, with Bony as his concentration. It had been four years since his first Bony novel. But his literary future was still problematical.

Success—when it finally came—was spurred from the United States. As America entered World War II thousands of G.I.s went to Australia, deeply ignorant about the country but surely interested in it. They read Upfield, had their curiosity piqued and talked about this amazing author to the folks back home. Upfield's works were offered to Doubleday in the United States, who picked six titles and immediately published four. Once sprung from the sea-hold of Australia, Upfield's books became almost immediately successful.

Most critics saw quickly that Upfield had achieved in his detective Bony what most writers of crime fiction never achieve—immortality for his detective. The BBC once called Bony "a unique figure among top-flight detectives." Anthony Boucher, writing in the New York *Times* called Bony his "favorite fictional detective of the past twenty years." The Times *Literary Supplement* credited Upfield with "an extraordinary gift" of writing and "the half-caste Detective Inspector Napoleon Bonaparte...who steps alive off the page." Most reviewers applauded the detective and the stories. Few, however, saw beyond the obvious and comprehended the real extent of Upfield's creation. Some critics did. The reviewer in the Chicago *Sunday Tribune*, for example, congratulated Upfield: "The picture of isolated life in Australia's vastness is unusually captivating." The comment is right on the mark. The strength of Upfield's creations—though standing among the three or four most original detectives in all the literature—is not really the crown of his achievement. As detective stories, these tales are triumphs. But they are much more than detective stories. They are documentaries of Australia—of the primitive and frontier land down under, of the white's and of the Aboriginals' Australia. They teach of the geography, the topography, the meteorology, the anthropology of Australia. Though now there are other studies that supplement Upfield's, few exceed it. Upfield's cultural studies tell how life in Australia was lived during the first half of the 20th century, who the people were, how they lived, how they interacted with one another and with the two cultures, and with the climate and the land.

A writer's success depends, of course, on three things: the story itself (is is worth telling), development of the characters who enact the tale (are they credible) and the effectiveness of the style of writing. In all areas, Upfield was outstanding.

First of all, Upfield tells a rattling fine story. Experienced from youth in being able to keep a listener's interest, Upfield changes his pace from action to description, from nature on the rampage to personal meditation, from externalities to introspection, from White to Aboriginal, from people to geography and meteorology with skill and awareness of what the reader wants. These stories develop into an intensity which at times is almost unbearable.

Secondly, Upfield wraps his stories around his splendid character development of Inspector-Detective Bonaparte, called Bony. Bony, though a little reserved and perhaps stilted, is, as

American poet Edwin Arlington Robinson said about his character Richard Cory, "human when he talked." Bony is human and gracious, almost always smiling, disarming, well-rounded and flesh-and-blood. Bony lives! He lives in his language, his actions, his introspection.

And, third, Upfield's books live outside the extraordinary stories he tells and outside the captivating exploits of Detective-Inspector Bonaparte. One of the most outstanding strengths of the book is Upfield's ability to paint the outback and other varied and remarkable parts of Australia with a vividness that makes one wipe his brow because of the 120 degree heat in the shade and forces one to shake the sand from his collar blown there by the great windstorms that rage across the burnt-out lands of Continental Australia. Generally, Upfield sets the stage for his books at the very beginning of the book. Often the first chapter sets the stage in graphic terms, as for example the opening paragraph of *Winds of Evil.*

It was a wind-covered hell in which the man who called himself Joe Fisher walked northward towards the small township of Carie, in the far west of New South Wales.

Upfield gets more graphic:

Somewhere west of Central Australia was born the gale of wind this day lifting high the sand from Sturt's country—that desert of sand ranges lying along the north-eastern frontier of South Australia—to carry it eastward into New South Wales, across the Gutter of Australia, even to the Blue Mountains, and then into the distant Pacific.

His fantasmagoria in color intensifies:

Now and then the dark red-brown fog thinned sufficiently to reveal the sun as huge orb of blood. That was even a trough passed between the waves of sand particles forever rushing eastward. The wind was steady in its velocity. It was hot, too, but its heat constantly alternated, so that it was like standing before a continuously opened and closed oven door.

Or Upfield's description in *Man of Two Tribes* of an advancing wall of sand on the Nullarbor Plain:

The party stopped, to gaze in wonderment at what was happening. They could see neither the eastern nor the western limit of what appeared as a pale-yellow snake, alive and menacing, its body rippling in effort to digest a male. Here and there it bulged towards them, at places it rolled over and over, and at no place was torn asunder. Bony knew it could roll over a man and do no hurt, but it appeared to be as weighty as molten metal. (161)

At times Upfield's strength lies in his symbols, some brief and some extended, as in the opening paragraphs of *Bushranger of the Skies*, in a quote that bears repeating:

One of Nature's oddities was the grove of six cabbage-trees in the dense shade of which Detective-Inspector Bonaparte had made his noonday camp. They grew beside an unmade road winging like a snake's track over a range of low, treeless and semi-barren hills; and, so close were they, and so virile their foliage, that to step in among them was not unlike stepping into an ivy-covered church porch on a brilliant summer morning.

The symbolism of the church and snake's track indicating the nearness of evil is intensified a few words later as Upfield gazes out of his sanctum and sees a picture "roughly framed in the shape of a Gothic arch," that is the outlet framed by the spires of the cabbage-tree trunks.

Upfield's descriptions also have a compelling urgency about them that pulls the reader into the action. Such involvement occurs frequently in Upfield's books. When they do they are about as effective as such passages by almost any other author. And when they are the center of extended attention, they are as gripping as one is likely to encounter.

As excellent example comes from *The Will of The Tribe*, in Chapter 23. Throughout his career Upfield has discussed the role that clothing plays in the transformation of Aborigines into white life-style. Originally going naked all the time, the aboriginals gradually took on clothes as they assumed other white characteristics. When they reverted to their native state, they discarded the white-man's clothes. Thus clothes to Upfield is a strong symbol of the degree the Aboriginals have passed from one culture to the other.

*The Will of the Tribe* is a gripping story of a white family that tries to assimilate two Aborigines—a woman and a man— and how they are doomed to failure. In a dramatic scene the Aboriginal male, who never really did want to cross the line, is determined that the Aboriginal woman he loves shall not cross it either, that she will remain his lubra. In a remarkable scene, mixed with the tribal symbolism of clothing and a larger symbol of a giant desert crater called Lucifer's Couch caused in earlier times by a meteorite, the Aboriginal male is chasing the woman in order to bend her to his will of remaining an Aboriginal. Her panties became the symbol of the white-aboriginal conflict, and she sheds them as final capitulation to her tribal life.

The panties denoted the division Tessa is suffering. From her waist up she had become a member of the White community. She was brain, as Bony said dozens of times he was. From the waist down, Tessa was Aborigine. Significantly, as she returns completely to the aboriginal state, she discards her panties and gives in to her basic and nearly ineradicable instincts. Women reading Upfield's books might not like the apparent bias that Upfield shows in this scene. But experience, for what it was worth, had led him to believe that Aboriginals were better off in their pre-civilization stage than they were assimilated.

In language, at times Upfield's short figures of speech are hard and crystal clear, as for example this brief figure of a storm in *Bony and the White Savage* (Chapter 24):

The eye of the wind, having circled toward the Antarctic, had worked on the sea with spectacular results. The Front Door of Australia was now being savaged by all the white ghosts from the South, tearing at the feet of this monolith, leaping high as though to clutch the hair of a giant and pull him down for the lesser attackers to devour.

At times his passages are poetic, as in this example from *Death of a Swagman*:

The minutes were ticked off the sheet of Time by the moon's inevitable passage down the pale blue bowl of the sky . . . (116)

Or in this passage from *Bony and the Black Virgin*:

Old Man Drought was dead, battered and bludgeoned by little drops of water. (121)

Or again from the same book:

Death was whispering in his ears. (42)

At times Upfield's style is aphoristic, as in his statement about the good effects a drought can have on a population: "A drought is a good chastener," ( *Bony and the Black Virgin*, 77). Or in *Bony and the Mouse*: "Success is an edifice built on Patience." (48) The list goes on and on.

Aside from the fine descriptive and poetical passages, a work lives, of course, on the basis of its diction, its conversation, its trueness to reality. If the characters talk like books, if they have no sense of real-life conversation, if they are wooden in their actions and talk, then they have one foot on a greasy banana peel to begin with. But Upfield's conversation is very lifelike, his white characters speak Australian with an accent. His natives speak what closely approximates what other authors have said is their dialectical English. The strange and exotic, the drunken, characters all speak with an authenticity that approximates what they should be speaking, and undoubtedly what Upfield heard many times during the years he habituated the pubs and bars. Though it sounds a great deal like Cockney English, it is Cockney Australian, or the equivalent thereof. Once in referring to his language and the fact that he "never" used "bad language," in a comment made to Pamela Ruskin, Upfield made a generalization that might refer to all his style: "I only use Australian words!" And indeed he does. His language is Australian, whether that spoken by whites, by blacks, by sober persons or by drunks.

Though his regular language is straight-forward and generally idiomatic, direct and clear though not strikingly different from that of most other authors, Upfield's vernacular dialect is scintillating and very vernacular. For example, in *The Devil's Steps*, Bisker, a delightful misshapen Dickensian character, gets up early in the morning with a splitting hangover. As he turns to his daily chores, he reflects as he proceeds with one of his jobs, that of cleaning shoes that are put outside the doors of the guests of the chalet where he works so that he clean them:

> "Ha! Ha!" chortled Bisker, "The old bird! The old cat! The old—old—
> — .... Now lemme see. Number Five goes for a walk late last night. In he comes, has a drink or two—I must ask George about that—then toddles off to 'is room, takes of 'is shoes and plants 'em outside his door for me to clean....
> But that same argument can't be applied to the old cat. She wouldn't be out walkin' late last night, and yet 'er shoes are wet same as Number Five's. The old——Ah—yes, she could 'ave. A little bit of love, eh! Sherlock 'Olmes, me!"
> (14)

Throughout, Upfield's language has the rhythm of life. His "what" frequently becomes "wot," "them" is "'em," "for" often becomes "fer." When he compresses the sentence "Let's have a look," into "S'ava look," he is giving the language the vibrance and short-hand that it has in life. There are enough examples in the various quotes throughout this book to demonstrate Upfield's style in all its nuances.

Yet Upfield was always self-conscious about his writing style and working to improve it. In preparing a revision of *The Barrakee Mystery* for an American edition, to be named *The Lure of the Bush* Upfield made extensive revisions, all of which reveal his wished-for care and goals in writing his books. Upfield's friend Louise Mueller outlined in a nine-page letter to Philip Asdell the changes that were made. The changes outlined below are from Mrs. Mueller's words and those of Philip Asdell, discussing Mrs. Mueller's letter ( *Bony Bulletin*, No. 7, Oct. 1983).

"Basically," Mrs. Mueller wrote, "there is no change in the action, or story line. The twelve chapters which carry most of the action are unchanged." She then outlined numerous changes in diction:

> Then, too, when you analyse the changes, most are concerned with the language—changing 'nig' to 'nigger' to 'abo,' yet the term 'blacks' is still used in the new text. The first 'gin' used in Chapter 2 was changed to 'woman,' mainly to translate for the reader, because in later chapters 'gin' is used.
> Politics are out to some extent—and some of the Napoleon worship. Social attitudes are modified, and a better choice of words employed.

I can remember commenting to Arthur after first reading *Barrakee* that I thought 'Marie' a better name for Bony's wife than 'Laura': this was the type of oversight that Jessica would have caught had she been physically able. (See Chapter 16)

The use of italics was stopped. References to 'Little Lady' and the 'Darling of the Darling,' while deleted in early chapters, remained in full use for the balance of the book. Of course, you have noted the color change in Bony's face—I was amused to follow the lightening of color in the chronological order of the books.

Asdell outlines Upfield's changing of the Aboriginal vernacular:

In the opening chapters Upfield eliminated the Aboriginal pidgin 'bin' in several places, especially in William Clair's conservation with Pontius Pilate and Ned, King Henry's son, in Chapter 1. In one sentence Pontius Pilate tells Clair, 'Oh, but Sarah she bin leave old Mokis now....' In the revision 'bin' is deleted. But, inconsistently, a 'bin' is retained a few sentences on when Pontius Pilate says, 'Him bin do a get from a white feller wants killum...' and this seems to be the first of several inconsistencies in the revision which, one speculates, may have been a result of Upfield's poor health as well as his wife's inability to carry out her usual editing.

Upfield also modified his use of a cliche about stereotypical Aboriginal behavior. Asdell again:

In Chapter 2 of the original edition, the squatter, Mr. Thornton, discusses with his wife the shortcomings of Martha, their Aboriginal housemaid, who has once again lost her slippers. He says, "No matter how you educate them, civilize them, they all go back to the life and conditions of their forebears. And that's that." This attitude was quite common at the time *Barrakee* was written, and it is to Upfield's credit that he eliminated that comment entirely.

Upfield's use of such stereotypes got him into trouble with the Aboriginals of Australia. Though obviously it is the proper function of an author to mirror the stereotypes of a culture, and he can do that only by repeating them, it is unfortunate, perhaps, that Upfield did not comment somehow on the stereotypes as he used them, so that his works would now be acceptable to the Aboriginal population.

Upfield deleted some sharp remarks about absentee landlordism, which he despised. But in Chapter 9 he kept some conversation about "Sir Walter Thorley.... That scoundrel.... That absent owner of half Australia!" (Sir Walter Thorley seems to be Sir Sidney Kidman, whom Upfield severely castigated in *Follow My Dust*). Upfield also removed other paragraphs criticizing absent landowners and Government policies on land.

He toned down some purple passages in which Frank Dugdale reveals his love for Mr. Thornton's ward. One was;

> It was impossible, he knew, ever to crush his love for Kate, no matter if thousands of miles lay between them; equally impossible was it for him to remain in close proximity to her, no matter how much he avoided her society. His head urged him to go away. His heart cried out against the separation from that which made it leap at sight.

Upfield made a change in Chapter 7 which resulted in more normal English and clear style. He changed "pointing out the huger of two huge gins" into "pointing out the larger of two large gins," and in Chapter 8 he rewrote "but not to avoid it will I risk your life" with "except risking your life." Unfortunately at times he left some passages almost as awkward.

A large section of the Napoleon worship was removed, the inclusion of which was a blight on Upfield, Bony and Mrs. Thornton, the lady in the novel who shared Bony's apparent love for the French Emperor. It would have been better had Upfield removed more. As it was, the revised text was some 1900 words shorter, according to Asdell, and he speculates "that the revision would have been more careful and perhaps more extensive had Upfield been in better health at the time."

Such flaws as those outlined immediately above are simple ones that a first-class editor would have deleted or altered. They are too minor to mar the total impact of the book, especially as they became fewer and fewer as the books progressed.

And impact there was, everywhere but in the literary group of Australia. As Upfield outlines in the two novels that deal directly with the Australian literary establishment, *The Devil's Steps* and *An Author Bites the Dust*, those people despised him, and he consequently hated them. To him, they were far too slavish in their worship of "Literature" with a capitol L and in quotation marks. They were not writing for the multitudes, as Upfield was. They were composing for immortality and for the upper classes of people who appreciate great literature. He was not their kind of author, did not write their kind of literature, and never could be. The literary Establishment, he undoubtedly felt, looked down upon him because he did not have the proper background, was not university trained, had come out of the bush.

But in other circles Upfield's works had great impact. In its obituary, Feb. 14, 1964, the *Times* (London) recognized that a major writer had died and described his work thusly:

> Upfield, by pedantic literary standards, wrote rather badly: his grammar was liable to slip. But in Bony he created a unique and memorable character; in his approach to crime he shared some of Simenon's sadness and sympathy, and he had real descriptive power. Few other writers have brought a seemingly lifeless desert more colourfully to life or been more successful in communicating the unexpected beauty of Australia's hills and forests and rocky coasts.

The impact has continued to grow. During the 1970s Upfield seems to have gone out of print and was available only in hard-to-find second-hand copies. But in the mid-1980s there has been a resurgence of interest by readers which is forcing the publishers to bring out the books, too slowly to be sure but constantly, from title one to title thirty-four. The Upfield reading public is expanding.

His reputation is also solid among writers of crime fiction. John Ball, whose knowledge of crime fiction is encyclopedic and ability to write it dignified and supple, thinks Upfield's work "a notable achievement in the structure of Australian literature," as he says in his introduction to the Mystery Library edition of *The New Shoe*.

Tony Hillerman, whose detective fiction is in many ways a kind of American variant of the same impulses as those that drove Upfield, is effusive about his respect for and debt to the Australian. In his introduction to the Dennis McMillan reprinting of *A Royal Abduction* (1984), Hillerman says that in his youth "nothing had excited [him] as much as Upfield's landscapes and the people who somehow survived upon them." This haunting influence has continued through life. Hillerman attests to Upfield's lasting quality:

> I cannot honestly say that when I set about to write my own version of the mystery novel, Arthur Upfield was consciously in my mind. Subconsciously, he certainly was. Upfield had shown me—and a good many other mystery writers—how both ethnography and geography can be used in a plot and how they can enrich an old, old literary form. When my own Jim Chee of the Navajo Tribal Police unravels a mystery because he understands the ways of his people, when he reads the signs left in the sandy bottom of a reservation arroyo, he is walking in the tracks Bony made 50 years ago.

Those tracks still exist for all of us—authors and readers— because a stiff-necked man fell in love with the Australian outback in 1910 and tramped through it in every kind of weather until he became it and it he. Few writers have had better training.

But training and pragmatic ways of seeing the world are most fruitful in a writer when he/she is energized and propelled by a vision of what the world might be, of questions about why conditions are what they are and are not what they seem. Upfield was driven by such questions about the universe. In searching among them for answers, Upfield is bound to remind the reader of America's greatest Questioner of the Universe, Herman Melville, and his methods of searching for answers among questions that troubled Upfield. They had a great deal in common. Upfield did not have Melville's Transcendental visions nor his Biblical rhetoric which, like a storm, could tear down almost any opposition. But Upfield did have similar visions of the role of the hero, of the place civilization plays in the lives of people, and of the dignity and worth of mankind. He recognized, like Melville, the need to probe beneath the masks of appearance in order to identify reality. Upfield's Questioner was a mixed-blood, as one of Melville's,

Queequeg, had been. Bony stood somewhere between Queequeg and Ahab, not quite Ishmael but approaching him—imbued with the native strength of the mixed-blood energized in his questioning by the same kind of white blood that drove Ahab in his monomania. Ahab stabbed at the stars and the all-powerful Being; Bony probed deeply into man's relations with man. Together in their searching, Melville and Upfield comprise a broad and deep search. Such attitudes constitute pieces of heavy intellectual equipment very useful in mankind's effort to understand themselves and their world.

All of us are the beneficiaries of Upfield's efforts.

# Chapter 5
# Half-Castes

The role of half-castes in Australian society has always been ambiguous, especially in the outback of Upfield's novels. There is simply not enough known about them to make explicit and definite statements. Not enough is known, for example, of Tracker Leon Wood, the half-caste on whom Upfield based his character Bony, to know his role in society and the price if any he paid through being ostracized, shunned, etc. for being of mixed-blood. He seems to have been widely and highly respected by squatters. He surely had the right personality—reserved, dignified, slightly pedantic—to gain him respect. But Upfield does not record those aspects of Tracker Leon's career in his short sketches of his model for Bony. According to Pamela Ruskin, in her brief sketch of Upfield's career, Tracker Leon was the half-caste son of a station owner, was university-trained and "wholly civilized" but someone who felt the lure of the aboriginal way of life and preferred it to that of his father.

Bony, of course, being a tool in the hands of Upfield serves the role of being accepted or shunned as Upfield needs. Generally speaking he is accepted by all people he meets. Occasionally a white lady—generally a young inexperienced girl—will find that Bony is not the kind of person to be entertained and housed in the big house on the station. Sometimes the owner of a station, like McPherson in *Bushranger of the Skies* will view Bony suspiciously and be unwilling to admit him to full citizenship in the world of equality. But these rebuffs come because people are looking upon Bony's obvious lineage and not upon his personality. When he is allowed to be an individual personality, as he always becomes in the books, Bony invariably bewitches and endears himself to everyone he meets. But Bony is unique among half-castes. The lives and fates of the real half-castes on the Australian frontier was somewhat different, though at times apparently not all unpleasant.

Needless to say there were numerous half-castes in Australian frontier society. From the earliest English settlers in Australia on, for many whites the idea of interracial sex with the Aboriginals was abhorrent. Such white settlers looked upon the Aboriginals as scarcely more advanced than animals, who therefore should be shunned. But from the earliest days, there was a desperate shortage of white woman in Australia, and sexual contacts by white men and even white women with native women and men did occur, with consequent half-caste children. Obviously not all whites thought the Aboriginals animals. Upfield has one of his women characters, Mary Gordon in *The Bone is Pointed*, realize that the Aboriginals were "not all children; nor were they semi-idiots or mere savages." On the contrary, they were educable and could be raised in culture to behave just like the whites they associated with. In *Bushranger of the Skies*, (10) Upfield has Flora, the white young lady whom he admires, defend the Aboriginals' accomplishments and potentials, saying, "if the blacks had been given the chances the Maoris got in New Zealand they would today have been as cultured and as good citizens."

John and Mary Gordon in *The Bone is Pointed* provide these chances to Jimmy Partner, a young Aboriginal who lives with them as their own child. He is living proof of what can happen to the Aboriginals if you start educating them while they are young. Jimmy sat well at the table, ate with politeness. He spoke better than many of the white hands on the station, his voice was mellifluous and "free of the harsh accent to be heard in the voices of many university professors and other literate Australians." He read, understood and discussed the issues raised in the weekly journals. He was, in every way a "crown of achievement". (183) In *The Bachelors of Broken Hill* Upfield has an aboriginal named Ted Pluto who was "quite a smart fellow. He could "read comic strips and the sporting pages, and he could write and even work out the simpler crossword puzzles." (183)

But despite this living proof to the contrary, Upfield voiced one of the apparent stereotypes about the Aboriginals' character, one that is held against him among the Aboriginals today. In *Bushranger of the Skies* Bony says: "Educate him as you will, influence him as you may, you cannot eradicate his supreme indifference to tomorrow." (71)

Just as beauty always lies in the eyes of the beholder, the attractiveness of aboriginal women seems to have been debatable. Among many early English settlers, and even today in the popular lore of the Coastal urban whites in Australia, such women were not handsome. Their features—coupled with their unfamiliar manners and dress—made them nominally at least unattractive to whites, especially white women. But thoughtful white women, and men, cast different looks on the more primitive females. Mary Durack, for example, in her account of the adventures of her grandfather and father, *Kings in Grass Castles*, tells of the loneliness of the un-womened men in Australia and she sees as quite natural the allure of what she calls the "soft-eyed native women," whose "only terms were the right to live and to serve." (381-2) Such women, and frequently the Aboriginal men also, were becoming "entities with human attributes and likeable ways." (38) That is, necessity was the mother of recognition of virtues, and as the Aboriginals were needed for physical as well as sexual reasons they became more acceptable to the people who needed them, with qualities and characteristics all their own but capable of being accepted and shared by the whites.

As in the ante-bellum American South, and as in all societies where people of two races live with each other, in Australia there was some sexual intercourse between white women and black men, no matter how shameful it might be held in both societies. In *The Barrakee Mystery*, Upfield's first Bony novel, the story turns on Ralph, the presumed half-caste son of the station owners, who had not yet turned black, the child of a white woman and King Henry, a very attractive Aboriginal who was "the finest specimen of an aboriginal, wide of chest, narrow of hips, with powerful legs and arms." In Upfield's novels, however, as probably in real life, most of the sexual intercourse is between white men and black women.

There were of course strict Aboriginal laws against such intercourse. Death was supposed to be the sentence; Tracker Leon's mother and Bony's mother were apparently killed by their tribespeople for mothering them, and Bony, according to his account of his birth, presumably would have been killed with his mother had he simply not been overlooked when the Aboriginals carried out their law against his parent.

Among the whites, the Aboriginals' virtues—or at least acceptable attributes—could, of course, increase. Mary Durack, in *To Be Heirs Forever* (93) quotes a passage from George Fletcher Moore (183) which is a kind of backhand negative compliment but indicative of his and others' feelings: "The natives are not so despicable a race as was at first supposed. They are active, bold and shrewd, expert in thieving, as many have experienced; they are courageous when attacked. . . ." But Durack for herself found that the Aboriginals became lazy, listless, indifferent—but after they had become dependent on the whites, thus in effect backing Upfield in his statements that assimilation must be gradual. In another instance, Durack, in *Songs in the Saddle* (444) wrote of an individual who "spoke movingly of the mixed and outcast people of other areas and of his hope of saving the fine, virile full-bloods of the north from the corruptive influence of white society."

But the proximity of the men and women turned sex into a desperate lure. Often there were tragic consequences. Mary Durack in *Keep Him My Country* has a story which marvelously touches on this problem.

In her story, Rolt, a heroic White who is holding together a cattle station and a whole rout of Aborigines through circumstances thick and thin recognizes that he loves Dalgerie, a young aboriginal women not over sixteen. Durack's description of the young woman is lyrical:

[Perhaps] her father was an Afghan hawker who used to move about the country with a camel team. She was not as black as many of the other women, but the skin colour of the Territory natives, mixing for centuries with seafaring Malays and Islanders was as varied as their features. Even among his own station people Rolt could distinguish the high cheek bones and flattened nose of the Malay, the narrow, slant eyes of Chinese and Japanese, the clear-cut features of Afghan and India. Dalgerie with her dreamy, slightly tilted eyes and fine bone structure might have been a mixture of them all, if such existed in the Territory, she might have been pure Aboriginal. Her skin was chocolate dark and sometimes in the sun she would appear limned in gold, her small, proud head haloed by sun-bleached strands of hair. (p. 56)

One of his other Whites told Rolt of the true value of the Aboriginal woman:

You get a lubra like that occasionally...Don't seem to go for the men much at all and then get one fella and stick to him through thick and thin. Finest type of woman in the world—a good lubra. They got courage and intelligence and don't you believe anyone tires to tell you they don't know the meaning of love. (57)

But in this story Rolt delays stating his love and commitment, and when he does he finds to his surprise that Dalgerie thinks she prefers to stick with the marriage that she has been promised in. She runs away from the cattle station and Rolt. Later, Rolt finds her just before she dies. The beautiful girl of yesteryear is now withered, disfigured and dying. She turns her "glazed eyes that had passed beyond sight and suffering" toward Rolt. Rolt asks here why she ran away from him, and she replies: "Jullungul...He bin kill me...I down now." "Why did you go away, Dalgerie? I wanted you." After this exchange the woman dies. And Rolt manages to survive the death, though hard-pressed and dazed.

Jessica Hawke (122-3) recounts a real-life experience of Upfield's that all too vividly illustrates the dilemma. One afternoon in the outback, Upfield came to a lonely station where only a mother and her daughter about nineteen were at home. The girl was "pretty, plump and emotional." The mother explained to Upfield that the daughter had fallen in love with an aboriginal youth and that the mother and the daughter were going to move to the city to escape the entanglement of the interracial love-affair. That night the daughter, apparently learning of the forthcoming forced-separation, took strychnine and died in Upfield's arms while he was forcing saline water between her lips and she was vomiting and trying to live. So Upfield knew first-hand the feeling of both the white parents and the emotional entanglements of the young people.

The pathos of the unbridgeable chasm between races, classes, colors, is of course the very backbone of many good stories. Folklore is rife with Lovers' Leaps where disconsolate lovers have ended the heartbreak they could not bear; faced with broken hearts or broken bodies, lovers, at least according to sentimental stories, chose the latter.

Upfield wrote about many women, some strong, some weak, some realistically presented, some greatly romanticized, including several lubras, or aboriginals. When they are mere background, they are called "lubras," or "gins" apparently from Australia to New Zealand. When he is making a point about their contribution to the civilization on the cattle stations or when they are contributing to the conflict between the Whites and the Aboriginal males, or even when they are causing it, Upfield creates his women as very attractive and appealing. In *Bony Buys A Woman* (107) Meena, a woman who is an integral part of the story is described as: "clean as a new pin. Her clothes are right..." Tessa, in the *The Will of the Tribe* (34) is an even greater part of the book. In fact the story, or one of the main stories in the book, turns on her. In Upfield's description of her Tessa is obviously an attractive person "Today she is almost fully assimilated," Bony says. "Her dress sense is excellent, her pose is very good. Her conversation is intelligent and lucid." "Her demeanour, her table manners, her dress sense were all tributes" to the mother and wife in the Brentner family. In *The Widows of Broome*, (93) Upfield makes his only reasonably realistic statement about the looks of the Aboriginal lubra. Irene, a half-caste woman, is described as "a slim girl about twenty, and had her nose not been so broad she would have been good-looking." Bony's half-cast wife has her characteristics described many times, but never her appearance. In this case, apparently her sweet, understanding and loving nature is all that seemed to matter to Bony.

Apparently the most alluring lubra in Upfield's books is Lottee, in *Bony and the Virgin*, (185) where she is described as "sweetly beautiful" with eyes that "glowed like black opal."

The story surrounding Lottee is poignant. This beautiful black woman has fallen in love with the white scion on the cattle station, and he with her. As happens in several of Upfield's stories, the white and the black seldom get married and live openly ever after; society is not that simple. Generally the marriage has to be kept under cover to avoid dire consequences. In *Bony and the Black Virgin* the circumstances become dire. Eric, the white man involved in the romance, is not strong enough to marry the Aboriginal and face down public opinion. He did marry her, that is he went through the tribal ritual, but he could not openly acknowledge the ceremony. Thus Eric had yielded to what Bony calls "The Spirit of the Bush" but is not sufficiently strong in personality to face the consequences. The consequence of the weakness of both the white man and the black woman is they died in each other's arms.

Despite the apparent approving comments on the beauty of the Aboriginal woman, there is considerable obvious sexist talk, perhaps representing the actual need and feeling of the men on the Australian hinterland. Tessa, just described as a kind of model black woman, one whom Whites could well emulate, is still learned and wily in the ways of the aboriginal, and nature. She "knows how to ravish a bloke," Bony is told. "You know, looks at you with both eyes wide open and an adoring look in 'em...She's one of the tabbies who has to work on a man or bust." (77) And she waggles her behind in order to attract men. (170)

So the sexual aspect of the Aboriginal was always close to the fore in the minds of White Australians. Such a position indicates not only the vulnerability that prudish Victorian women seem always to feel but also the physical and psychological need for women of any sort on the frontier.

One of the favorite pastimes of the Aboriginals is the so-called "Walkabout," that is the activity of the tribe when they simply decide that it would be pleasurable to move to another part of the country, in search of food (this out of necessity) or simply to see new territory. Upfield uses the activity of the walkabout to reveal certain aspects of the Aboriginals—often their irresponsibility in White eyes, never being where they are needed when needed, their lack of discipline. Another activity he uses in several books to denote savage and pleasure, is the activity of running. Frequently the Aborigines, in Upfield's books, simply use running as a kind of coquetry and vamping, and as a prelude to sex. In *Bony Buys a Woman* (83), for example, Meena, described above, vamps her man Charley in a kind of coquettishness that is as old as men and women. Meena

wakened Charley by nudging him with her toes and calling him a lazy black bastard. She turned and fled, fled to the lake, and he raced after her and joined battle with splashing water. She danced about him, shouting with laughter at his attempts to grab her, shrieked with pretended terror when he succeeded. Together they fell and writhed in the foam, and eventually came walking back to camp hand in hand.

In *The Will of the Tribe* (23) this physical running is carried out in one of the most powerful and dramatic sequences in any novel by Upfield or anyone else. After a long chase, the aboriginal lady and man have sexual intercourse. The union is not rape. The point is that it was done in a great flurry of physical motion.

Perhaps the most sentimental story of the beauty of the lubra comes in the novel *Bushranger of the Skies*. Mr. McPherson, a very strong and heroic though self-denying man, is running all the activities of a cattle station. It is a very difficult task. In addition he is being harassed by his son—an ebony black half-caste who was the child of Mr. McPherson's marriage to an Aboriginal named Tarlalin. This offspring grew up a tortured individual. Little wonder since theirs was an ill-fated marriage from the beginning. As a child and young adult, McPherson was kept by his parents on the cattle station, out of town and away from all contact with other whites of his age. Knowing nothing but aboriginal men and women, McPherson eventually falls in love with Tarlalin, and proceeds to marry her. Both his mother and father disapproved of the marriage, feeling that it was a kind of miscegenation that could never prosper. Their disapproval drove their son and his wife to live in a separate house and live their separate lives. Eventually Tarlalin died young and sweet, and McPherson, becoming very secretive and taciturn, buried her in a grave with a beautiful memorial, remaining as faithful to the memory of her beauty and sweetness as was possible for any one to remain. He was fighting...to preserve his name from being soiled and Tarlalin's memory from scorn and derision. He was fighting an evil spirit, threatening Tarlalin's memory and his own name.

The evil spirit is, Rex, their child. It seems clear that in this instance Upfield, though he uses the opposite approach, is indicating that the union between Whites and Aborigines, no matter how pastoral and beautiful, results in misbegotten monsters who are the scourge of the earth.

In this book Upfield is as romantically lyrical about the question of love between Whites and Aborigines as possible. Not content to state this lyricism once and develop other aspects of the story plot, Upfield apotheosizes the relationship again and again. Once he capsulizes the tragic story of love between the Whites and the Aboriginals as lyrically as possible:

Tarlalin! One aboriginal woman of all the countless women who, down through the ages, had been little better than beasts of burden, been used carelessly and cruelly by men: regarded without honor, without value, save the questionable value of producing children that were seldom wanted because of the hard-won food they would eat and the precious water they would drink. Of all those numberless women but one had been loved greatly in life and greatly honored in depth. (70)

There was in Upfield's mind in this instance, in fact, little difference between the Aboriginal woman and her White counterpart. Except for color they were suitable companions. After all, as Upfield says in *Bushranger of the Skies*, (36) "A black girl can love as passionately as a white woman." Tarlalin may have been a dunce but she was beautiful and a lovely wife. There was also, at least in Upfield's mind, very little difference between the white and the aboriginal male. McPherson was "a man as near to the aborigines and their philosophy as Burning Water (an aboriginal) was to the white race and its philosophy." Bony had put on the veneer of white civilization, and McPherson had put on the veneer of the aborigines' mentality. (60-61) Upfield is saying that all people are the same under the veneer. As young Lacy says in *The Bone is Pointed* (70-71) "the more you know about the blacks the less superior to them you feel."

Half-caste children took a little more getting used to, naturally, among both the whites and the blacks. Durack, in *To Be Heirs Forever* (p. 91) reports that in colonial Australia the young men of the colony "had to look for their women outside the genteel parlors of white society." The result of their actions sometimes caused consternation among the black women, who understood nothing of physiology and conception. Even in these early days, Durack reports,

> black mothers in the outlying camps, puzzled by their pale-skinned babies, were rubbing them with charcoal and when this proved to no avail sadly returning them to their spirit ancestors.

The women too often suffered for their illicit actions, for they were breaking the tribal laws. Often they were killed for their transgression. Upfield has Bony tell nothing of his mother because she was killed at his birth, presumably for having broken the tribal law, and he had been left on her corpse, again presumably to die. On several occasions Bony speaks of the result of the sexual transgressions of black women with white men.

Through necessity, however, apparently the Aboriginal tribal customs bent to the inevitable and the blacks accepted their half-caste children, looking upon the whiteness that the babies had at birth and for years afterwards (Bony says until they are up to 30 years old) with a mixture of curiosity and religious awe. Acceptance among the Whites of the mixed-blood babies also took some time. Durack, again, in *Kings in Grass Castles*, quotes her father at some length over the feeling he had on seeing the first half-caste strapped to the back of its mother:

> It is greatly to be hoped [he wrote] that such is not to become a commonplace in our community for the strain resulting will be no asset its being common knowledge that the half-breed inherits the worst characteristics of both races, nor would I feel disposed ever to trust or to employ one of the kind. The problem will therefore inevitably arise as to what can be done with such unfortunate unemployables who through no fault of their own are brought

into the world in evidence of the unlicensed and irresponsible conduct of the poorer products of both black and white societies. (p. 372)

Durack records that her father was voicing the consensus of the conservative "right thinking" people of the day. But in fact such half-castes, called "yella-fellas," proved excellent specimens, "better adapted," as she says,

to the environment than the white man and better to the new way of life and philosophy than their full black brothers.

She quite properly attributes this superiority to the fact that

The men who fathered them were after all mostly hard individuals with guts and staying power and their mothers selected from the more attractive and healthy specimens of black womanhood. (p. 382)

But the fathers of some of the half-castes were not always of premier stock, at least to some individuals, though apparently the mothers were often considered superior. Durack herself, in *Keep Him My Country* (172-3), tells of a man who persists in calling a half-caste a "blackfellow." When told that the term offends the individual concerned, the white remarks:

I got a lot of respect for the blacks... Well you tell him from me his mother belongs to one of the finest races in the world, but his father was poor trash what I know of him. You've no business making him ashamed of his dark blood. (p. 173)

To some observers, especially those who came after the actual living conditions experienced by those early pioneers, the possible gentility of interracial couplings is not seen as having been so bucolic as others might claim. To the analyst and critic of white domination of Aboriginal rights, Frank Hardy, who wrote scripts for the television series about Bony (in *The Unlucky Australians*, 1968, 35), the interracial escapades of the whites amounted to, quoting from the manuscript of Frank Stevens, almost animalistic sexual domination of aboriginal groups by frontier type cattlemen, which even in recent years has included a sexual traffic in aboriginal girls as young as seven years of age.

So, apparently the practice is not over—nor the problem. To races seeking assimilation, interracial sex is proper since it reduces the differences between the races and tends to melt them all in the common pot. But to a race that insists on its own autonomy in racial characteristics and customs, that has determined to maintain its separateness because it sees racial, economic and cultural reasons for the distinctness, interracial sex is abhorrent. Surely the feeling of superiority of one race over the other and therefore the holding of certain sexual "rights" is intolerable.

The case of casting some people because of their mixed blood somewhere between "pure" and "mixed" blood continues to be a haunting problem.

# Chapter 6
# Clothes and Nakedness as Metaphor

Clothes to the Australia Aboriginals were alien and foreign artifacts. To them nakedness was the proper and natural way to present the body. Originally the Aborigines wore nothing at all. Accounts of the Aboriginals in the eighteenth and nineteenth centuries, and even documentaries as late as 1930 show them completely naked. But the Europeans as their influence spread forced the Aboriginals to adopt the European use of clothes. So the Aboriginals went from complete nakedness to the pubic tassel for both men and women and finally to the complete dress code of the Europeans. The use of, or restraint from the use of, clothes and the development of these clothes among the Aboriginals became a kind of metaphor, especially for Arthur Upfield, on the degree to which the Aboriginals, fortunately or unfortunately, had been civilized—clothes became a symbol of the civilized and nakedness one of the non-civilized.

From complete nakedness, the Aboriginals, under European prodding, went first to the breechcloth for both men and women, the women going without top covering. Subsequently, lured by the bright colors of whites' clothes, the Aboriginals graduated to brightly colored clothes and presented a gaudiness in clothing that some whites found amusing. Others, however, like Upfield and Bony, were saddened by this display of gaudiness, for it demonstrated a degeneration of the Aboriginal. In *The Widows of Broome* Upfield contrasted Bony with the Aboriginal race:

Standing on the outskirts of the crowd, Bony was sad, for his race was dying, and the remnant here clothed in rags and gaudy finery presented the dreadful tragedy of a once rigidly moral, supremely free people being devoured by an alien and stupid civilization. (193)

Upfield recognized the unconscious power of clothes and color to help disintegrate the native culture.

So powerful was the lure of clothes that Aboriginals, like whites though probably for different reasons, easily adapted to the dress of their vocations. In her excellent account of her family's history in Australia, *Kings in Grass Castles,* Mary Durack quotes the manager of a station in Aubergne, T. K. White, on the Sunday attire of the men and women Aborigines on his far-out-back station:

The many-coloured dresses of the women have now given place to skirts, moleskin pants and stockwhips slung across their shoulders. They are not now easily to be distinguished from the stern sex but for their fuller posterial curves. (371)

From these starts and stabs the Aboriginals developed into wearing precisely the same clothes, often hand-me-downs, that the whites wore. But when they wanted to revert to their former status, when they wanted to "go native" again, invariably they cast off their clothes and went back to total nakedness, sometimes with ceremonial feathers on their feet.

Upfield, like Thomas Carlyle and many others before and after him, uses clothes and nakedness as a dominant symbol in depicting freedom vs. restraint, Aboriginal culture vs. civilization, happiness vs. unhappiness. Nakedness is natural; wearing clothes is unnatural. Nature as well as man knows and observes the distinction. In Upfield's *The Will of the Tribe* the great Australian distances make a traveler feel vulnerable and naked: "Crossing the great elbow of the desert gave the sense of nakedness induced by limitless spaces." (72) In *Bony and the Virgin* Upfield says: "Fear of the unknown—the dark. Fear of nakedness—the light." (67) Nature in its most sublime aspects stands alone, naked. In *The Will of the Tribe* Upfield describes Lucifer's Couch, the mountain bed that is to play a prominent part in the book as "isolated, remote, majestic," which gave one the sense of "complete nakedness." (39) The natives when they went native removed their clothes for their activities, because they were strongest when naked, having all the mystic power of their sorcery and their ancestors. In *The Will of the Tribe,* when

Aborigines are slinking around the house threatening some kind of underhand activity, they are completely naked. In *The Bone is Pointed* the Black who is pointing the bone at Bony "was completely naked save for the masses of feathers about his feet." (139) In *Bushranger of the Skies* when the Aboriginals are chasing the airplane that Rex, the half-caste, is flying away, they all start out in the chase fully clothed, but riding their horses like madmen after the plane and into a reversion into their native state, they shed their clothes piece by piece as they ride, in what becomes a major metaphor of Upfield for the slipping of the Aborigines from civilization back into primitivism

Upfield established his notion of the difference between European clothes and Aboriginal nakedness early. In his second Bony novel, *The Sands of Windee*, he made his position quite clear:

I have heard that call [of the bush] with the blood of countless nomadic ancestors in my veins! I left Sydney when I was twenty-two and went back to North Queensland, where I first saw the light. And my body craved for complete freedom from the white man's clothes. I wanted to go ahunting as my mother's father had hunted, and I wanted to eat flesh, raw flesh, and feast on tree grubs, and lie down in the shade and go to sleep, fed full and feeling the wind play over my naked skin. (65)

Again, in the next book, *Wings Over the Diamantina*, Upfield through Bony continues to speak of the inhibition of clothes and the joys of the sensuousness of nakedness:

Bony inhaled deeply. The hot sun already was striking on their backs. The sleeves of Bony's shirt were rolled above the elbows, and its neck was wide open. He was feeling that delicious sensation of being wholly free, and he wanted badly to lapse as he had done the previous evening. The aboriginal instincts he had inherited from his mother urged him to cast aside all the white man's clothes,...His blood burned with the desire, but his brain pounded down the impulse. (89)

Bony is strongest when on the land of the Australian out-back. When he leaves the land he is vulnerable. In *The Mystery of Swordfish Reef*, when Bony is at sea, Upfield admits that on the sea Bony is out of his element and is in some danger. Upfield is therefore presenting his symbols in their starkest strengths. His clothes metaphor is especially strong. Mr. Rockaway, a Jekyl-and-Hyde character whose obsession is, significantly, swordfishing, is trying to destroy Bony. He has thrown the Detective-Inspector into a cabin below the water line trussed up and behind locked doors. Bony, however, has escaped from his bonds and through the locked door, and is sneaking toward Rockaway meaning to destroy him for the pain and suffering he has inflicted upon other people. Bony's passion and mission in this instance are quite unusual. Ordinarily he remains cool and detached in his detecting, indifferent to whether a person is punished for his crimes. But in this instance, Bony has slipped his civilization moorings and has reverted to the Aboriginal civilization of his mother. Bony's garb is the ultimate in reversion to the natural state:

> His general appearance was the antithesis of that of the being known to his colleagues. The veneer of civilization, so thin in the most gently matured of us, was entirely absent. He was wearing nothing. A film of oil caused his body to gleam like new bronze. His hair was matted with blood. His eyes were big, and the whites were now blood-shot. His lips were widely parted, revealing his teeth like the fangs of a young dog.

Here is a reversion from "civilization" to the "natural" state. But once the blood lust is satisfied, Bony is able to readjust the veneer, dress himself and come back to the civilized state. The picture Upfield draws is almost too stark. But it was not unique for him.

In *The Sands of Windee* Bony reverts to the naked savage. In a scuffle between two sets of natives, Bony's throw-back to the aboriginal state is easily accomplished:

> Excitement made Bony speechless. His blood was aflame with ecstasy, and he was moving back along the branch to reach the main stem by which to get down to join the fray, when from almost below them the reports of a double-barrelled shotgun very nearly caused both him and Withers to fall to the ground. (79)

A more extended and dramatic treatment of the symbol is used in *The Will of the Tribe*. It bears being repeated here for illustration. On a station in the bush the kind and civilized Brentner family, with two daughters of their own aged 5 and 7, have taken into their family a beautiful Aboriginal girl named Tessa, aged seventeen. The family plans for Tessa, who is treated like all white people, to go to college, which is unheard of for an Aborigine, and to become a school teacher. As a school teacher she can serve as a "bridge" between the white and Aboriginal culture and thus help the people of her civilization. A young male Aboriginal named Captain two years older then Tessa also lives and works on the station, and is treated almost like a member of the family, surely with the same respect that other members of the working crew receive. Tessa and Captain, like members of the family, dress in white.

Nakedness and naturalness, or the lack of it, is the dominant motif in the plot of this novel. The countryside around the farm is described as "naked," therefore natural though barren. The aborigines are always being reprimanded for walking around naked, even without feathers on their feet.

Tessa and the Captain represent two degrees of nativeness. She is trying to get away from it, the Captain trying to conform to it and retain it. Yet in her reluctance to be entirely separated from her background, Tessa collects legends of the Aborigines. The Captain is writing a history. She is treating the subject romantically, he is treating it realistically. Bony, as the plot unfolds, is torn between the two. He commends Tessa for her accomplishment, and calls her a remarkable girl. Bony reaffirms that he has tried at times to constitute a bridge spanning the gulf between the Aboriginal and the white. Somewhat out of character Bony states that if Tessa realizes her ambitions she might "well build a far stronger bridge" than he had built because Tessa would be "thinking as a white woman."

The Captain has already decided to serve his people. In fact he never toyed with the idea of working with any other, and he resents the fact that Tessa, whom he considers his woman, is contemplating making a breakaway. Tessa, though the sweetest of individuals and trying hard to be white, cannot wear her two traditions without much conflict. She dresses and acts immaculately, yet—like an Aboriginal woman, Bony says—she is likely to swing her hips around men to attract their attention. She admits she is vain and enjoys being stared at. The Captain, loving Tessa, thinks that the clothes she wears keep her too far from him, representing too much civilization for a young Aboriginal woman.

Bony himself is torn between these two forces. His head tells him that one serves best by being outside the tradition. His heart asserts that one serves best within a part of the system. The solution of the plot turns on clothes as a symbol.

The tension of the book is released in one of the most dramatic and bizarre episodes in literature. The Captain, caught as being guilty of having killed the white man found in Lucifer's Couch nearby, turns a gun on Bony and Tessa, telling her that she is his lubra, his woman, and that he intends to kill both. Tessa frightened, not sure that she wants to give up civilized life, starts to run from Captain. He follows. Now the role of clothes in the plot becomes dominant.

Running hard to escape from Captain, Tessa realizes that she has become soft wearing white woman's clothes and shoes. The clothes that she used to treasure now are impediments to her safety. She kicks the shoes off. She throws the skirt from around her legs. She pauses a moment to pull her slip over her head, and with it she pulls off her bra. Now she feels free, her lungs able to take in plenty of air.

Freed from the artificial white woman's clothing she runs for what seems like hours from the maddened Captain. She flees toward the desert and to the magical Lucifer's Couch, but they offer no protection. She has long since realized that the protection afforded her by the White's house no longer holds in this real world. She realizes that

the clothes she had worn for so long, the books and the study, the ambition to become a teacher, it hadn't been real after all. It was a story told her by someone... She was an aborigine.

With fear of Captain but also with doubt that she really wants to cease being an Aborigine, Tessa finally succumbs to her ancestral ways. Running wildly from Captain dressed only in her "beautiful panties," she makes her choice. Dressed in these "beautiful panties"—bright colors always bewitched the Aboriginals—Tessa reluctantly stops and gives in to her primeval urging. She pulls off her panties and turns to face Captain. She

obeyed the command given by women to their maiden daughters down from the Alchuringa times. She collapsed upon the sandy ground and clawed the sand over her breasts and between her thighs.

Captain runs up and collapses on the sand beside Tessa. Fully naked, she recognizes that she wants Captain. They get up from the sand and walk away.

Bony witnesses the flight and Tessa shedding the pieces of her clothing. To him the symbol of the clothes is just as dramatic as it is to Tessa. From a distance he sees Tessa when she is wearing only her green panties, and to him "she is divided midway by the green panties she was still wearing." In other words from her waist up she is "white" in inclination—to Upfield reason is a white person's characteristic. From the waist down she is Aboriginal—primeval. It is natural then for her to pull off her panties and give in to her ancestors' inclinations and callings.

Bony is satisfied with the solution of the conflict. But he wants to give Tessa another chance to renounce the life of the Aboriginal—to allow her the option of being sure that she has done with Captain what she really wanted to do. He brings her another set of White clothes and she puts them on. But a permanent change has come over Tessa.

without the foundations [of White clothes and also of the pretensions of White society] the smartly-cut skirt and the light-blue blouse—as bright enough to lure any simple lubra—made her look pathetic. (160)

She tries to wear the clothes. She squats down on her haunches, lubra style, but then remembers and sits flat on the ground and pulls her feet under her skirt.

So though Tessa and Captain have run together into "Eden by the back door," and each had his or her will with the other, Upfield does not sentence Tessa to renouncing life in the White style. She has just properly proportioned it. After she and Captain are married, she remains at the homestead to help out, in a position hardly changed from that she had held before the great trauma.

But now she is a life-long Aboriginal, not a Black trying to escape her role in life.

What does this episode in what is perhaps Upfield's strongest book really mean? This is his next to the last book that he finished, and his concluding statement on the subject, after a lifetime of observing and worrying. Was Upfield a sexist? Did he believe that a woman's place was on the reservation? This is his most obvious and powerful statement of such an attitude. But it is not unambiguous, and the conclusion is not emphatic one way or the other. Surely he is saying that civilization is not beneficial for the aborigines, or fast assimilation. He had said these things often. In *Man of Two Tribes* he says that "Eighty per cent of tribal strife has its origins in white interference. (16) He is certainly interested in advancing the cause of the Aborigines, Bony's great ambition in life, and he may well believe that the cause can best be served by working from within. It would seem that he is denying Tessa the goal in life that she at least at one time thought she would enjoy and deserved. He is not saying that the two races cannot mix; Bony was himself a half-breed and knew many others, like his wife and children, who were exemplary and useful citizens. And he painted many full-blooded aborigines who were exemplary. One thing is clear. Despite a life of wandering the Australian continent, or because of it, Upfield, like Bony, seemed to prefer order to chaos. Bony admired General Napoleon Bonaparte, for whom he was named, because Napoleon "never lost a battle because he planned against the future." Upfield may have felt it was easier to plan ahead in one's established role in society, to work from the inside out, evolutionarily rather than revolutionarily. As he had declared earlier, in *Bony and the Black Virgin*:

complete assimilation isn't achieved by the aborigine via swift passage from one state to another.... Assimilation is gradual and requires several generations. (144)

Yet Upfield is never absolutely sure of himself and his opinions; he is not one to say never. Sometimes aborigines can wear clothes as naturally as anyone else and achieve the dignity that clothes bring. Tessa, and some other lubras in his stories, do. In another instance he awards all the dignity possible to an Aboriginal and his White clothes. In *Bushranger of the Skies* Upfield has Flora, the leading woman in the story and one that Bony admires, say of Burning Water, one of the heroic Aboriginals, that he "wore clothes as naturally" as anyone. He was "never a travesty in clothes." But though dressed in White's clothes, Burning Water is not trying to lose his Aboriginal identity and become White. It is only when the clothes become permanent barriers between the Aboriginal and his culture that Upfield objects and finds them obnoxious. In this society more than in others where the differences between two races was less, clothes became a significant symbol.

# Chapter 7
# Pubs and Booze

Life on any frontier has always been lonely and difficult both physically and psychologically. With all kinds of recreation and mind-lightening activities devastatingly in short supply men and woman have always turned to the one solace that somehow always seems to be supplied—booze, and the houses which supply it. In outback Australia the pubs and hotel bars supplied the access and the material—and in great quantity. The variety of drinks spread from whiskey to beer, but most people seemed to prefer beer—at least in the outback. In *Mr. Jelly's Business*, Upfield estimates that one man has drunk ten thousand gallons of beer. In *Bony and the Mouse*, Melody Sam, owner of the pub and musician, takes out his fiddle and plays, and "Australia rocked on beer" so happy that all ignored the mandatory closing hour of 6 p.m.

In outback Australia pubs and bars were numerous. In the so-called "Golden Mile" linking Boulder and Kalgoorlie in Western Australia, established in 1893, by 1900 there were 8 breweries, 93 pubs, for the 30,000 citizens. In Wilcannia on the Darling River, called the Queen City of the West, in 1911 on the main street there were 19 pubs, 12 stores, banks and private houses, with more pubs along the west bank of the river. In even the smallest communities there had to be pubs where the hard-working swagmen could drown their troubles.

Owners and publicans in these pubs worked hard, for the customers drank hard. In *The New Shoe*, Upfield describes a barman who is

working flat out. It was ten minutes to the fatal hour of six, and the enforced National Swill was in full flood.

"The National Swill" was the rushed drinking by the customers as the hour approached 6 p.m. All bars closed at 6 p.m. and therefore workers who came by the bars after quitting time at their jobs at 5 or 5:30 had only a half hour or an hour at most to get their fill. They therefore often consumed vast quantities of beer or liquor in a short time, thus getting deeply drunk. In Australia now there is no longer a "National Swill" because the pubs stay open until 10 p.m.

Upfield describes the size of outback towns and villages by the number of pubs available. In *Venom House,* for example, the place of Manton is a "four-pub town," Edison is a "one-pub town." In a description that is fairly typical in ratio of pubs to other buildings in a town, Edison has "one pub, two churches, three banks," and the average number of drunks, till-ticklers, scandal-mongers and snobs. In other words, you can get a profile of a town by the number of certain kinds of buildings present.

Pubs were great democratizers. Snobbishness tended to disappear in a pub, and that was one of the great benefits of the pubs, and of drinking, in Upfield's Australia. This was especially true if the only licensee in a town, as in the village of Carie in *Winds of Evil,* happened to be a strong and democratically-minded individual. In this book the only licensee is a woman who will not tolerate any challenge of her order of democracy in her pub and her town.

One of Upfield's longest and most explicit statements of the habit and methods of drinking in outback Australia comes in the novel *The Sands of Windee.* A Mr. and Mrs. Bumpus are two Dickensian characters who own the hotel and pub in the town of Mount Lion. In language and action they could have stepped straight out of the pages of Charles Dickens' fiction—or for that matter straight *into* the pages. Two whimsical characters who play into and disrupt the eccentric habits of the Bumpuses are called Dot and Dash, whose names come from their physical similarity to punctuation marks and sounds in the Morse Code: Dot is an American who is short; Dash, naturally, is a tall Englishman. They perhaps best exemplify one of the attitudes of the drinking Australian about the booze they consume.

They call beer "Australia's greatest resource."

They also tell how it is cooled in the torrid heat of the Australian outback, and they bless the person who discovered the art. Beer is put under wet porous bagging and as the water evaporates from the bagging the beer is cooled. In a country where the temperatures can reach 120 degrees Fahrenheit in the shade, any degree of coolness is a blessing.

Pub-hopping to Upfield's characters was highly desirable though they often discovered that it was an exercise in futility, only a fondling of fools' gold. As an old-timer in *Death of a Lake* (23) says, one finds when you've drunk at one bar you've drunk at all, and when you have demonstrated the futility of trying to drown your sorrows in booze you have demonstrated the scenario in perpetuity: "Australia is just a pancake dotted with pubs wot are all alike." Nevertheless, the pubs and the booze of old had been superior to and more important than they were to the youngsters and newcomers. The old-timer in the novel just mentioned thinks that

the coming generation is too sap-gutted with fruit juices and milk in their tea, and nowadays if a man has a go of the horrors he ain't liked. Once upon a time, if a man didn't have the horrors he wasn't reckoned a man's shadder. (23)

So in Australia, as in America and elsewhere throughout the macho-oriented world, the pub was the board of democracy, and drinking the mark of how high a man stood.

Perhaps no better proof of the attraction and need for pubs and booze in Australia can be found than an anecdote involving Upfield himself. He had been working on the vermin fence at Momba station for more than twelve months when he realized that the solitude was getting to him. He had developed the habit of talking aloud to imaginary companions. Once he had argued vehemently with such an imaginary companion about his choice of beer being better than the companion's choice of "plonk," and had even set a place at his table for his companion to eat. Four days later he reached the main homestead and related the incident to his manager.

Realizing that the affliction was not unusual and had only one cure—getting away from the solitude—the manager said:

Time to take a spell, Upfield. Only two antidotes for that type of lunacy. Either go get a job driving a tram, or go on the booze at Wilcannia. (Hawke, 81).

Apparently many lonely men took the second option, and returned later to court lunacy for other long periods of time.

On another occasion, Upfield had diagnosed the same cure for himself. In 1924, when he was 36 years old and had been in Australia 14 years since first coming, Upfield met Mary and Angus, a couple holding a small station, for the second time, and in talking with them revealed that he was about to go crazy; he knew the cure was to go "to the city and have a good old bender," but the city did not appeal to him anymore, nor apparently did the sure cure for the blues.

In another incident Hawke, undoubtedly paraphrasing Upfield, described the meeting of the bushman and his booze. After six months to a year in the bush the refugee from loneliness went to the nearest pub and wrapped himself around all the liquor he could buy and drink—starting out bleary-eyed but dry when the bar opened, having to be poured out of the bar at closing time, dazed and moronic looking. Hawke apotheosizes them:

Australia belonged to them! The pub was their own. They were the hosts, gracious and generous. All for twenty days. The long-pent dreams of good living, endless days of thirst quenched by milkless tea, long weeks and months on monotonous rations, were banished for three weeks at the cost of two station checques totalling almost a hundred pounds when a pound was a golden nugget. (97)

At times Upfield merely touches on booze and pubs in passing. For example, in *Bony and the White Savage* when Karl Mueller sees Marvin Rudolph, the giant who devastates the countryside, he thinks he has had a touch of the "horrors," that is delirium tremens. In *The Sands of Windee*, Bony thinks that Luke Marks, the man who has disappeared, was drunk when he wrecked his car, and therefore as Bony says "Drink, I believe, is the foundation of the whole affair." (7)

At other times, Upfield uses drinking as a source of amusement, and of showing a man's heroics, as the Old Timer mentioned in *Death of a Lake*. In *Death of a Swagman*, for example, at a wake in a pub a Mr. Jason sets a record in drinking and holding his breath. He fills his lungs with four breaths of smoke and holds it for 2 minutes 37 seconds, meanwhile drinking four mugs of beer, with smoke leaking out of nose and mouth while he talks. Indeed he is a giant in this exercise.

At times Upfield uses booze to develop and enrich his character development. In *The Devil's Steps*, for example, Bisker is a Dickensian character who has sunk in life because he drinks too much. And he always regrets his boozing, especially when it is time to get up at five-thirty every morning. He curses the drink for what it is and himself for drinking it.

In this same book, Clarence B. Bagshott, the Upfieldian character introduced as a writer of popular fiction, is a hard-drinker, who always wants to stop at the first pub.

Sometimes Upfield uses booze to develop deeply tender and poignant characters. In *The Widows of Broome*, for example, Mr. Dickenson is a richly-developed Dickensian character who is temporarily impecunious three days before his quarterly check arrives from the government and has to resort to some other kind of drink than whiskey. So he drinks highly-diluted battery acid. But he is always a gentleman and maintains his dignity. Another Dickensian character given to boozing is Mr. Simpson in *The Mountains Have A Secret*. (16) He always has a "dry throttle" and begs for whiskey, and one of the leitmotifs in the book is Bony's unceasing promise to get him booze.

Occasionally Upfield uses booze as a source of all evil, or at least as a vice indulged in by wicked people. In *The Mountains Have a Secret*, (70) for example, the Nazi conspirators are all heavy drinkers, who take over a pub, beat up Bony and destroy the democratic camaraderie usually found there. At times drink turns people into monsters who have nothing to do with politics. In

*Madman's Bend*, for example, the villain is a drunkard and wife-beater named appropriately William Lush.

At times Upfield develops his stories more neatly around booze, the pub, or some related activity. In *Wings Above the Diamantina*, one of his early books, for example, Upfield has a fine physician in the Australia outback whose only solace is drinking. He uses an airplane, as he must, in visiting his patients. And he always tries to get drunk before flying the plane. He has had three accidents while flying, and all three while "stone sober," as he says. In his first flight in this book, he crawls into the cockpit with face "tinged with colour" after at least six drinks. But flies perfectly and soberly. He is a source of constant amazement to his fellow Australians.

The story is even more intricately bound in with the characters in *The Battling Prophet*. The prophet is a meteorologist who is able to predict years in advance whether the seasons will be wet or dry. He, named Mr. Wickam, is 75 years old. He spends most of his time with his friend, Mr. Luton, who is 84 years old, and they have spent most of their lives on drinking binges. Sometimes these binges last 3 weeks, 6 weeks, even at times 2 months. Mr. Wickam is murdered while in a fit of delirium tremens induced by a 3-week binge.

Upfield had first-hand knowledge of what a binge really was. He had spent his share of time holed up at the pub, handing the bartender his check from working on the station and drinking until the money was gone—then being tossed out on the road with only a half-bottle, to wander back to his job and remain lonely until the next break and binge.

But hard as these bouts with booze were with Upfield, they were not of the same magnitude as those he had seen on other people. Once, for example, while cooking at Wheeler's Lake, Upfield had been sent as a man to help out during a shearing spree a drunk who had just been thrown out of his latest pub. Forced to become sober cold-turkey, the man, named Sto... Bird, was having his troubles. After only three weeks on the bottle, he was brushing imaginary creatures from his hands, his arms, his neck and face. With his face glistening with cold sweat, he took up an empty soup bowl and "swiped hard at something perched on the sugar bowl." As the case of delirium tremens progressed, Storm Bird fought against all kinds of monsters, climbed from the table to the cross-beam above him, where he stayed, despite all coaxing and arguing, for two hours. Finally, exhaustion drove him to sleep. The whole experience tired and disgusted Upfield, but did not drive away his sympathy and understanding.

In *The Sands of Windee* Upfield draws another character who is delightful and outlines one of his practices. He is Father Ryan who tries in his pragmatic way to keep people out of the Slough of Despond and on the road to heaven. One way he helps out the drunks is by fining them for their drinking. Father Ryan understood why people from the lonely deserts came into Mount Lion and went on their binges that generally wound up in delirium tremens.

In the bigness of his heart Father Ryan loved all these lonely men, many of whom were without family or family ties. He knew the stagnancy of their existence and mental depression with which the bush afflicts them, and he forgave them their lapse into very occasional drunkenness as did his Master. He placed them all in one of two classes, which he called 'Gentlemen' and 'Drunks.'

Though he forgave them, Father Ryan charged them up front for his forgiveness. When a "gentleman" came to town, Ryan demanded half a sovereign for his benevolent fund to support those who could no longer support themselves. When a "drunk" blew in Ryan demanded three, four or five pounds for his fund. These funds were subsequently spent on those poor wretches who had drunk themselves into food-starved, mentally crippled wretches who had to be rehabilitated before going back into the bush for another six months.

In two books Upfield uses episodes in pubs to set the stage for further developments of character and action. In *Sinister Stones* two Irish giants, named Breen, intimidate all other guests and monopolize the whole house. The alert reader will of course recognize that these giants are going to be at the hub of the villainy in the novel. But good drinking buddies cannot be all bad in Upfield, and at the end of the mystery, Bony will not testify against the guilty person because this kind of people have "never done a bad turn." (106)

One of the rowdiest and most delightful barroom brawls occurs in *Mr. Jelly's Business.* In the township of Burracoppin there is a pub run by Mr. and Mrs. Wallace. He is a meek man, she a "she-bull," who is described as "a liner steaming slowly out of the harbor." Mrs. Wallace brow-beats and physically abuses her husband. He curses her under his breath. When this pair is confronted by the heroic actions of Mr. Garth, whom Upfield calls "The Spirit of Australia," all suds break loose. Garth beats all the men in the pub, Mrs. Wallace beats him. All beat Mr. Wallace, and everybody loves the evening. The scene of this bar-fight is a classic equal to that of most American westerns all combined. Dickens never created a better scene.

But of all the scenes and developments having to do with pubs and booze, perhaps Upfield's story in *Bony and the Black Virgin* is his most complex and richest statement on the subjects. The story begins in the town of Mindee on the Darling River. The town has three hotels with bars. Downer, a little wisp of a man who owns a cattle station in the surrounding outback, has spent a month in the town on a binge, as he does every so often. His son Eric is now engaged in his usual activity of trying to find his father, who is wily and experienced enough to slink out the backdoor of each hotel bar as his son walks in the front door inquiring for his father. Downer is not a wicked man. He is a typical Australian squatter who drinks too much. In other words, he is a typical Australian White man.

His son Eric is an exemplary man, sober, conscientious and hard-working. His only trouble is that he is love with Lottee, an aboriginal girl on his station. Eric and Lottee feel that they have always belonged to each other, and they intend to love and marry despite the laws and customs and frowns of the two peoples who oppose their liaison.

As the story develops, it becomes clearer and clearer to Eric and Lottee that they are not going to be allowed to love and live together happily ever after. So they plan their joint suicide. They get in a boat, row out to the middle of a lake, pull the plug in the boat and in a final embrace sink into the water. Locked in an embrace, they demonstrate that the East and the West—the white and the Aboriginal—can and should meet. But the ending of the story says much more.

Upfield obviously is making a statement here that he makes nowhere else. Throughout the 29 books in which he appears, Bony describes himself as a person who is knowledgeable in the Bible but is otherwise skeptical, a doubter and unbeliever. Yet in the ending of this book, Upfield shows himself and Bony leaning toward Christian humanism. Upfield ends this book with two Christian symbols which are unmistakable. The passage needs to be quoted in its entirety:

> The boat disappeared, and for a moment the man and the woman appeared standing on the water. Robin turned from Bony to Sefton [the three persons on the shore witnessing the event], and the tall policeman slipped an arm about her, and pressed her face into his uniform shirt. Swiftly the lovers sank, still fast in that embrace. The birds were drawing in above them. The man and the dog were motionless on the dune.
>
> Somewhere a tree stood waiting with its branches wide.

The first symbol is perfectly clear. In their embrace the two lovers become Christ-like figures who for a moment stand on the water, as in the Bible Christ walked on it, before sinking. But the action of the lovers apparently has failed on the face of it, at least with the whites. Robin, the white lady on the shore witnessing the double suicide, turns from Bony, the symbol of the black race represented in the drama by the drowned Lottee, to her white companion, Sefton, the tall policeman, who slips an arm about her, joins her to him and demonstrates that he and his office will protect her in the future. So the actions of the whites on the shore have demonstrated that the two races will not be joined. They will remain sundered.

The finality of the statement is saddening. Though there is no evidence that Upfield knew Herman Melville's novel *Moby-Dick* the similarity of the statements concluding the action in the two books is so close that they must be compared. On the third day of the hunting of the whale Moby-Dick, Ahab and his ship the *Pequod* are sunk by the giant whale, with nature attesting the destruction:

Now small fowls flew screaming over the yet yawning gulf; a swollen white surf beat against its steep sides; then all collapsed and the great shroud of the sea rolled on as it rolled five thousand years ago.

Just as there was one who survived the sinking of the *Pequod*, Ishmael, but was unable to do anything about the disaster, Upfield has man and nature witness the sinking of the potential liaison between the two races and make absolutely no move to assist: "The man and the dog were motionless on the dune." They were passive witnesses, perhaps confirming the inevitable.

The most enigmatic of Upfield's concluding statements is the final one: "Somewhere a tree stood waiting with its branches wide." Two possible choices for interpretation present themselves. The first is that the living tree—representing nature and the future— is waiting to embrace, nurture and develop with the two lovers. So the conclusion is hopeful and optimistic. The other possible conclusion is, however, exactly the opposite. It is entirely pessimistic. If the tree with open arms does not represent the tree of life, then it clearly symbolizes the Cross, waiting for yet two more persons to be hanged from its trunk. Perhaps even that could be an optimistic statement, for with Christ on the Cross there has been hope throughout the ages. So there may be hope yet for the assimilation and future of the Australian people. But given Upfield's general disbelief in the teachings of the Bible, and his many statements against the need and hope for assimilation of the Aborigines in Australia, the tree seems one that will be short-lived, serving more as the symbol of death than of life.

In this final symbol in this book, then, Upfield seems to be standing on both sides of the issue of the White vs. the Aboriginal Australian controversy. The older Downer, with his Australian customs and attitudes symbolizes one attitude of that conflict—the Whites-forever side, with not necessarily any antagonism left but with the assumptions that the Whites should be the ruling class. The younger Downer occupies the other side, looking ahead toward a policy of assimilation of the Aboriginals, with the inclusion of them in the society. Upfield, although he has throughout his books insisted vehemently that he is against assimilation, seems at this point to be wavering, to be sentimentally relaxing his attitude, or to be cloaking his feeling on the subject in ambiguity. The message is not clear here, and seems doubly clouded in light of Upfield's generally held opinion.

In this particular instance, however, Upfield's attitude seems to be clear. In the couple he has seen a meeting of the two civilizations. The East and the West met in their union. In their death they sanctify their union. It is a long way from the drunken pub-hopper of a father to the Christs on the Cross. But the symbols seem to stretch over both and to speak a message of reality and hope.

Indeed such apparently was the symbol that the pub or bar and its booze flashed to the people of Australia. It was spa and oasis in a very dry land. But it was much more. It was the great democratizer in a country that insisted on universal equality. It was the American West, mostly without the American violence, transported to a country as a whole.

On perhaps no other continent has the flow of booze been so important to everyday life as it was in frontier Australia. For that reason, perhaps if for no other, a glass should be raised for the institution and the liquid which floated it.

# Chapter 8
## Caves as Symbols

Anyone reading Upfield's works, the Bony series as well as the others, is struck by the use of cave sites in at least six of the novels. Obviously, then, although the cave-lore and action are natural and quite in place in keeping with the physical surroundings, the caves clearly mean more than they might seem. They are used for symbols of larger topics.

At first, in *A Royal Abduction*, the caves surely have a sexual connotation. But in all, even in *A Royal Abduction*, the cave-symbols also have birth and growing up overtones, as well as Christian symbolism. At times these symbols are developed separately, but usually they are tied together intricately, at one point emphasizing one aspect, at another point emphasizing another.

Elsewhere in this study I have commented on Upfield's unusual background and training in human and sexual relations. Anyone growing up as he did in a Victorian background dominated by old people—old ladies as well as old men—is pretty certain to develop some sexual hang-ups. Upfield had the usual young-man encounters with women and sex while still in England, but, according to his own accounts, managed to escape or avoid any sexual liaisons. Although after being demobbed after World War I, he married and fathered a son, he called this marriage "a disaster." In later life, when speaking of sex Upfield said that he hoped he was not a prig, but the truth is that he was at least somewhat prudish.

Jessica Hawke, in her biography of Upfield twice mentions Havelock Ellis in a context which indicates that she is saying that Ellis' studies of sex had a profound influence on Upfield. Hawke recounts one of Upfield's admitted encounters with a prostitute and his rather unusual behavior. The story bears repeating. It goes that when he went to town once as an escape from the solitude and loneliness of life on the outback, he was enticed into a brothel by a pretty young prostitute. He paid his pound for the privilege but went into the bedroom, sat down on the bed opposite the pretty woman and when asked if he was going to "have" her said that he would instead like to talk to her. They talked until the purchased time ran out. Upfield then invited the woman to go to the races with him the following afternoon, and to dinner afterwards. During dinner they talked unceasingly. Hawke's account of what happened after two nights and one day of the company of the young prostitute is highly suggestive. She says that "What he paid was little for the feminine society which no man can do without." Then she adds the even more suggestive sentence: "When he became normally human, he was broke."

The implication here is that Upfield stayed with the whore until his money ran out. So, once his inhibitions were released—and he got through with his compulsive talking—he was actually sexually self-indulgent.

Although Upfield does not mention Sigmund Freud—or Havelock Ellis, for that matter—obviously one is invited to give Upfield's frequent and wide use of caves a sexual connotation.

Upfield will use caves in six books altogether, five of them in the Bony series. But the widest, most grand, and most sexual is to be found in Upfield's fifth published novel, not one in the Bony series, *A Royal Abduction*.

This is a far-fetched Victorian adventure. Earle Lawrence, an Australian crook, plans to kidnap Princess Natalie of Rolandia when she visits Australia and hold her for ransom. To assist him he enlists the aid of a rich American crook named Van Horton, whose daughter, Helen, Lawrence covets. Princess Natalie is young and beautiful, and as it turns out playful, capricious and democratic. The Princess and her entourage are taken from a train and whisked off to gigantic caves twenty miles east of Eucla, on the Great Australian Bight, beneath the Nullarbor Plain.

There is beneath the Nullarbor Plain a gigantic cave with some dozen large chambers in it, through which the various people in the party, sometimes together and sometimes separately, live and wander for days. Obviously, as Upfield's very learned explanation of some of the physical features of the cave illustrates, the caves are first of all actual phenomena of the Nullarbor Plain, and are treated as such. But the alerted mind must be forgiven for seeing possible sexual implications in the underground adventure also. The first meal in the caverns initiates the sexual overtones of the whole affair. The chapter in which the goings on develop is entitled "A Mixed Gathering." Princess Natalie and Helen Van Horton have dressed for dinner. As the gong is struck announcing the evening meal, the two women step into a large cavern which is roughly circular. Hanging from the central peak or arch forty-feet above, shimmering in a cluster of lights is "The Sword of Damocles!" as Helen announces. The fetishistic nature of the Sword is revealed in Upfield's description, as seen through the eyes of the two women:

It hung from the cavern roof half-way to the floor, a glittering needle-pointed stalactite, reflecting the electric light in every tint and shade of the spectrum. It was a peacock preening its feathers, for once oblivious of the hen birds as represented in duller colours by crystallized lumps of rock set in the limestone walls that sent back gleams of brown and the slate blue from their irregular polished surfaces ( *A Royal Abduction*, 121-22).

The sexual overtones in the whole episode are emphasized later on when the whole party is touring the various caves. At one spot "a man with a big black moustache" who "took his soup with much noise" "leered at the maid." And Lawrence, the Australian crook who engineered the whole affair, answers Natalie's question if they are "in the earth deep" with the words that urge further exploration:

'No, Princess, a mere fifty feet or so.... There are passages, however, which lead down to caverns at least a hundred and fifty feet below the surface. They are well worth exploring. Sometime we must go on a tour.' (125)

There are other sexual passages in this adventure, such as the description of two streams of water, one rising from a fountain on the right and one on the left, which eventually flow into and form one river. The passage is symbolic and suggestive. Surely the suggestiveness of the sexual symbolism of the caves is present.

But there is an even more important though very subtle overtone in Upfield's use of this cave. Though it is not as clearly developed as it will be in later books, a theme developed in the symbolism of the cave is that of birth or rebirth. In this instance it is a rebirth on the part of Natalie, the Princess of Rolandia, from the restrictions of royalty to the freedom of democracy and equality. After all the people who have been harassing her have been killed or converted to her side of the struggle, Natalie realizes that she loves a commoner, and "at long last she was free," (288) and she flies to her lover's arms, to live happily ever after. The development is a little melodramatic, but the symbolism is clear.

A cave plays an entirely different though allied role in *The Mountains Have a Secret*. In this story, Bony is in the mountains south of Melbourne looking for people who caused the disappearance of two girls who were hiking through the mountains. Disguised as a sheep-rancher on vacation, Bony has to play his role carefully. Beset by a bunch of Nazis in a pub there, Bony is saved from severe physical harm by an American named Shannon. Neither Bony nor Shannon is aware of the true role of the other until one day Bony slinks into a cave and prepares to pursue his subjects. Shannon has seen someone enter the cave and follows him, there to be confronted by Bony with a pistol and the threat that he will shoot the Texan dead if he does not prove that his intentions are honest. Shannon then undergoes a confessional and he and Bony cement their alliance. So the cave in this novel is used as a place of confessionals, when the two "good guys" reveal their purposes, Shannon says that he loves one of the lost girls, Mavis Sanky, and their alliance is sealed for the solution of the crime. Though the symbolism of the cave is thinly developed, it is significant as the first use by Upfield in the Bony series, and it anticipates much more sophisticated and significant uses in later books.

Use of the cave as symbol is much more profound in *The New Shoe*. This is a story about Bony going down the coast south of Melbourne to investigate the murder of a man who has been found naked sealed in the wall of the lighthouse. From the beginning it is clear that this book is about rebirth, emergence from the womb and religious apotheosis.

The book begins with a half-grown penguin that has been drowned in the sea because it didn't have sense enough to realize the danger of the sea. It was "the foolish one." Bony very carefully buries it above the high-water mark on the beach.

He then immediately looks up from the beach above the cliffs of Eagle Rock that rise sharply from the beach. At the base of the right cliff two caves "offered cold shelter." From his position he could see all of the lighthouse in which the body had been found "save its foundation upon the grassy sward, a tapering white stalk holding aloft the face of glass beneath the cardinal's red hat." That is his attention centers on the religious symbolism of the part of the lighthouse that sends forth the light.

In beginning his search for the murderer Bony goes into a cave at the foot of the cliff and there finds a "treasure-trove" of the clothes and belongings of the murdered man. Then he is faced with the task of climbing the cliff above him, a sharp and dangerous cliff which scared him almost to death in the descent, "via that ledge to life and eventual triumph." (68)

Climbing from the cave up the cliff is actually symbolically climbing from the womb and being born. It is a difficult birth. But Bony keeps struggling up the cliff. "Red rain was falling down his forehead, down his nose." After he finally achieves his rebirth and is lying on the grass, with the toes of his shoes thumping the soft turf, he is cleaned by his mother:

An animal whimpered and a hot tongue caressed the nape of his neck. (69)

Reborn with the information he had acquired in the cave at the foot of the cliffs, Bony must be reborn yet again in order for Upfield's symbolism to be complete.

The murdered person in the lighthouse has been the casualty of most of the people in the small town and his death has created a conspiracy of silence that can only with difficulty be broken. Bony, though disguised, is recognized as a threat to that conspiracy, and is treated as an enemy. The events take a sinister turn, when Mr. Penwarden, one of the fine law-abiding conspirators, takes it upon himself to eliminate Bony. Penwarden lures Bony into lying down inside a coffin that he has just built, closes the top, and tells Bony that he, Penwarden, knows Bony's purpose in the community, that the people intend to thwart him, and that Bony must "make [his] peace with the Eternal" since he is now in his tomb (167), as Christ had cautioned the thieves on the Cross.

But Bony manages to tell Penwarden the truth of his mission, and Penwarden releases him from the coffin-cave-tomb, having fallen down on his knees and begged for forgiveness. Bony rises from the coffin—again in a parallel with Christian symbolism—just as though he has been reborn a superior person. As indeed he has, since he declares that the murder of the individual was in fact a justifiable homicide and should not be pursued further.

This birth symbol of the cave is carried on even more explicitly in *Murder Must Wait*. The plot of this book turns on the fact that babies are being kidnapped from the hospital and from their cribs, with no apparent cause or consequence. As it turns out they are undergoing a new kind of re-birth. In witnessing this ceremony Bony is mounted on the limb of a tree when the whole scenario unfolds beneath him. The Aboriginal Medicine Man goes through hours of ritual which will summon a baby from the mysterious Otherworld. Meanwhile, of course, a real baby has been kidnapped especially for this purpose. The recipient of the re-born baby is a woman who has longed for a child, been unable to have her own, but is prepared to pay for the child. She has been doped and hypnotized and placed in a hollowed tree preparatory to the great event of the coming of the child. As Bony witnesses the event unfolding beneath him, he charts the role the cavern has played in this event:

Within the tree cavern it was totally dark, and he knelt and found the woman lying on her side, the infant resting in the cradle of her arm. (173)

The parallel with natural, even spiritual, birth could hardly be more explicit.

As obvious as the cave-symbolism is in the preceding works, it gets even more complex and useful in *The White Savage*. In this book Upfield uses the cave as a sign of weakness and of rebirth.

This story is an account of a giant of a man named Marvin Rhudder who after a happy and congenial youth grew up into a cruel rapist and murderer, and after serving a term in prison breaks out and returns to his old community. Bony is sent to locate him.

Sadie Stark is a Romantic lady who has always needed love. She loves Rhudder, who in their youth says he returns the love. When he comes back into the community, he promises to live up to his former promise to marry Sadie. She hides him in a cave and feeds and takes care of him. But when he disavows any love for her and abuses her, she murders him. She buries him in the cave, sets up a rock altar and returns frequently to reassume the clothes she had worn when she was young and Marvin was normal and loved her. The cave she has buried Marvin in is threatened by the sea when storms rage. Bony enters the cave and sees Sadie's reenactment of her youthful love for Marvin and talks to Sadie about the murder. Sadie confesses that she killed Marvin. As they leave the cave, Bony urges Sadie to climb the dangerous cliff before him because he wants her to be sure to escape the angry sea that threatens to wash both of them out to sea. She is safely up but a giant wave threatens to wash Bony away, when Sadie with considerable threat to her own life reaches down and grabs Bony's hand and thus saves him.

So she has taken one life and saved another. But the cave means more than this. It means a loss of her innocence. She has grown up by killing in the cave and being reborn by talking with Bony there. Subsequently Bony talks sharply to Sadie about her world of Romance, of her Knights and Ladies and her Dreams, and makes her be reborn into the world of reality.

> Long before then she had created a suit of shining mail for him [Marvin], and despite all the crimes he committed, she continued to regard him as her Knight in Shining Mail.

But reality forced Sadie to kill the monster. Upfield's conclusion is that hard diseases require hard cures, and Sadie's act, especially if it caused her to grow up, is justified. Upfield's conclusion is that he is surprised that Sadie shot Marvin only three times.

In *Man of Two Tribes*, Upfield uses the same caves, or the same kind of caves, he had used in *A Royal Abduction*, the vast underground caves under the Nullarbor Plains. Here however they are used quite differently.

In this novel Bony arrives at the Weatherby station on the Plain looking for the disappeared Myra Thomas, who stepped off the train at a station on the Plain and simply disappeared. Bony is searching the plains for Myra when he is lowered into a vast set of caves under the Nullarbor Plain by Aboriginals. In the caverns Bony finds a group of men and Myra Thomas. All have been guilty of murder, all have served some time in prison, have been released on parole. Since they are all nasty and independent murderers, life in the caves is not tranquil and pleasant. One of their number has already been murdered by one of them. Myra, being the only woman in the group, apparently is vamping all the men, keeping them hot and overwrought, suspicious of one another, and ready to fly at one another's throat at a moment's notice. Bony tells them of their terrible plight under the Nullarbor Plain, how if they were out they would be 200 miles from the nearest mark of civilization. Nevertheless, they find a way out, and all are willing to risk the dangers of walking 200 miles through the heat, all except a certain Dr. Havant, who is too ill to make the trek. The group gets out of the caves, walk across a very hostile and dangerous plain until they arrive at the home of Charles Weatherby, the man who apparently at the instigation of his wife generated the conspiracy to catch as many murderers as possible of the type who had been let off too easily for their crimes, and to imprison them in the caves until they died. These had been released only through the skill and the determination of Bony, who, of course, could handle the situation.

Earlier while they were in the cave and not sure of their escape, the murderers had inducted Bony into their fraternal organization, making him a Fellow of the Released Murderers' Institute. Now that all are out, the murderer of the one man killed in the caves identified and going to stand trial, the group has really changed very little. They are still fractious, surly, dangerous and intractable. Myra Thomas is still vamping all, now planning to sell the adventures of which she has been a part to some movie producer or writer for a fortune. The only decent, almost human, attribute that these murderers have is a kind of democratic comradeship. They are still members of the Released Murderers' Institute, and proud of it. At the end of the book they are planning their first "annual get-together," and asking Bony if he will attend. He says that since he is a member,  he will look upon attending as a duty. "Fellow of the Released Murderers' Institute. I really earned that...." (215)

It is easy to read much meaning into final statements in books and other entertainments. But one must work hard at finding any profundity in Bony's concluding statement. That he has recognized that all people are the same under the skin, that all are potential law-breakers, even murderers, placed in the right circumstances seems obvious. That all murderers need protection of fair treatment under the law, and that once the law has been served such people should be viewed as having paid their price seems, again, obvious. That Bony, though an officer of the law, is not superior to associating with these ex-prisoners seems again clear. But other than that, Upfield has not made great use of the potential symbolism of the cave. Using them as part of the locale for his story, and as part of an exceedingly entertaining tale, he wrote a fine story. But he did not weave into his story nearly all the symbolism possible, much of which he had used before in other books.

So, apparently caves meant either of two things to Upfield— simply geological formations which could be used for underground development of plot, or symbols of other, deeper and more profound statements. In both areas, Upfield used the formations with great effect. They enrich and deepen the effect of the novels. And they reveal a man who worked in both areas of human experience, the conscious and real and the allusive. In both he was effective.

# Chapter 9
# The Role of Women

Women, of course, play a major role in the works of Arthur Upfield, as they do in any novelist's writings, and for the usual— and somewhat unusual—reasons. On the frontier women assume an exaggerated role because of their great importance in the maintenance and perpetuation of the human race, and because of the romantic feeling men have for them, especially when they are scarce or absent. If absence makes the heart grow fonder, it also intensifies sexual longings and washes away warts and other blemishes. In Upfield women have three roles, two perhaps exaggerated, and one very realistic. We should examine all three closely.

In Upfield and to Bony women remained something of a mystery in all three roles. Perhaps Upfield did not understand women. Some readers of his works feel he did not. Betty Donaldson, a keen and avid reader of Upfield's works, had two reactions to Upfield's depiction of women. During her first reading of Upfield's works she felt that he had done a "passable job," probably "no worse, but probably no better," than other male authors of popular and, especially detective novels. On her second and more systematic reading, however, she concluded that he

provided his readers with a whole gallery of strongly delineated women with quite separate and distinct personalities. ( *Bony Bulletin*, #16, Feb. 1986)

Detective novelist John Ball feels that Upfield's vast experience did not include enough with women. Upfield, himself, in several books, asserted that he did not understand women—but then, he thought, no man does.

Nevertheless, there was no question in his mind about the role that women had played on the frontier and in developing Australia. *The Beach of Atonement*, his third novel, is dedicated to "Australian Women," and in a short story called "How They Waited for the Rain" Upfield asserted "The Real Pioneers of these days—are the women." Respect them and their contribution to the growth of Australian society, he did. Understand them he apparently did not.

Perhaps his background accounts for some of his failure to understand women. Upfield grew up in the world of the real Queen Victoria—and surely she was enough to tilt some people's attitude— and his maternal grandmother Way and her two unmarried sisters, "who always dressed like the Queen, even inside the house." These elderly ladies were to have a significant influence on young Upfield short-range and probably long-range also. Another set of influences was the Grandfather Upfield family, consisting of Grandmother and an unmarried Aunt, with whom young Upfield, in order to make room for the succession of brothers who followed him, went to live. All these women, as well as the men, were strong-willed, clever people who could weave their way through life with considerable effectiveness. Little wonder then that the young impressionable Upfield developed an attitude which held these women, and by extension women in general, in awe and respect. They were generally untouched and untouchable.

Through Bony's admissions, Upfield reveals that he does not know and understand women. In *The House of Venom*, for example, Bony is perturbed when admitting how little he knows of feminine psychology. In another book, Bony thinks that women "can think and look deeper than men" (*White Savage*, 36), and he is pretty sure that it takes a woman to know a woman, thus voicing a kind of male chauvinism that probably is without foundation, but is an excuse for men in their unwillingness to bother to try to understand women. Bony feels that women have intuition "stronger than men, and Aborigines have it stronger than white women." (*Bony and the Black Virgin*, 141)

In *The Widows of Broome*, which concerns a psychopath male whose career has been blighted through fear of and hatred for women and who therefore has an obsession about female's undergarments,

Bony admits that he is stumped and needs to know more about women than he does:

I am finding so much femininity in this investigation that often I wish I were a woman, with all a woman's knowledge of other women, and all women's knowledge of men. Women can see deeper into others of their own sex, and much deeper into man than men can.

But then Bony's world, as well as Upfield's, is pretty much tilted toward that of the male.

Bony's knowledge of men vis-a-vis women, as this novel demonstrates, is deep enough to allow him to understand a psychopath's motivations and actions and to apprehend him, in conjunction with a woman to be sure. Mr. Ross, the criminal, is described by Upfield as having overweening ambition and honor and finding that such attributes and attainments were not what attracted women. Women, Ross discovered, according to Upfield "are themselves a Science, and only the ardent acquires the counter-science." Ross did not understand women and, like Jack the Ripper and his countless imitators who plague society and fiction even today, he murdered those women whose activities (that is women who gave away sex and power) and whose sex tormented him.

Upfield and Bony also, to a certain extent, seem threatened by women. Upfield is not married during the writing of at least some of his books, but Bony is, to a half-caste like himself named Marie, who seems to be everything a husband could want—sweet, understanding, a homebody, a reader of popular fiction and piano player: the perfect wife. But on several occasions Upfield refers to women as the force which disrupted the bliss of the Garden of Eden. As he says in *The White Savage* (90):

With the coming of the First Woman universal misery was introduced among men.

At it s most extreme, this misery is represented by women who stand out as being forceful and powerful females.

Sometimes this strength is for good, though evil might result. In his first Bony book (*Mystery of Barrakee*, 11), Upfield sketches a strong woman, Mrs. Thornton, wife of the squatter on whose station the events take place, as "a woman who invariably had her own way," and who dominated her husband. "It was that trait of dominance in her character which attracted him." In other words, Thornton knew that to succeed on his cattle station, and he had succeeded, he had to have a strong-willed wife. Yet it is her strong will that causes all the trouble. She is determined to mother a child, and when her own child dies at child-birth, Mrs. Thornton adopts the child of her cook, born within 48 hours of her own. She does not tell the child, and raises him as her own natural child, who at 18 returns from college an apparent success but soon goes astray with tragic results.

Bony, although he might not be able to read the female mind, knows a strong-willed woman when he sees one. He immediately recognizes in Mrs. Thornton that he has a worthy friend or a formidable adversary:

In her disposition he recognized gentleness and firmness, a wide charity of outlook and a great breadth of mind, apart from the capacity to dislike. He read, too, in her firm mouth and chin a powerful will, to which opposition was rather a spur than an obstruction. (137)

And she was great as an Australian democrat, which made Bony respect her. Mrs. Thornton "forgot his colour and his apparent station in life" and she and he

talked as equals, without condescension on her part or presumption on his. Nowhere but in the bush could that have been so. (136)

In fact Bony pays Mrs. Thornton the ultimate in compliment and heroizing. He tells her husband,

If she, and not the poor Empress Josephine, had been the beloved of the Emperor Napoleon, today the nations of the earth would be a peaceful and prosperous World Federation. (320)

But strong women sometimes work to the detriment of society. *Mr. Jelly's Business* (161), for example, is the story of a woman who conspires with the foreman on her cattle station to murder her husband and take over his considerable fortune then live happily ever after with the lusty younger man. She is, of course, discovered and is about to be turned over to the law. But in one of his several respectful statements about the strength of the Australian pioneer stock, Upfield allows this caught killer, Mavis Loftus, to prove her stock and strength and her superiority to her fellow-murderer by committing suicide:

'Now they won't hang me,' the woman said with a vicious laugh. 'I have descended from the pioneers.'

She is superior to her paramour who has risen "from the gutters." Mavis has the courage to commit suicide but he hasn't "the manhood to follow." She poisons herself, he is thrown into the arms of the law for his justice.

The grudging respect that Upfield holds for this strong woman does not extend to all the other powerful women in his books. One he finds particularly offensive, Mary Answerth in *Venom House*. This book is about three perverted characters, two women, one retarded man whose life has been tyrannized over by the two women. The women are studies in contrast: Janet Answerth, a syrupy python character who wheedles her way into your confidence with her feminine wiles only to destroy you. But Bony and Upfield are even more frightened by her sister, Mary. Mary is as dangerous as her sister but has this danger wrapped in an unnatural package. One of the characters describes her to Bony as

'Quite a tartar, sir. Lives too late, in my opinion. Should have lived a couple of hundred years ago when the scum knuckled to their betters.' (13)

She's described as a "he-woman. She's ruddy dynamite." (16), and "An Amazon. She offends my sense of what is a woman." She is big, muscular, strong, loud-mouthed, demanding. She is physically so strong that she literally beats up, or down, all the men she opposes. In fact, Bony is the only person she has not managed to man-handle and overpower.

Other women come in other packages. In *The Will of the Tribe*, Myra Thomas who has killed her husband, is pictured as a tease sex-pot, interested only in herself and in teasing men. In the setting in which the story develops she is placed in an awkward position. She and six men who likewise were convicted of murder but released from prison prematurely, at least in the eyes of one man, are thrown into a cave in the Nullarbor Plain and kept prisoner, presumably until they die, thus serving out their term for taking another's life. There she seemingly encourages the men to fight over her, apparently enjoying seeing men kill other men over her. To Bony she protests that she is not interested in teasing men into murder over her, and apparently Upfield agrees with her. After the escape from the cave, Upfield develops her into actually much more than a mere sex-trap.

At his extreme Upfield develops two women who are actually only females in perpetual heat alluring men and enjoying seeing them writhe in sexual frustration. In *Death of a Lake*, Mrs. Fowler and her daughter Joan are well-drawn characters. They are the only two woman at a cattle station situated on a lake that is drying up in the intense summer heat that can reach 120 degrees in the shade. The mother is young and virile enough to be her daughter's sister. The daughter is interested in only one thing: men. Each of the females fights over the same man's attention, any man's attention, even to the point of destroying one another for the sake of the prize. They are like women from Erskine Caldwell's *God's Little Acre* or *Tobacco Road*. *Death of a Lake* is one of Upfield's most powerful novels, intensely compressed, unbearably centered on heat and the drying up of a lake and the corpse that this dead lake is bound to reveal. The heat of sex compounds the discomfort.

Diametrically opposed to this kind of woman is the saintly, the heroic, the better-than-life kind of female character. Of these there are several in Upfield's books, two white women and two aboriginal (whom we will take up later).

Bony had been correct in saying that he did not understand women, and this attitude often got him into trouble with them. Another aspect of his character got him into trouble with women. After a wild love affair with a girl in his youth, he had lost her but had subsequently found Marie, whom he married. She was apparently suitable in every way. She is like Bony, a half-caste, she is sweet and understanding, completely supportive, and has mothered his three sons. Therefore he seems to be inclined to accept women as being superior beings. When this respect for women is tied in with the pride which serves as the backbone of his being and accounts for not only his motivation in life but also for his dogged determination to succeed, and women recognize his pride and superiority, or when he cannot fail to recognize women's superiority because it would betray his trust—then Bony gets into situations where he may put more regard into women than reality would warrant.

Such is surely the case with Kate Flinders, in Upfield's first Bony novel, *Mystery of Barrakee*. In addition to Mrs. Thornton, whom Upfield draws fully developed as a strong character, he sketches in the Thorntons' niece, a girl who lives on the station and becomes affianced to Ralph, their son. Though Kate is presented as a very likeable and natural young lady, who comes to love Bony and eventually to cause the ultimate happiness of her uncle, Upfield cannot allow her to be without guile. She should not be accused of what Upfield calls "hoydenishness," but she

was the kind of girl who regards all men as willful boys, and sometimes she took keen delight in arousing them. (61)

Such is also the case with Marion Stanton, daughter of a bluff squatter with whom Bony worked to solve the mystery of a man named Marks. *The Sands of Windee* is Upfield's second Bony mystery, and he is working out some of the details in the character of Bony. The picture of the half-caste detective presented here is therefore in its first mold, and differs somewhat in the degree of sentimentality and restraint that both Bony and Upfield treat the detective in later books. But in outline the character is not untrue to the later one.

Therefore when Bony talks about being thrilled by the "spiritual beauty" of Marion Stanton, he knows intuitively that she had had nothing to do with the disappearance of the man. She presents Bony with a dilemma:

The tip of one horn represented pride; the tip of the other, a fierce admiration for the pure and beautiful. (174)

And Upfield adds to the rather embarrassing picture of Bony in this feminine presence:

for the first time since he had renounced the love of his youthful sweetheart he had met a white woman who never looked down on him from a higher plane, who aroused in him the ecstasy of the worshipper of beauty, who had made him forget his inferior birth and status, and who recognized unreservedly his spiritual superiority. (176)

She was his "white goddess." The degree of his capitulation to her charms can perhaps be best described in Bony's own words:

"To me, Miss Stanton, you have been most kind,' he said, and would have taken her hands had she not drawn back. 'You have been kind in a way which no white woman has been kind before. To use a well-worn phrase, yet one very apt, you have stooped to conquer. From an Olympian height you have bent down to one in the mire, and my feeling for you has more of spirituality in it than of earth.' (177)

In *Wings Above the Diamantina* Elizabeth Nettleford is a paragon of virtue, loves her father, loves her housekeeper, loves the stranger they find in the plane, but is cold toward Bony when they first meet:

But to accept a half-caste detective as an equal was quite another matter. When Hetty had awakened her to tell of the arrival of Dr. Knowles and a detective, who was an Australian half-caste, and that this detective even then was with the doctor and her father in the latter's study, and, above all, that Mr. Nettleford had given orders that a room be prepared for this half-caste detective, Elizabeth felt that it was really too much. (60)

Upfield sets up the contrast so that Bony can be built up in his conquering the women. But it is an artificial situation.

In *The White Savage*, Bony goes one step further in his treatment of Sadie Stark. But then his treatment of Sadie Stark in this book demands an unusual treatment. *The White Savage* is a book very much about earthly individuals, yet Upfield manages to turn it into something like a modern myth, with other-worldly men and women living in a world that is somewhat divorced from present-day reality. Given Upfield's proclivity to romanticize and sentimentalize women at times, there is little surprise that in this book he makes Sadie a creature who is so ethereal that she hardly touches the ground as she walks. Sadie is a woman verging on thirty, whose "body had the resilience and hardness of contours of a woman much younger." She walked

with the elegant freedom of a mountain lass, her back straight and shoulders strong, and her legs springy and confident. (124)

From this strength she soared into atmosphere more rarified than normal. Bony received from her

the impression that she had read every book in the world, that she had lived for a thousand years, that she had dissected the mind of ten thousand men and knew with unshakable conviction that all of them were children. (137)

Bony did not love this "Mona Lisa," so he had to respect her. Bony rhapsodizes and mythologizes Sadie more than any other character in the book:

'If only all Australia was like this forest,' Bony said when driving again. 'So cool and silent and waiting, as it has been waiting for a million years and won't mind waiting for another million. Waiting for what? Sadie? Dress Sadie in close-fitting moss-green clothes, give her a green felt hat to wear, have her sit on top of a fir-tree, and you'd see one of the Little People who might tell you what the forest is waiting for. Sadie of the mysterious smile, of the all-knowing, pitying eyes, Sadie who has lived for a million years.'

Sadie is an Alice in Wonderland, a female Peter Pan child who is fey, but she is lovable, and will pull out of her otherworldliness. So, luckily, will Upfield and Bony. In one other book, *Bony and the Kelly Gang*, Upfield attempts to dive into the magic of Ireland and the charm of Irish characters, with some more, though by no means complete, success.

If Upfield has some trouble with his women in over-romanticizing some of them, he had even greater difficulty with his fictional female children. They were not little people. They were creatures all their own, and he like many men before and after him, Nathaniel Hawthorne for example, obviously did not know how to handle them. He tended to draw sentimentalized pictures of little Dickensian characters who were cuddly but not much more promising of a useful future. In working with them Bony leaves a great deal to be desired in the adults with whom they live. In *Mr. Jelly's Business* for example, Dulcie, called "Sunflower" by sister and father, makes Bony act and seem like something of a fool. She flits and twits around the farm, bewitching people whose acquaintance with children has been long-distance, and exacts from a Detective-Inspector on serious business of discovering criminals some rather foolish behavior and promises.

In *The Death of a Swagman*, Rose Marie, the daughter of the local constable who jails Bony when he first arrives in town, is so pixieish that she is unbelievable. As soon as Bony is put into jail for vagrancy and impertinence to a law officer, Rose Marie appears at the door with her playthings, starts playing toys with Bony, and then releases him from jail, after she has made him promise not to run away. After releasing her father's duly arrested prisoner, Rose Marie sets a tea for herself and Bony:

With the precision of an experienced hostess the little girl set out her service of cups and saucers and plates. They had two blue stripes. It was evidently not the first occasion that Rose Marie had served afternoon tea. (6)

Rose Marie holds the center of attention far longer than reality would seem to dictate.

Interestingly this episode exactly parallels one that happened to Upfield himself as a child. One day a glass marble fell through the skylight of his father's place of business, and his father strongly suspected that son Arkum-Willum (Arthur William) had fired the shot with his catapult (slingshot). Because young Upfield would not admit his guilt, his father sent him to the local Constable, who, again because Upfield would not admit his obvious guilt, threw him in jail. But Arkum-Willum was not to suffer long. Almost immediately the Constable's fat and red-faced wife, who clucked over the youngster's fate precisely as Rose Marie was to do in Upfield's book, set for him a lovely tea of buttery muffins, and then sent him off home, with the maxim ringing in his ears from both Mr. and Mrs. Constable that one should always tell the truth. In the real-life situation the incident seems credible; in the fictionalized version with the role-reversal, it sounds somewhat forced.

Linda Bell, in *Bony Buys a Woman*, is perhaps even more sentimentalized than the earlier two little girls. On the cattle station run by her widowed mother, Linda Bell is the darling of all the workers around her. She is precocious in conversation and actions with her dolls, and constitutes the very backbone of the novel. She is every worker's princess, every Abo's goddess. She is the fulcrum of the novel. By the end, fortunately having endured some trying times and fear, she has not matured very much beyond the shy, demure stage.

The remainder of Upfield's female characters have a large amount of realism in their character and development. Some are obviously heroic, some are ordinary, some are really insignificant but show how Upfield draws minor characters.

His first "normal" character in the Bony series is Mrs. Watts, in *Mystery of Barrakee*. (63) She is the wife of a manager of one of the stops on the many stations on the Cattle Station. Though she plays only a minor part in the story, she is described as a solid-rock individual the likes of whom had made Australia great:

A large pleasant-faced woman, a little more than thirty, opened the gate leading into the miniature garden... Mrs. Watts was a bushwoman, one of the small band of heroic women who live cheerfully and happily in the semi-wilds of Australia.

At least two characters are really outstanding. In *The Widows of Broome*, Bony is faced with a difficult situation. There is a strangler of women loose in the small town. He has strangled four women already, is obviously a dangerous menace and is about to strike again. Bony realizes that the only way he can direct the man's next act is to set up a trap and get some woman's cooperation in what is clearly a life-threatening situation. He chooses the most competent accomplice, Mrs. Sayers, a widow living in a large house with only a helping man around who sleeps in an adjacent building. As Bony sets the trap, with Mrs. Sayers acting as the bait, Bony sits back and utterly admires her actions. He says, "Mrs. Sayers was superb" (227) and

Her eyes were bright with an excitement and she gained Bony's complete admiration when he failed to see a sign of fear.

She is big, strong, knows ju-jitsui, can defend herself, is loud-mouthed, but fearless. She is more than a match for most men. Yet there is not the least trace of distaste for her person or personality by Bony in the same way he would dislike Mary Answerth in the later novel, *Venom House*.

Another outstanding character is Bony's twice used assistant, Alice McGorr, a police woman. Of all his accomplices he seems to prefer Alice, and of all his heroes he finds her just about as admirable as any other. In *Murder Must Wait*, Upfield introduced her and described her background and virtues:

Coming from low down on the pecking order of society she worked hard, cooking, making beds, sweeping rooms, and studying in the meantime. She had the knack of baking good bread and 'spinning threads of information into patterns. ' (25)

But her skill as a policewoman is most admirable:

She could fight like a tiger before she entered the training school for women, and when she passed for duty she could master the instructors in ju-jitsui. They put her into the worst districts, and she was never hurt. Attempts to cripple her were made by thugs, and the thugs were crippled by their own. A gunman shot at her, and the gunman had his face slashed. A low type once told her what he'd do to her, and the bad man's wife bided her time and emptied a potful of boiling cabbage over him. No one seemed to know why...

Apparently she was able to enlist a great deal of assistance from the residents of the tenderloin district.

Alice is even more fully developed and more effective in the later novel *The Battling Prophet*. Here she is in the midst of some very heroic men and some very nasty Hungarian spies who are killing right and left in order to get their way with useful secrets. Stymied by the magnitude of the job, Bony calls for Alice to be sent out, as his niece, to assist him in his task. She is more than equal to the task. As a matter of fact, she acts somewhat like a frenzied Amazon swinging her mighty right and left knocking over men as though they were tenpins. Faced with intimidating gunmen, Alice reacts like a giant spring:

> It was as though Alice McGorr was shot out of a gun at a fair. She sprang from the floor to the gunman. The gun exploded and arched through the air to land on the floor beside Bony. The gunman rose in the air, too, as far as the ceiling would permit. He was coming down most ungracefully when each ankle was grasped by a hand, and each leg pulled as far apart as a human frame can span. Then he was on his back, and the instep of a shoe was gouging hard into his throat. He began to object, but the split of his legs was widened a fraction beyond possible. He did shout something before realising that surrender was indeed the best policy.

For such heroic acts, Bony approves with the words,"Bravo, Alice!" It is almost as though such feats deserved more applause. But there is no doubt that Bony approves of Alice, Alice admires Bony, and the two make a wonderful team. It is too bad that Upfield did not use her otherwise. (187)

In addition to these rather unusual women, Upfield has a whole series of women who people his novels as ordinary, everyday realistic women. Generally speaking they are treated as women and human beings. They are not romanticized or sentimentalized. They are etched in as best Upfield can create them, and generally he is successful in his efforts.

One of the most successful is in his early novel *Winds of Evil* who is named Stella Borraday. She has her own quiet dignity, she treats Bony as an equal and he treats her generally as his equal. She, however, is caught up in Upfield's development of Bony's tragic flaw, his vanity, and she like most of the other women in Upfield's novels, comes to respect and admire Bony. Stella early on gazes closely at Bony and comes to admire him. As Upfield catalogues his urge, it is a sentiment that is to be repeated in most of his successive books:

> Through the smoke of her cigarette Stella watched the dark face now animated and lit with the lamp of enthusiasm. She tried very hard to keep out of her own eyes the increasing interest in this half-caste who behaved and spoke as well as any man she had known. His vanity was obvious, but the interest was not based on his fine face and modulated, cultured voice. Just what it was based upon puzzled her. (122)

Diana Lacy in *The Bone is Pointed* is another sensible girl who "looked as though she had stepped from the pages of a society paper." But she is polite, reserved and very much her own mistress. Upfield likes such women. Though Bony was ostensibly Diana's "enemy," Diana's

feminine sympathy claimed her heart as she watched him lift his hat to her, then slide down from the horse's back, and advance with his peculiar gait, leading the mare. (62)

Her evaluation of Bony was particularly high: "I think he's the bravest man I've ever met." (229)

Flora, McPherson's niece in *Bushranger of the Skies*, is a beautiful and clever woman, under thirty, who accepts Bony as an equal:

She had evinced no hostility towards his mid-race, had accepted him without question. (21)

She is strong enough to resist her half-brother Rex, the mad bushranger of the skies, to demand to face her share of the problems and dangers Rex raised, and to front them with uncommon strength and pluck.

Something less than halfway through his list of titles, Upfield drew one of his most sympathetic characters. In *An Author Bites the Dust* she is Janet Blake, the author of numerous best-sellers under the name I.R. Watts, and wife of Mervyn Blake, who has been murdered. Upfield sketches the features he likes and respects in women, perhaps especially in female authors:

The deep bosom lifted a fraction, pushing back the shoulders. The fine feminine head went upward as the wide mouth and the firm chin were recast by strength, leaving nothing of weakness. The wide-spaced dark eyes beneath the deep dark brows became occupied only with Bony. Her voice gained steadiness. (216)

In subsequent books, Upfield rounds out the characters. In *Sinister Stones*, Kimberley Breen is a very attractive minor character, who is perhaps a bit overly sweet and weak for her age, but she is attractive. In her, Upfield manages to picture the naive, country cowgirl who wants to go to Brisbane to visit Mrs. Bony and to achieve some sophistication. Upfield does not use Kimberley to picture the evil of civilization, as he has done with several other characters; instead he uses her to point out the value of civilization, as seen in urban districts.

In *Will of the Tribe*, Mrs. Brentner is a sensible and attractive cattle station wife who adopts Tessa, the lovely Aboriginal girl who is going to become all white and serve as a bridge to her race until she fulfills Bony's prophecy that no Aboriginal can ever fully leave her race, and she reverts to it, at best more Aboriginal than White.

At times Bony's obvious and outright respect for women regardless of how they might have gone against the law is manifest. Such is Jill Madden in *Madman's Bend*, (7) who thinks she has murdered her father-in-law who has been beating her mother. Bony does not think she is guilty, and sets out to prove her innocent. But regardless, he admires this strong, powerful girl who is willing to kill to protect her beaten mother. Bony carries his admiration even to those women who are guilty. Mrs. Wessex, in *The New Shoe*, (184) poisoned the son she had loved dearly after he went bad, but she is in Upfield's eyes a noble and restrained woman.

There is at least one other kind of female whom Upfield pictures and admires. They are strong, a little Dickensian eccentric, but amusing, not only because of the strength they try to project but also because they are off-balance and worthy opponents/allies.

They are no doubt drawn from all the picturesque grandmothers he grew up with and the Dickens he was steeped in. One is the eccentric lady, owner of the pub and virtually everything else in the town of Carie. She is aged but by no means old.

She is short and stout and something over seventy years old, remarkable for the beauty of her snow-white hair and the brilliance of her dark eyes. Her appearance denoted the essence of respectability, her movements bespoke eternal youth, her personality claimed the ever-alert business woman, never to be defeated by circumstances or daunted by advancing age.... It was as though her portion of the upper veranda was her throne from which she ruled Carie.

In a later book, *Bony and the Kelly Gang*, Upfield draws another old lady with a somewhat similar situation who rules over all the people she has mothered and the valley she has created, and this time Bony finds himself playing with this old citizen, himself becoming a professional Irishman for the occasions. Grandma Conway is

A tiny woman wearing a white lace cap, a high-necked black bodice and white lace cuffs about her wrists. (25-6)

She has a sense of purpose and an iron will, but she also has a sense of humor, can be gulled, but is essentially the figure of Mother Ireland in Australia. She and Bony become inseparable friends.

Just as Upfield's conflicts often involve the clash between Aboriginal and white civilizations, frequently his books involve to one degree or another sexual relations between Aboriginal women and white males. Bony's attitude toward the subject apparently fluctuated. He himself was the result of such a sexual union. The mixture of the two races accounted for the great strength he possessed in deductive reasoning and primitive intuition. Clearly then the union between the two races was something Upfield liked to dwell upon. Though generally he was against such sexual union, he was not as adverse to it on all occasions as on some.

In his first study of Bony, *Mystery of Barrakee*, Upfield made it explicit that he felt such union was nasty miscegenation. As a result Bony did not honor his father or mother:

Because they did not honour me. My mother was black, my father white. They were below the animals. A fox does not mate with a dingo, or a cat with a rabbit. They disobeyed the law of the wild. In me, you see neither black nor white, you see a hybrid.

But nevertheless,

I am what I am. I am not ashamed of it, because it was not my fault. But I feel sometimes as if black and white are at war in me, and will never be reconciled.

Just as fury, real or potential, boiled in Bony's body, so did it also boil in the body society when Aboriginals and whites mated. So it has been throughout Australian history, as Mary Durack's historical records reveal. So too it was in Upfield's books. Yet, the physical need of white man for Aboriginal women in the Australian bush caused Upfield to cover the subject several times.

In his first book, that microcosm of most of the subjects that he would deal with at great length in later books, Upfield took the subject up fully. Ralph, the "son" of the squatter family, is really the half-caste son of the Thornton's cook and a handsome Aboriginal, the likes of whom Bony had never seen among Aboriginals.

Thus instinct drew Ralph to his black woman—or *lubra* or *gin* as Aboriginals were called in Australia. Upfield insisted that escape for Ralph was impossible. Upon his return from college at age 18 he soon started assuming the ways of the Aboriginals, such as dressing in bright and bizarre colored clothes, and according to Upfield Ralph would have started turning black by his middle thirties, as Bony says in this book he had.

Against this background, and his hatred of mixed-marriages, Bony and Upfield describe Aboriginal women in various ways, most of the time not complimentary. The girl Nellie that Ralph fell in love with was described at length. She was probably around 20 years old, with

an unusually lovely figure for a lubra, for somehow the angular awkwardness of the aboriginal girl changes with startling rapidity to the obesity of the gin.

But clothes make the aboriginal woman, as they do the white female:

She was dressed in a white muslim blouse, a neat navy-blue skirt, black stockings and shoes. She wore the cheap but well-fitting clothes with the unconscious grace of a white woman. When close, she looked at them fearlessly.

Nellie was an exception to all generalizations about aboriginal women:

According to the white man's standards it cannot be said that the Australian
lubra is anything but ugly. This girl, however, was a rare exception. Her face
was oval and flat. Her (43).

In other words, she would have been a pretty lady "if she were
white." (56) After he falls in love with her, Ralph, of course, thinks
she is beautiful.

Upfield has several other Aboriginal women who play very
important roles in his novels, and generally they are described in
pretty much the same terms as Nellie.

*Bushranger of the Skies*, for example, is the story of half-caste
who has gone wrong and is determined to conquer his father, The
McPherson as he is called, and through him to gain power in order
to reverse all the evil discrimination that has been waged against
the Aboriginals from the coming of the first Whites. The Aboriginal
woman in this story is named Tarlalin. McPherson had been kept
by his parents on the cattle station throughout his formative years,
was not allowed to go to college or even to the city in order to
see what other people his own age and color were doing in life.
He fell in love with the local Aboriginal lady named Tarlalin. His
father did not object to the marriage between the two, but his mother
did after marriage. McPherson was therefore forced to move from
his ancestral home and with Tarlalin live outcast lives. Their child
was Rex, one of the evil half-castes who, Bony said, often result
when a white stoops to the folly of marrying an Aboriginal.

Upfield, and Bony's feelings about the marriage are mixed.
There is no doubt that the union was a mistake. But an
understandable mistake, under the circumstances. In his salute to
the Aboriginal lady, Upfield described her as mentally weak and
one of very few "greatly loved in life and greatly honored in death."
McPherson had enshrined her in his heart and in a beautiful burial
plot.

At times Upfield is precise about the beauty of Aboriginal girls.
In the *Widows of Broome*, for example, Irene, a half-caste woman,
is "a slim girl about twenty, and had her nose not been so broad
she would have been good-looking. (93) In *Bony and the Black
Virgin* (185), Lottee:

...wore only white shorts. The dilly-bag of crimson silk divided her breasts.
She was sweetly beautiful and her eyes glowed like black opal.

Meena, in *Bony Buys a Woman* (107) is "clean as a pin" and "her
clothes are right." And she has beautiful feet: "If white girls had
been there to watch Meena, they would never wear shoes." (85)

Of all the Aboriginal women Upfield developed most fully
Tessa, one of the main characters in *The Will of the Tribe*. She
has been adopted by the Brentner family, lives with them as a
daughter, is going to be sent to college to prepare for becoming
a teacher so that she can then go to the tribes and serve as a bridge
between them and white civilization. She apparently is beautiful,
"her dress sense is excellent, her poise very good. Her conversation
is intelligent and lucid." (34) and she has excellent demeanour and
table manners. (67)

But despite their beauty, these women are not far from their
origins and their tribes. They cannot escape their instincts, and
generally will run off to the tribe when "something inside compels"
them. Further, they like women in general apparently, are compelled
to exercise their feminine wiles. Tessa, for example, "knows how
to ravish a bloke....You know, looks at you with both eyes wide
open and an adoring look in 'em....She's one of the tabbies who
has to work on a man or burst." She waggles her behind in order
to attract men. Meena, in addition to being beautiful, is a tease,
determined to play the sex-game and to give in when it pleases
her.

Upfield's knowledge of the actions of young people, black or
white, surely was perceptive. His recounting of the teasing by Meena
was exact. Teasing Charlie, her boyfriend, Meena played coy but
capitulated.

No author who writes of such a large gallery of women as
Upfield did in his 34 books can be as ignorant of them as he at
times tried to appear. Women of both colors are in Upfield's novels
in all their natural variety and characteristics. Because of their
appearing in the exotic and largely-unknown setting of outback
Australia, sometimes they seemed to be stretched out of all
proportion. But the fault, as is often the case, is more with the

reader than the writer. Upfield's women just need to be better known. Then they become largely natural.

An aboriginal lady

From *Follow My Dust*, courtesy Don Uren

# Chapter 10
## Supernatural as Symbol

Upfield's strongest statements and most effective books incorporate to one degree or another the Christian or primitive supernatural. Bony, it is made very clear time and again by Upfield, is a pagan and is not susceptible to religion. Yet, as Upfield makes clear in *The Sands of Windee,*

There was certainly a good deal of the mystic in Bony, although he seldom admitted it. Of all the great world religions he was skeptical, but where several religions agreed he agreed also. Which is to say he believed in the fundamental existence of God. Of all things spiritually beautiful Bony was a worshipper. (67)

In *Mr. Jelly's Business* (121) Bony says he is not a Christian but he has read the Bible and believes in the Old Testament's philosophy of an "Eye for an eye."

In *The Sands of Windee* (197) in the great forest fire that almost destroys him, Bony obviously relies upon and receives divine assistance in escaping. Bony becomes, as it were, somewhat along the lines of Wordsworth the British poet, one with nature and God, and in so doing is actually saved by Grey Cloud, the horse that he has tamed and trained, and his own natural instinct. There are other manifestations, though subtle. Though Bony usually has some kind of helper in the solutions he arrives at in solving the crimes, they are never his equal; again and again he says that he is the greatest detective Australia has ever produced or perhaps the world has ever produced. Yet in *Death of a Swagman* (105), Bony makes a rare admission that is almost out of character:

There is a much greater detective than I, one with whom I have allied myself
to a very great degree. I refer to Providence.

Thus Upfield is set for Christian, or at least supernatural, symbolism
in his books. He uses it rather extensively.

*Bushranger of the Skies* is such a book. A bushranger is an
outlaw. In Australia, as in America, there have been many outlaws,
operating sometimes locally in the outback, sometimes, of course,
in the urban areas. A bushranger of the skies, that is one who used
an airplane as his means of transportation and operations, was,
however, apparently somewhat uncommon. But in the distances
that make up Australia, the airplane is a most important, indeed
vital, means of transportation. The distances are awesome, even
to Australians living in the urban areas along the coasts. They
are still bemused by reports which they frequently read and hear
about how people at the cattle stations in the outback are not lonely,
and find plenty to keep them busy even though their nearest
neighbors are 150 miles away. In 1986 one story was making the
rounds that someone asked a lady at a cattle station if she wasn't
lonely since she had no neighbors. She minimized the loneliness
of her eixstence by saying that she had a close neighbor who lived
only 100 miles down the road to the crossroad and then 70 miles
east.

In *Bushranger of the Skies* the airplane is a demonic agent,
used by an outlaw madman to destroy people on the ground. Its
introduction into the scene of the novel is given as violating the
sanctity of a natural cathedral on the ground. The opening
paragraph of the book unfolds the sacredness of the surrounding,
as we saw in Chapter Two. The symbol of the cabbage-tree-cathedral
is strengthened by the fact that this tree has been through the years
one of Australia's most useful plants, with the leaves used for
protection against the sun and for food.

Bonaparte, safely inside the cool of this natural grove looks
out at the events transpiring outside through the picture "framed
within a leafy arch of Gothic type." While around him two crows,
aware of his existence but fearing him far less than the approaching
terror, caw and flutter. Then as the plane dropped a bomb inside
the grove the crows "shrieked defiance" as the plane passed low

above them, and the crows "left their sanctuary, and fleeing as though pursued by ten thousand hawks." (23) Bony, stunned though unhurt, reacts naturally and animal-like to the attack of the silvery-grey, unmarked plane in which one person sits. Bony's "fine lips were drawn taut, revealing his white teeth in what was almost an animal snarl of fury." This is the kind of gesture Bony makes throughout the canon and shows that Upfield has drawn the lines for developing the story between the human-animal cunning of Bony and the devil in the supernatural airplane.

Upfield's second use of a supernatural symbol is of a different kind, less Christian but more heroically supernatural, and this book, *The Will of the Tribe*, living up to the promise of the symbol is perhaps his most powerful. The book turns on Bony's greatest problem, whether as mediator between the two civilization, white and Aboriginal, he should give in to one or the other. In other words, the tug between the two cultures which he and his author read as wrenching the country and the two cultures apart every day threaten everybody's existence. This book is Upfield's most anguished examination of the struggle, and in it, though not in the other books, Upfield and Bony come down on the side of the Aborigines.

This indigenous civilization manifests a belief in and practice of a different kind of supernatural, a supernatural that was not strikingly different, except with needed local modifications, from that of primitives throughout the world.

The reality of sorcery and its effects, its reality, among the Australian Aborigines seems to have been complex and very manifest. Aborigines believed, and believe, that most people die not from natural causes but from sorcery, and that hatred, revenge, tension, a hundred things, can be the cause for sorcery. Kenneth Maddock in his *The Australian Aborigines, A Portrait of Their Society* (1982), states that

...As sorcery consists in physical operations that can be carried out (such as singing, uttering spells, making gestures or throwing or pointing an object), the possibility of its occurrence cannot be displaced... Aborigines, then, accept the reality of sorcery and are afraid of it, even if they cannot name anyone who will admit to knowing the art. (47)

And Maddock insists that evidence supports the contention that people who have the sorcery projected upon them may be so severely affected that they will die. He gives an example of a young man who would not fulfill obligations imposed upon him, and for his offense the offended people "sang him," with the result that the young man apparently became demented, went into the bush, and eventually died there; whereupon his body would not be touched by anyone for fear of being killed by the poison which obviously killed him and still persisted in the corpse.

In the same vein Mary Durack, in *Keep Him My Country* (1955), tells a somewhat longer though equally informative anecdote. She recounts how a young man named Wondritch is obviously wasting away and will die because he has been "sung," and nobody will have anything to do with him; even his wife will not feed him. He believes that he is dying, and aided by society he will in fact die. The young man says that his enemies have driven a spear into his heart and he is slowly bleeding to death. The white hero of the incident, knowing how powerful the spell is, examines the victim. Then, agreeing that the man has been condemned to death, he scratches his back enough to draw blood, and then he begins to draw forth strands of dry grass, saying

"They stuffed you up all right... Hallo! They even put stones inside. No wonder you don't feel too good."

He pretends to draw forth a spearhead which he covers in blood and shows to the surprised dying man.

"We got something here. I can feel it coming down into my hands.... There it is, nasty looking thing too."

Showing the physical object to the man convinces him that he has been cured of the curse and gives him the will to live again. Willing to live, he immediately drinks a healthy draught of brandy and eggs, and literally "life and hope come flowing back, a look of heavy contentment clouding the glazed eyes." (147-149) The cure is as old as the hexes: one recognizes the hex and reverses it, casting a heavier spell to counter it or, as in this case, physically removing the cause, something like modern surgery!

One of Upfield's more powerful books, *The Bone is Pointed*, pulses and quavers with this same motif. Bony the great skeptic is nevertheless closely allied with the Aboriginals through his mother's blood. The Aboriginals knew that Bony could not break this bond because their blood flowed through his veins.

Their beliefs and their superstitions were implanted in the very marrow of his bones, and all his advanced education would not make him other than what he was. (136)

So he was susceptible to their magic, and through that magic vulnerable to them. (127)

Upfield is detailed in elaborating the process of the ritual and its effect. As he says:

The act of pointing the bone was, of course, merely a theatrical show, having a psychological effect both on the bone-pointers and the victim. The power to kill lay not in the outward show but in the mental willing to death conducted by the executioners. (137)

Bony knew that the hex was weak or powerful depending on the mental power—in other words, the charisma—of the executioner. He also knew the best shield against the hex:

If the victim could conquer inherited superstitions, and then if his mind were stronger than the minds of the bone-pointers, he might escape death long enough for his relations to find out who was pointing the bone and at once exact vengeance. (137)

Interestingly, Bony who could and did always win in other contests of the will or of skill, could not win against this ancient medicine of the Aborigines. When he is hexed, he becomes dizzy, and he wants to sleep, in fact finding sleep irresistible. His body becomes wracked with pain, he wastes away into a mere shadow, and is in fact about to expire. But the curing individual brings the curing medicines in time and Bony is saved.

The curing process is exactly like that described by other authorities on the subject. To cure Bony the medicine man put Bony down on the ground, told him that he saw little bones and eagles' claws in his back and sucked on the back for a full hour. After that process, the man drew from Bony's insides six little bones and two eagles' claws. He showed them to Bony, then buried them. Then he counseled Bony that he was cured: "You goodoh, bimeby," he assured Bony. "No little bones and eagles' claws in your insides now.

Afterwards, naturally, Bony feels much better:

> By degrees Bony took stock of the remarkable change within himself. He was astonished by the absence of pain from his body, for no longer did the darting pain-arrows shoot him like white-hot comets. Timidly he moved himself on the stretcher bed, and instead of pain there was that delightful desire to animate muscles. (238)

With the absence of pain, clouds of weakness and doubt dissipated, and Bony's clear and ebullient spirits returned.

In other books, Upfield incorporates various other bits of Aboriginal lore into a plot to one degree or another. In *Bushranger of the Skies* he has a character named Itcheroo, Rex's companion in crime, who knows how to point the bone but even more important is proficient in "among other things, in the less sinister practice of mental telepathy." He was able to

> project through space mental pictures to be received by minds open to receive them,

and he was capable of receiving as well as sending such telepathic messages:

> he was able to clean his mind, like a slate is cleaned of writing by a sponge, and so receive thought-pictures projected by a distant mind. (55)

In one other book, *Murder Must Wait,* virtually the whole plot turns on the Aboriginal belief about where babies come from. In this story somebody is stealing babies, and the reason and destination of the babies is unknown. As we have seen, as Bony uncovers the scenario, however, it becomes very plain that the whole mystery of birth according to the mystery of the Alchuringa is reenacted, but it is aided, as it always has been, with the strong arm of practicality. In order to assist women who do not have babies in having them, real babies are stowed in a hollow tree, the woman who wants one is doped and hypnotized into thinking that she will be provided one. The all-powerful medicine man then goes into hours of voodoo practices and theatrics, and when the childless woman wakes up she discovers that indeed she has an infant—which often might be observed by the careful eye to be somewhat old for a just-born natural infant—in her arms. Upfield's account of the ritual is detailed, fascinating, and lengthy.

Bony is unable to vitiate the power of the two bloods that course through his veins. Upfield is unable to avoid recounting and using many of the beliefs and practices from both the white and the black cultures which direct and at times control their cultures. No picture of Australian life would be complete without such pictures.

# Chapter 11
# Attitude Toward Non-Australians

Upfield apparently loved Australia from the time he arrived there. He also came to respect the Aborigines, to learn what was being done to them by outsiders, and to see that the original people of Australia were not getting a fair shake from the late-coming whites. We have seen how Upfield railed against these individuals, the civilization they brought with them, and its consequent vitiation of the Aboriginal's life style.

Not all foreigners were viewed with the same attitude by Upfield. At times he praised the civilization brought to Australia by his countrymen, the English. At other times he thought it was the beginning of a continuing curse, which would end only with the total destruction of the Aboriginal race. Upfield genuinely longed for the pure and simple life of the pre-invasion Australians.

About Americans Upfield's attitude was consistently more affirmative. He had always wanted to come to America but had never been able to make the trip. Bony confessed that there were

two things he wanted to see in America: Death Valley and the Grand Canyon. There were three things he wanted to do: to be the guest of an Indian chief, to fish for marlin off the California coast, and to meet the Chief of the Federal Bureau of Investigation.

Upfield was the only foreigner up to his time to have been given the Mystery Crime Writers Award, an American institution, and he sorely wanted to come to the United States to get it. But his health prevented it. In addition, apparently, he felt that Americans' presence in Australia had not been as detrimental to the health of the Aboriginals and the continent as that of other people, and so he generally was positively inclined toward Americans and their contributions to the growth of Australia.

He drops an American or two into a few of his works without fleshing them out very much. But in *The Mountains Have a Secret* he develops an American character to a considerable degree. Bony nearly always uses an assistant of some sort, to one degree or another. Often it is a police constable, who might or might not remain in the background. Twice it is Alice McGorr, a policewoman sent out at his request to assist him. In *The Mountains Have a Secret*, the assistant is an American from Texas. In developing this character Upfield pretty much sticks to the stereotype of Texans and when he enlarges it he creates Texan characteristics that exist only in the minds of people who do not know Texas or who willfully distort the picture.

*The Mountains Have a Secret* is a story about Nazi spies operating in the mountains just south of Sydney. Two hikers have disappeared from their walk in the mountains. Bony has come to see if he can locate them. There he discovers the Texas sweetheart of one of the hikers, Glen Shannon, who it turns out is something quite different from the stereotype Upfield assumed as a working principle. Shannon is sensible, courageous, humorous and hospitable. In his own way a giant and hero, Glen Shannon is allowed to represent America and Americans favorably.

But not all foreigners are quite so well received. Upfield had been widely read and favorably reviewed in Germany. Perhaps that is one reason that he wrote for the post-World War II Germans a rather savage picture of the Nazis in the same novel in which he developed the favorable picture of the American. The Nazis are in Australia, of course, to sabotage the country and to establish a kind of tyranny of their own. They are wicked individuals. Not only do they kidnap unwary travelers in the countryside but they put them into a kind of prison where they have to serve the Nazis, as custodians, cooks, etc., in slavery. The Nazis do not kill or otherwise harm their prisoners. But they do use them as slaves. The Germans are not the only evil persons in this conspiracy. There are several Australians who likewise have joined in the threat against their homeland. In their little Nazi land in Australia, they mill around in their various activities, "like the Valkyries of the Norsemen to carry the remains of heroes into the Halls of their Valhalla" (1) and play German songs on a giant organ that sends music reverberating throughout the large hall in which it is situated and across the countryside, playing "a portion of Wagner's tetralogy, the Ring of the Nibulung," and concluding with "Deutschland Uber Alles" which pours over the company "like a fluid of sound" as the Nazis stand and the curtains slowly move to contact at the center. The scene is enough to make every good Nazi genuflect and good German reach for the flush bucket.

Totalitarian governments must have made Upfield—with his yen to be free of all trammels—quiver. In two other books, *The Battling Prophet* and *The Devil's Steps*, he writes of a conspiracy by outside forces.

*The Battling Prophet* is about a fine Australian weatherman who although despised by his fellow Australians is admired and treasured by Americans, but who is envied by a gang of communists, who see that any weatherman who can accurately predict weather would be a marvelous force in their efforts. Though the conspirators are too much for the C.I.D. and official police force, Bony and his assistant capture and overpower them.

*The Devil's Steps* turns on another conspiracy's effort to subvert and take over an institution. This time the action is in a writers' retreat just east of Melbourne. Bony himself is on retreat there until he is confronted with a murder that looks unusual and is forced to deal with foreigners who are trying to usurp the good land of the good Australians. Bony will not stand for it.

In many ways Upfield's attitude was similar to that held by most of us. He was quite free to criticize and condemn the actions of the British in Australia and the destruction they continued to cause to the people native to the land. They might not have been the best. The Americans, for example, perhaps because there were fewer of them in the land, were not like their British cousins. The Americans were more benign. But though he might have wished that the British had not come, they were there, and they were far superior to other nationals who were determined to set up totalitarian governments. They were far more evil than the resident British.

# Chapter 12
# A New Discovery: *Breakaway House*

Recent interest and scholarship in Arthur Upfield has brought to light the manuscript of a non-Bony novel, called *Breakaway House*, that was not known to exist before. Since I got to read it in manuscript after the present book was typeset and the new book does not really affect any of the preceding study, I shall take it up here as a kind of supplement.

It is difficult to tell precisely what location Upfield in mind for the setting of this novel. He mentions that a cook passed through the garden gate and "crossed the Myme-Magnet track," and was "on the lip of a Murchison breakaway, colourful space with far-flung foundaries." It would seem then that the general location for the setting of the story is north and slightly east of the real town of Mount Magnet.

There seem to be few if any facts about the composition date of *Breakaway House*. There is a note on the cover sheet which reads: "Offered for the author by: Geo. Frankland, Farnham Royal, Slough, Bucks." and Upfield is cited as "Author of 'Sands of Windee'." Publishers Angus & Robertson, North Ryde, Australia, who provided this bit of information, also write that a date of "the early to mid-1930s has been suggested" as the date of composition of the new novel.

That supposition is perhaps as good as any other. There is strong internal evidence that the book was written soon after *The House of Cain*, Upfield's first published novel, possibly while Upfield was still brooding about what to do with *The Barrakee Mystery*, which he worried over while trying to get his detective legs under him. In *Breakaway House*, the motif of brother taking

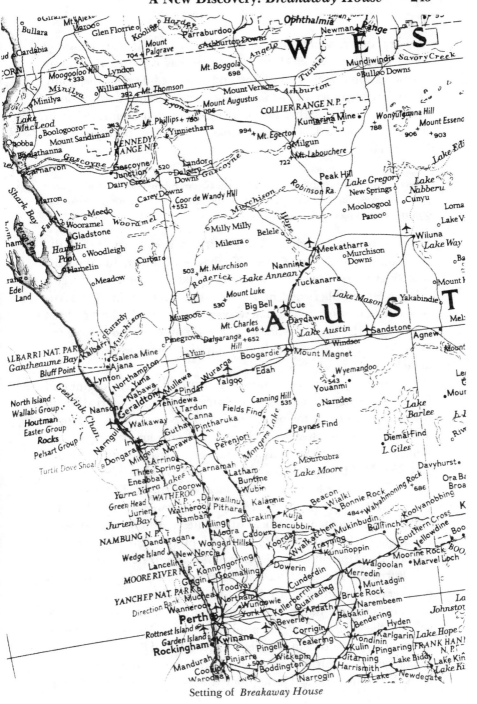

Setting of *Breakaway House*

care of brother, which predominated so strongly in *The House of Cain*, is still at work. Harry Tremayne has come to Breakaway House station to search for his lost and presumed-dead brother John. Harry Tremayne is almost as heroic in appearance and action as Monty was in the earlier novel. Tremayne is handsome, debonair though unpolished, a practical jokester, a prize policeman and fighter. He has

powerful shoulders, slim hips, and feet encased in riding boots...wide-spaced grey-blue eyes, the features chiselled as though from the dark wood of the omnipresent mulga itself.

He likes women though he stands a little in awe of them, especially the beautiful and strong ones. Tremayne's brother, for the brief span he appears in the novel, is totally unlike the effete and protected brother Martin Sherwood in *The House of Cain*. John Tremayne is a ferocious tiger made that way by the fact that he has been forced to perform slave work in a cave for an extended period and he is determined to revenge himself on his captors, as he does with demonic fury.

Upfield's respect for beautiful and strong women, begun and furthered to an extreme in *The House of Cain*, is carried on in *Breakaway House* in the person of Frances Tonger, niece of Morris Tonger, owner of Breakaway House and obvious participator in some kind of nefarious activity. Frances is sensible, strong, brave and worthy of being the love of such a hero as Harry Tremayne.

If Frances looks back to the ideal woman of *The House of Cain*, Violet Winters, an Amazon of a woman who can beat up virtually any man, looks forward to later creation. She becomes the first, fairly-well sketched, heroine of physical strength and courage that Upfield was to develop more roundly in his later works.

But if *Breakaway House* reads close to *The House of Cain* in several ways, in several it seems far removed. Internal evidence demonstrates how much Upfield had learned about his craft since writing the first book of his published career. He is much better at character development. His heroic Tremayne of *Breakaway House* is not nearly as caricatured as his equivalent, Monty Sherwood, is in the earlier book. Throughout this book, unlike *The House of Cain*, the characters are real, credible, and the story is both interesting and entertaining.

In physical setting, *Breakaway House* is not much different from that portion of *The House of Cain* which dealt with the outback. In *Breakaway House* the setting is the Murchison plain on the gigantic breakaway crags leaping toward the sky. As he did in *The House of Cain* and was to do even better in later books, Upfield approached and described the setting with considerable awe:

> Here, on the lip of a Murchison breakaway, colourful space with far-flung boundaries so overwhelmed one with a panorama of scintillating tints—an intoxicant to the imagination and a vision of freedom known only to swift birds—that a solitary man was lost in the grandeur of his surroundings.

Though the book will develop awash with sea images, Upfield makes it clear in the second paragraph that this is a land story, where he was most at home and most capable of speaking authoritatively:

> This was the rock-bound coast of a sea that never was. Never had the ocean roared against the rock-strewn foot of this curving, hundred-foot cliff which swept away to the north-west to end in a mighty headland of black and brown stabbing into a sea of dove-gray saltbush, and, to the south, curved out to westward to end in an escarpment of ironstone and granite rubble amongst which specks of mica reflected the sun as though an escaping thief had thrown away all the jewels of India.

The real setting for this novel apparently is some 80 miles from the sea, north of Perth in Western Australia, northeast of the real town of Mt. Magnet. It is gold country. Into the area Harry Tremayne's brother John has come to investigate the rumor that a gang is stealing gold. John, though disguised, had been discovered and has disappeared. His father, who is a policeman, and his brother, also a policeman in Perth, fear that John has been murdered. Harry is therefore dispatched by his father to investigate the disappearance. Harry, though nominally a policeman, continuously floats back and forth between being on the force and being just-resigned, as suits his immediate purpose.

On the sheep station at Breakaway House, Harry discovers that Morris Tonger, the owner of the station, is unusual and acts in unaccountable ways. Also he seems to have more financial resources than a person in his position in life should have. He also has a niece named Frances who is very attractive to Harry.

In addition to the beautiful craggy terrain that surrounds the area and plays an important part in the story, another aspect of Australian landscape, caves, is introduced into the story, though more as a place of action than as a symbol. In *The House of Cain* caverns had been used with heavy sexual and political symbolism. In *Breakaway House* a cave is merely a cave. As the story develops, John Tremayne has been kidnapped and forced to work for a gang hiding their operations in a cave near the sheep station. Living there has pretty much reduced John to the mentality of an animal, a kind of forecast of what will happen later to Bony when under the heaviest stress. So the cavern is a place of evil people and evil acts. In no other story will Upfield utilize the cave in precisely this stark way.

The people in the story are more realistic than those in *The House of Cain*. The wicked are not unmitigatedly evil. In fact, some know that they are not acting in the way best suited to advance civilization and humanity, and they at least occasionally are remorseful, though they do not change their ways. Such remorse is not a soft-heartedness on the part of Upfield. When he wants to be tough, he is tough.

In addition to the use of geography and caverns, aspects which will continue to be important to Upfield, there are certain other aspects of Australian life as he knows it which are introduced here that will continue to be his staples, and which look forward rather than backward in his writing.

For example, booze and drunkards. As we have seen, booze was a staple on the Australian frontier. Here it is also. Some people drink to excess, or just enough to be at their most proficient. Here, for example, the cook turns out the most delicious foods when he is dead drunk. So, Harry and others want to keep him drunk so the good food will continue to flow. The booze, Upfield makes clear, is cooled, as it was before ice or refrigeration was available, through the use of evaporation.

Several other aspects of this novel look forward rather than backward. Harry rides a sensitive and intelligent horse, one that recognizes evil persons are around before Harry does, and when they are attacked by the evil gang in the mountains sacrifices her life in order to save that of her master. In this book too Upfield's love of a good fight, a brawl, is developed, this time on stage, as it were, as it will be in later books. Upfield loves to have strong heroic people engaged in a democratic brawl. Upfield's concern with foreigners is evident here, also, this time in the person of a Russian, who is tied up with the gang Harry has come out to investigate. As had not happened in *The House of Cain* or *The Barrakee Mystery*, Upfield's first Bony book, but would happen in several later ones, Upfield discusses various foreign idealogies—in this case Bolshevism—at considerable length.

Finally, there is unmitigated evil in the actions that the gang overrunning the neighborhood have taken. They are exporting some 700 pounds of cocaine per shipment of wool to Britain. They conceal the cocaine in the bales of wool that Tonger ships to Britain after each sheep-shearing. Upfield, expatriated Briton that he is, resents this evil that is being imposed upon the people of England.

All in all, this is a successful statement of Upfield's writing talents, regardless of the date of its composition. It is somewhat less intense and less effective than the books in the Bony series, but it is successful as an early effort of Upfield's treatment of the Australian outback. Its discovery after all these years is remarkable, and the book is a fine filling-in of Upfield's skill as a novelist during his early years.

# Chapter 13
# Conclusion

As we look back upon the life and the works of Arthur Upfield, what conclusions can be drawn? In many ways he was a simple and direct individual; in many ways, however, his books are complicated. Surely he was ambivalent.

He was first of all, it seems, a Britisher who had gone Australian. As a Britisher he undoubtedly was proud—at least off and on—of his heritage. But he was even prouder of his Australian persona. He generally detested what the British represented and what they had imposed upon Australians, especially the Aboriginals. He was in this characteristic more Australian than the Australians.

But he was also undoubtedly very British and very Australian, at the same time, in his fierce independence. He loved the freedom of the Australian Outback, he respected the Aboriginals for their freedom in living in this Outback. Though he envied their freedom he really did not want to become a part of it. He could work in it and enjoy it for short periods of time, but when a job was finished, he wanted to go back to his semi-White, or all-White, existence, with his half-caste wife, their three children and their little home. His life style was what he preferred, perhaps not superior to the Aboriginal's, but one that he preferred.

Did Upfield present Australian Outback life and culture comprehensively and fairly? The answer has to be in the affirmative. Few observers had seen more, had experienced more of life's varieties, and tried to present it fairly, though not dispassionately. He knew the cattle station owner, the squatter, Britishers of all kinds, and he knew the Aboriginals in all their manifestations. He had lived among them all, had been a keen observer, and wanted to be a truthful reporter.

Of the British, nobody has ever accused Upfield of not presenting them fairly and objectively. He, being one of them, could read them and report his findings.

But what of the Aboriginals, those people whose land Australia was originally and from whom the British had wrested it? Did Upfield picture them as they were? The answer has to be an unequivocal affirmative. He knew them as well as any non-Aboriginal probably could ever know them. In picturing them as living human beings, warts and all, he at times projected them in less than favorable lights. Like their White counterparts, the Aboriginals were sometimes ugly, evil, selfish, ignorant and stupid. So were the British. At times Upfield presented the Aboriginals in the shorthand of stereotype and cliche. But it should be remembered that Upfield was writing for a literate—that is largely non-Aboriginal—audience. He wanted to write the "great Australian" novel. That means he was writing for literate Australians, and for other English-speaking peoples around the world. That does not mean that he had license to falsify the Aboriginals, but it does mean that perhaps he can be excused for having used the stereotype and cliche in his effort to get along and tell the story. He was, as he repeatedly said, primarily a story-teller.

His stories have the ring of truth about them. Many people throughout the world have learned what they know about all aspects of Australia from Upfield. Perhaps even some Aboriginals have learned a great deal about their own land from Upfield. But many have not responded affirmatively to what they have learned. Have they responded properly to Upfield? The answer from a White cannot of course have the feeling of full truth. Only one who is a member of the race can have the full feeling. But it does seem that perhaps the Australian Aborigines may have censored Upfield prematurely. In banning Upfield they may in fact be banning parts of their history and their lives.

Upfield wrote some of the finest and strongest novels of crime fiction of all times and all places. His Bony stands as one of the half dozen most outstanding crime investigators of all time. Upfield stands as a gem in the Australian crown. If he failed to be utterly and completely objective at all times, perhaps he was a victim of his own upbringing. He was never quite able to cast aside his British blood and British point of view. Perhaps that was his weakness as well as his strength.

# Chapter 14
# Glossary of Australian and Aboriginal terms used by Upfield

In using Australian and Aboriginal terms in his works, Upfield naturally employs some words and phrases which are not familiar to the non-Australian reader. Almost never does he explain them. Included here are the main ones that the reader of Upfield's works might want to have explained. Fuller explanations are to be found in the various issues of Philip Asdell's *Bony Bulletin*, which I follow here, and in various books on the subject.

Art—Australian Aboriginal art, according to Elkin in *The Australian Aborigines*, is highly symbolic, a ritual activity, "corresponding with chanting, dancing and acting," not intended to be beauty for its own sake. Since there were few colors available, the Aborigines used primarily red and yellow ochre, white pipeclay and black charcoal. Some rock art, which occurred in caves and overhangs, was done by incision or by coloring the surface. "Wood and stone churingas" (or "tjuringa") were "symbolic representations" of ancestral associations of "Dreamtime," that is of the creation and beginning of mankind.

Barcoo sickness—spews, vomit.

Bardee or Bardee Grub—a large round-headed tree borer, which is the larva of a beetle. Savored by some people.

Billabong—The word, about whose origins there is some dispute, may have come from two Wirehuri Aboriginal words: "billa," meaning water or river, and "bong," meaning dead. However,

Surveyor-General Thomas Livingstone Mitchell, a nearby explorer of central and western New South Wales, says it came from a river which he discovered in 1836 which the natives called "billagang." The term means a portion of a river bed that has been abandoned by the main flow of the river. So it is a pond, a slough, a body of dead river.

Billy—Probably any kind of container that could hold water and be heated over the open fire, an indispensable part of the daily equipment of any Australian.

Bonzer—means "excellent, first-rate, delightful." Probably derived from the American term "bonanza."

Boomerang—Upfield, in *The Barrakee Mystery*, is explicit about the kinds and uses of boomerangs: "There are three kinds of boomerangs... The Wongium, which returns in its flight to the thrower; the Kirras, which does not return; and the very heavy Murrawirrie... The Central Australians employ the last two—the Kirras for throwing and the Murrawirrie for use as a sword... The Kirras is, or was, in general use all over Australia; but there is a sharp difference in the carving. The eastern blacks always flattened one side; the Central Australia blacks never flattened either side, but kept the weapon round." He was able to identify the one that had been thrown in the book as being a Kirras.

A majority of boomerangs, despite common understanding, were not the returning type, which, used nowhere but in Australia, were restricted to the eastern and western parts, and were, according to Asdell, "considered playthings." It has been suggested that the returning boomerang was developed to be used over water, when one that did not return would obviously be lost in the water. A. H. Reed, in *An Illustrated Encyclopedia of Aboriginal Life*, says that there is a fourth kind, the so-called "warradulla," which has a hook on one end, which in case someone tries to shield himself from it will catch on the shield, turn around it and inflict a heavy wound.

Boomerangs

Burial of the dead—There was apparently no common system of burial of the dead countrywide. Various ways were used: interment, cremation, platform or tree disposal, mummification or desiccation and exposure. A. H. Reed reports that in some places "to keep the spirit warm at night" fires were built over the places of burial.

Ceremonial ground—Generally called "bora ground," "bora" being the word for "initiation rite," at least in New South Wales.

Churinga—see Art

Cicatrices—Weals made with stone or shell knives, with ashes rubbed into the cuts to raise the scars. These initiatory rites demonstrated the male youth's passage into manhood and his indifference to pain.

Corroboree—Originally a dance, festive or warlike. Later any social gathering or public meeting.

Crook—"To go crook," means to become angry, to express annoyance, to voice dissatisfaction.

Damper—unleavened bread, flat cakes baked over the ashes of a fire.

Dijerdoo—Upfield comments on this musical instrument: It "was thick as a man's leg, and so long that the end rested on a sheet of bark beyond Canute's outstretched feet. The mouth end was but little smaller than the end opening, and from it issued sounds which to ears accustomed to white man's music would be meaningless."

The Dijerdoo or Drone-Pipe, which was used only in the Northern Territory and in the eastern Kimberleys, was usually made of hollowed timber or bamboo soaked in water. Some were smaller at one end. But they were difficult to play. It was necessary to achieve a constant drone-like sound. This was done by the player filling his cheeks with air and taking short, quick breaths through the nostrils. Generally Aboriginal music was mainly vocal. Besides the Dijerdoo all other instruments were percussion.

Dilly bags—Form of Aboriginal suitcase or carry-bag, tightly woven from fiber and grass and bark string, most were suspended from the neck, on women generally falling between the breasts. Some were so tightly woven that they could carry water and other liquids.

Earth-Worms—Giant earth-worms with an average length of six feet but which sometimes reach 12 feet. They are about three-quarters of an inch in diameter, though can reach several inches. They "bark" by moving through their elaborate burrows. They are now an endangered species.

Generosity—The Australian Aboriginals, like primitive people everywhere, held things in common. Nothing belonged to an individual. If a person "gave" something to another individual, it might not remain long with the second person, for he/she would easily pass it on to yet a third. This concept of not owning material goods has brought the Australian Aboriginal, as it brought the American Indian, into various circumstances where they unwittingly "gave away" things to non-tribal members.

Gilgie; Gibber—"Gilgie" means saucer-shaped depression hiding water. "Gibber" (both pronounced with a hard "g") means a barren country covered by stones and boulders.

Gin—Probably of white origin, means aboriginal woman.

Goanna—Lizard-like reptile.

Humpy-Gundy, gunyan, mia mia, quamby, wurley—all mean "A small native dwelling supported by three forked sticks (about three feet long) brought together at the top in triangular form: the two sides toward the wind covered by long sheets of bark, the third...always left open to the wind."

Jackaroo—a novice learning sheep-or cattle-farming. Probably derived from association of Johnny or Jacky Raw with kangaroo.

Kangaroo—Origin of the word is shrouded in history and folk etymology. The legend that Captain Cook asked the natives what the jumping quadruped was and was told "Kangaroo," meaning "I don't know," is probably false. Apparently, the word "kangaroo" was a general term used for all animals except the dingo. Kangaroos range from the large grey, which stands taller than a man to the small rat kangaroo, which is usually about a foot and a half in length.

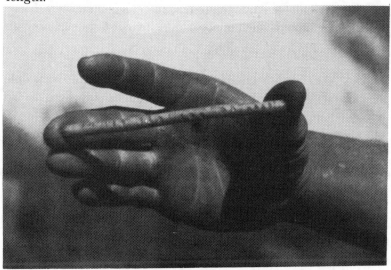

From *Follow My Dust,* courtesy Don Uren

Letter-stick—Upfield describes the letter-stick at some length: It was "about six inches in length, and had been scraped by a quartz or granite chip, scorched by fire and polished by sandstone mixed with saliva. Two encircling cuts gave the stick three divisions, and within two of the divisions short cuts had been made, the third division untouched. It was a...ceremonial letter stick." A. W. Reed suggests that early on it was thought that the carved notices, dots and bands on such letter sticks constituted some sort of hieroglyphic language, but lately it is felt that they comprised a mnemonic device which aided the messenger in delivering an accurate message. Reed reports that also such letter-sticks were used for ceremonial purpose—to announce a corroboree, death or mortuary rite, and such sticks may have sacred symbols on them and might have been decorated with feathers.

Lubra—Aboriginal word for woman, known throughout Australia.

Menu—Upfield, in *The Sands of Windee*, describes Aboriginal's food at a corroboree as "quartered kangaroo, sheep's offal, iguanas, yabbies, hush yams and enormous emu legs." Apparently the Aboriginals, being nomadic, ate any and everything they could find that was in any way edible.

Nardoo seeds—A fern seed which can be ground into rough flour and which provides some nourishment.

Offsider—Derived from "offside" of an animal team, in Upfield it means "assistant" or "mate."

Rainstones—Apparently artifacts used in incantations to summon rain. In *Bony and the Black Virgin*, Bony says: "dig up your rainstones and make rain, pretty quick."

Relationships—Family relationships among primitives are always complicated, interwoven networks devised to protect and help care for various members. Australian Aboriginal systems are often confusing. A. W. Reed explains them thusly: "It requires the training of a qualified anthropologist to penetrate the ramifications of kinship in Aboriginal life and tribal lore. Essentially, everyone with whom a person comes in contact was a relation. Prescribed rules had to be observed in speech and in their mutual attitudes." In this society all brothers were equal to all brothers, all sisters to all sisters. Reed explains further:
"Thus a mother's sister was regarded as equivalent to a mother and was so called. However, the first degree of kinship existed between mother's brothers, not with sisters. Similarly, a father's

brother was a father, therefore the sons of father's brothers were also brothers, not as we know them, cousins. Conversely, a nephew who was the son of a brother was not a nephew but a son... As a result of these classifications the children of a man's sisters were not sons and daughters but nephews and nieces. His sisters' children regarded him not as a father but as an uncle because he was their mother's brother. Her sister's children, however, were their brothers and sisters. The same principle extended back a further generation."

To run-bankers—obviously a term meant for a river in flood stage.

Smoke-signalling—A. W. Reed is skeptical about the wide use of smoke-signalling by Aboriginals. It was more widely used to indicate a site where a person could be found than in other more sophisticated means of communicating messages.

Squatter—Borrowed from American usage, first meant to "squat" and occupy land. In Australia, in the early 1800s "squatter" referred to a freed convict who built a hut on unoccupied land. By 1840 it meant "one who occupied a tract of pastoral land as a tenant of the Crown." By the end of the 19th century, W. S. Ramson in his *Australian English* says, "squatter" meant "a pastoralist with large freehold property."

Station—Probably originally a military term, came to mean a tract of land in Australia on which were run sheep or cattle.

Sundowner—Trapper who shows up at sundown, too late to earn his keep for the night.

Swag—Widely used for all kinds of things that an itinerant could bundle up and carry with him. Probably with the Australian wanderer meant everything he owned.

Tea—Outback tea was generally made from any kind of available water, heated in a "billy" and served without cream or milk or lemon. Apparently it was a standard drink whenever it could be brewed.

Tea-Tree—A name given to several species of the genus Leptospermum, a member of the myrtle family. Not the source of present-day tea leaves, though the leaves might have provided "tea" in the early days of settlement.

Tjuringa—see Art.

Totemism—Totemism goes back to Aboriginals' "Dreamtime," that is the beginning of all things, when the spirit heroes and heroines distributed their "spirit totems" all around. These spirits, according to Asdell's summary which is as succinct as necessary, "were in human form, some in animal form and some in both. The spirit totem linked each baby with the Dreamtime and, as the infant grew older, imposed social restraints and obligations. For instance, a woman was not permitted to marry a person of the same totem, and people were not permitted to kill or eat their totemic animal." These totems afforded cross-tribal links, for a person entering a new territory claimed brotherhood with this new tribe because all members of a clan or totem were automatically related.

Waddy—A straight tapered stick used for hunting or warfare, or perhaps in corporal punishment.

Walkabout—Collectively or individually to take a long walk for pleasure or to search for food.

Wandering Millie—Australian wanderlust.

Willy-Willy—"those tall and drunken spiralling columns which march across hot Australia" (Hawke, 141). Circular wind upsurging sand and rubbish, generally still inside, like the eye of a tornado. Larger than American wind devils but smaller than tornadoes.

Witchetty grub—A moth larva found among acacia trees, a prized Aboriginal delicacy.

Yarby—In New South Wales, Victoria and Tasmania a freshwater crayfish.

# Bibliography of References

Any study of an Australian author is incomplete without constant references to other works on the country and the people. I have found the following books to be useful, especially for references to Aboriginals

Asdell, Philip T., ed. *The Bony Bulletin* 5719 Jefferson Blvd., Frederick, MD 21701.

Brown, Hosanna. *Death Upon a Spear*. London: Victor Gollancz, 1986.

Corris, Peter. *The Winning Side*. Sydney: George Allen & Unwin, 1984.

Durack, Mary. *Keep Him My Country*. London: Corgi Books, 1983.

Durack, Mary. *Sons in the Saddle*. London: Corgi Books, 1983.

Durack, Mary. *To Be Heirs Forever*. London: Corgi Books, 1979.

Hardy, Frank. *The Unlucky Australians*. Sydney: Pan Books, 1978.

Hawke, Jessica. *Follow My Dust! A Biography of Arthur Upfield*. Melbourne, Heinemann, 1957.

Maddock, Kenneth. *The Australian Aborigines*. New York: Penguin, 1982.

Reed, A. W. *Aboriginal Stories of Australia*. French's Forest, NSW, 1976.

## Upfield Editions Used in this Study

Because Upfield's works are coming to be available in several editions, I append here the bibliography of texts I used in this study. I assume that page numbers will differ among the various editions available. I have numbered the books to correspond to the map which gives the general areas of the stone's. I have given an asterisk to indicate fictitious settings for stone's.

*An Author Bites the Dust*. Sydney: Angus & Robertson, 1983.
*The Bachelors of Broken Hill*. Sydney: Angus & Robertson, 1983.
*The Barrakee Mystery*. London: Heinemann, 1972.
*The Battling Prophet*. Sydney: Angus & Robertson, 1981.
*The Beach of Atonement*. I did not see.
*The Bone is Pointed*. Sydney: Angus & Robertson, 1981.
*Bony Buys a Woman*. Sydney: Pan Books, 1984.
*Bony and the Black Virgin*. New York: Collier Books, 1965.
*Bony and the Kelly Gang*. Sydney: Pan Books, 1983.
*Bony and the Mouse*. Sydney: Pan Books, 1984.
*Bony and the White Savage*. Sydney: Angus & Robertson, 1984.
*Breakaway House,* Sydney: Angus & Robertson, 1987.
*Bushranger of the Skies*. Sydney: Angus & Robertson, 1980.
*Death of a Lake*. New York: Scribner's, 1982.
*Death of a Swagman*. New York: Signet Penguin, 1945.
*The Devil's Steps*. New York: Charles Scribner's Sons, 1982.
*Gripped by Drought*. I did not see.
*The House of Cain*. San Francisco: Dennis McMillan, 1983.
*The Lake Frome Monster*. London: Pan Books, Ltd., 1966.
*Madman's Bend*. Sydney: Pan Books, 1984.
*Man of Two Tribes*. Sydney: Angus & Robertson, 1981.
*The Mountains Have a Secret*. Sydney: Pan Books, 1983.
*Mr. Jelly's Business*. Sydney: Angus & Robertson, 1981.
*Murder Must Wait*. Sydney: Angus & Robertson, 1984.
*The Mystery of Swordfish Reef*. Sydney: Angus & Robertson, 1983.
*The New Shoe*. New York: Scribner's, 1983. *
*A Royal Abduction*. Dennis McMillan, 1984.
*Sinister Stones*. New York: Scribner's, 1982.
*The Sands of Windee*. Sydney: Angus & Robertson, 1980.
*Venom House*. Sydney: Angus & Robertson, 1985.
*The Widows of Broome*. New York: Charles Scribner's, 1985.
*The Will of the Tribe*. Sydney: Angus & Robertson, 1983.
*Winds of Evil*. Sydney: Angus & Robertson,˙ 1980.
*Wings Above the Diamantina*. Baltimore, Md: Penguin, 1965.

## Books and Settings

The action of some Upfield novels is set on homesteads (cattle and sheep stations and other places) and in small fictitious towns. The locations of these fictitious places can generally be inferred. Because location of setting is important for the development of plot, I have given here geographical pointers for the locations. These designations are given by number on the accompanying map. Asterisk indicates the locale is fictitious.

1. *House of Cain.* Melbourne and northwest New South Wales.
*2. *Breakaway House.* Murchison breakaway, western Western Australia.
*3. *The Barrakee Mystery.* Barrakee Station, River Darling Basin, N.S.W.
4. *The Beach of Atonement.* Dongerra, Western Australia.
*5. *The Sands of Windee.* Windee Station N.S.W.
6. *A Royal Abduction.* Eucla, Western Australia.
7. *Gripped By Drought.*
*8. *Wings Over the Diamantina.* Coolibah Cattle Station, west Queensland.
9. *Mr. Jelly's Business.* Burracoppin, south western Australia.
*10. *Winds of Evil.* Wirrigatta Station, near Broken Hill, N.S.W.
*11. *The Bone is Pointed.* Opal Town, St. Albans, Queensland.
12. *The Mystery of Swordfish Reef.* Bermagui on the Tasman Sea.
*13. *Bushranger of the Skies.* McPherson's Station, 80 miles n.w. of Shawo's Lagoon, South Australia.
*14. *Death of a Swagman.* Merino, west N.S.W.
*15. *The Devil's Steps.* Wideview Chalet, Manton, Mount Chalmers, Victoria.
16. *An Author Bites the Dust.* Yarrabo, Victoria, near Melbourne, valley of the River Yarra.
17. *Widows of Broome.* Broome, Western Australia.
*18. *The Mountains Have a Secret.* Dunkeld, Victoria.
19. *The New Shoe.* Split Point, Victoria.
*20. *Venom House.* Answerths Folly, Edison, Queensland.
*21. *Murder Must Wait.* Mitford, N.S.W.
*22. *Death of a Lake.* Porchester Station, Lake Otway, N.S.W.
*23. *Sinister Stones.* Agars' Lagoon, 240 miles south of Wyndham, Western Australia.
24. *The Battling Prophet.* Mount Gambier, South Australia.
25. *Man of Two Tribes.* Nullarbor Plain, southwest South Australia.
*26. *Bony Buys a Woman.* Mount Eden, Lake Eyre, South Australia.
27. *The Bachelors of Broken Hill.* Broken Hill, western New South Wales.
*28. *Bony and the Black Virgin.* Mindee on the Darling River, N.S.W.
*29. *Bony and the Mouse.* Daybreak, Western Australia.
*30. *Bony and the Kelly Gang.* Bowral near Sydney, N.S.W.
*31. *Bony and the White Savage.* Rhudder's Inlet, Leeuwin Lighthouse, Western Australia.
32. *The Will of the Tribe.* Wolf Creek Meteor Crater, Western Australia.
*33. *Madman's Bend.* White Bend, N.S.W.
34. *The Lake Frome Monster.* Lake Frome, eastern South Australia.

General locations of Upfield's novels